MW01629954

WHERE *THEY* STAND

I have known Reb Yossy for many years as a gifted speaker and outstanding orator. He is a master at relating the Parsha to the contemporary scene and Jewish life today... Fluid and fascinating, riveting and relevant...succor for the soul.

From the Foreword by Chief Rabbi Israel Meir Lau, Israel

ℬ〜ℛ

Rabbi Yossy Goldman leads Johannesburg's Sydenham Highlands North Hebrew Congregation, one of the great synagogues of the English-speaking world. Rabbi Yossy is a rare and special talent. I remember vividly our first meeting, more than twenty five years ago, in his capacity as a Jewish radio producer. I was struck then by his energy and drive, his great gifts as a communicator, his seemingly effortless ability to connect Jews and Judaism and to make the ancient teachings of our faith accessible, relevant, contemporary and compelling. I loved his combination of learning, humanity, and a sense of humour. I remember how blessed South African Jewry was to have such a man in its midst.

This new collection of his words is a gem, witty and wise, learned yet accessible, like the man himself. Read it and enjoy it. It will make you smile, and better still, it will make you grow.

Chief Rabbi Lord Jonathan Sacks, UK

ℬ〜ℛ

My dear friend, Rabbi Yossy Goldman, has the unique ability to discover valuable insights and precious wisdom in the weekly Torah portions, and to present them in a concise and consumer friendly manner. His work makes the Torah what it was intended to be, a teaching and a guide for proper living.

The brevity of each sermon should not lessen its importance. When a person really knows what one wishes to say, one can do so in a few words. Rabbi Goldman is an expert at this.

Rabbi Abraham J. Twerski, MD, USA

ℬ〜ℛ

Rabbi Yossy Goldman, one of the most prominent rabbinic figures in our community, has written an engaging and insightful book which shows in a most powerful way the eternal relevance of G-d's Torah to our lives and our world. Rabbi Goldman has for more than three decades served the South African Jewish community with loyalty and excellence, and it is an honour for me, as a friend and colleague, to be able to pay tribute to him on the publica-

tion of this book, which gives a glimpse of his dynamic and inspiring way of reaching out to all Jews.

Chief Rabbi Dr Warren Goldstein, South Africa

⁎

Rabbi Goldman's columns, many of which have been published on chabad. org and its hundreds of affiliate websites, have greatly enriched our Parshah offerings. Indeed they are one of the most popular features of our Parshah section, eagerly sought out each week by many thousands of readers, rabbis and laymen, scholars and novices alike. Rabbi Goldman never fails to find a theme in the weekly Torah reading that is both illuminating and relevant. Events which occurred thousands of years ago are applied to contemporary life, and concepts introduced in the first generations of Jewish history are shown to be even more meaningful and practical than yesterday's newspaper. This collection will certainly prove a delight to both the soul and mind of all who peruse it. It is eminently usable for everything from a Rabbi's sermon to a vort *for your Shabbos table.*

Yanki Tauber, author and past Editor, Chabad.org

⁎

The world is an increasingly challenging place in which to live. How do we understand what is happening? How do we secure our family well being, education, old age, when decisions that can affect our present and future are taken on financial markets in nano-seconds, determined by factors far removed from our everyday lives? How do we build trust, dialogue and an ability to listen to and respect others, including those who hold different views? There are no simple or glib answers but it is a delight to read the life messages contained in Rabbi Yossy Goldman's "From Where I Stand." Pithy, humorous and thought-provoking, the essays are easy to read and provide a context within which to live our lives. Enjoy!

Gill Marcus, former Governor of the South African Reserve Bank

⁎

Rabbi Goldman represented the Jewish community in South Africa on the Religious Broadcasting Panel of the SABC and contributed significantly to shape the thinking of the role of a public broadcaster, in terms of human values and religious and spiritual matters.

The good Rabbi is watched by millions throughout South Africa and has reached audiences that are not only Jewish. Not only did he share witty and inspirational messages, but he believes that whatever we transmit must be simple and practical that changes lives...for good.

Yashika Singh, Head of Religion, South African Broadcasting Corporation

ଈୠ

My rabbi is one of the most outstanding communicators from the pulpit and is an articulate and engaging teacher, as all my fellow students of his Talmud class will happily testify. His written words will now make compelling reading as his spoken words have always made compelling listening.

Phillip Boruchowitz, Judge of the High Court of South Africa

ଈୠ

It is high time that Rabbi Goldman's thoughts and writings are finally being put together and published. His highly empathetic and thoughtful column which he wrote for the SA Jewish Report some years ago on "being a mensch" was so popular among our readers that they have consistently clamoured for more. The SA Jewish Report has immensely benefitted over the years from his friendship and insight, particularly in the context of a Jewish community living in the complex South African environment which, during his decades-long tenure as rabbi of one of the most important synagogues in Johannesburg, and a senior leader of the SA Jewish community, was transformed from apartheid to democracy.

Geoff Sifrin, former Editor, *South African Jewish Report.*

ଈୠ

How exciting that Rabbi Goldman has brought out a book on the weekly Torah portion! As a regular columnist for Jewish Life magazine, Rabbi Goldman never fails to make Jewish values and Torah wisdom accessible to anyone and everyone. Readers have commented to me that though they are secular Jews, they can always relate to Rabbi Goldman's articles, and I personally always learn something new. I especially love his ability to connect the loftiest concepts, mitzvot, mysticism, ancient texts and commentaries to ordinary everyday anecdotes and events, thus making the Torah's eternal truth real and relevant to life today.

Paula Levin, former Editor, *Jewish Life* magazine

From
Where I Stand

Photo: Ilan Ossendryver

From Where I Stand

Life Messages from the Weekly Torah Reading

Rabbi Yossy Goldman

With a Foreword by Chief Rabbi Israel Meir Lau

KTAV Publishing House
Brooklyn, NY

KTAV PUBLISHING HOUSE
527 Empire Blvd
Brooklyn, NY 11225
Website: www.ktav.com
Email: orders@ktav.com
Ph: (718) 972-5449 / Fax: (718) 972-6307

ISBN 978-1-60280-225-4

Library of Congress Cataloging-in-Publication Data

Goldman, Yossy, 1950-
  From where I stand : life messages from the weekly Torah reading /
Rabbi Yossy Goldman ; with a foreword by Chief Rabbi Israel Meir Lau.
     p. cm.
  ISBN 978-1-60280-225-4 (hard cover)
  1. Bible. O.T. Pentateuch—Criticism, interpretation, etc. I. La'u, Y. M.
(Yisra'el Me'ir) II. Title.
  BS1225.52.G6735 2012
  296.7'2--dc23

לעילוי נשמת אחותי

חנה לאה ע"ה בת הרה"ת ר' שמעון שיחי'

ולעילוי נשמת מורי וחמי

הרה"ת ר' שלמה שניאור זלמן ב"ר מיכאל

ת. נ. צ. ב. ה.

For Chanchy
who laughed and loved
and made us all do the same.
G-d bless your precious soul.
Keep smiling down on your family.

And for my esteemed father-in-law
Rabbi Zalman Kazen
a humble tzaddik

Contents

5. Sefer Devarim — The Book of Deuteronomy   191

Foreword

Parshat Hashavua, the weekly Torah reading, enjoys a place in Jewish life unlike any other part of our holy Torah. So absolutely central to a Jew's existence is it that it is studied daily, read every Shabbat in Shul, and taught in every Jewish Day School with children bringing home Parsha sheets with words of Torah to share around the Shabbat table. Rabbis are forever using its material in their speeches, whatever the occasion, not only on Shabbat but also during the week. Whether it is a Bris, Bar Mitzvah, Chupah, or, G-d forbid, a funeral, somehow there always seems to be an appropriate message gleaned from the Parsha of the Week. For millennia, it has been the Jewish People's endless wellspring; an inexhaustible source of infinite wisdom and inspiration for every possible occasion.

Indeed, it has always been fascinating to observe how relevant it never fails to be, with up-to-the-minute current events often finding a connection in that very week's Torah reading. And, always, there are valuable lessons with important insights to address the moral dilemmas of the day.

My dear friend, Rabbi Yossy Goldman שליט״א, President of the Rabbinical Association of South Africa, is a master at finding and extracting these ideas and relating them to the contemporary scene and to Jewish life today.

He was kind enough to share with me a collection of his essays on the weekly Parshah based on the sermons he gave in his Johannesburg congregation, the respected and well-known Sydenham Shul. These are now to be published in book form to be made available to a wider audience.

I have known Reb Yossy for many years as a gifted speaker and outstanding orator. As I perused his writings, I was greatly pleased to find succor for the soul with both new and traditional ideas presented in a literary style that is fluid and fascinating, riveting and relevant. I am confident that the publication of this Sefer will bring great benefit to many.

While reading the manuscript I came across a thought on פרשת בשלח (Parshat B'shalach) that I would like to expand on.

ויקח משה את עצמות יוסף עמו —"And Moses took the bones of Joseph with him" (Exodus 13, 19).

Rabbi Goldman asks: Since the remains of Joseph's brothers were taken along as well, why does the Torah single him out to the exclusion of his brothers?

The beautiful answer he gives us is that Joseph was unique. His brothers were only simple shepherds, but as Viceroy of Egypt, Joseph managed the affairs of state of the mightiest "superpower" of the time. Still, he maintained his staunch commitment to his father's Jewish way of life. Now that the Jewish People emerged from Egyptian bondage, they were suddenly confronting a new world order—as a liberated people and as free men and women. In this new reality, only Joseph could be their role model. Only he had the experience to prove that it was possible to adhere to the traditions of the Torah even while enjoying freedom and affluence.

I would like to ask two more questions.

First, Joseph was the father of two great tribes, Menashe and Ephraim. Why was it so important to Moshe that he take away this Mitzvah from them and perform it himself?

Second, our sages apply the following verse to Moshe's deed: חכם לב יקח מצוות —"He who is wise of heart takes for himself Mitzvot," (Proverbs 10, 8. See Talmud, Sotah 13.). Now, why is this act of Moshe's described as "wise"? It was undeniably kind, caring and compassionate. Clearly, it was also a righteous deed. But what was it that made it particularly wise?

It seems to me that the answer may be this:

Moshe's insistence on taking the remains of Joseph with him was most certainly deliberate. The great shepherd knew his flock well. He remembered how already on the second day that he "went out to his brethren" in Egypt, two quarreling Jews threatened to inform the authorities that he had killed the Egyptian taskmaster. Blessed with the foresight that comes from wisdom—"Who is wise? He who sees the outcome of things"—Moshe had a premonition of coming events in their impending great trek through the wilderness. He anticipated all the moaning and groaning, the complaining and the incessant kvetching. He foresaw the Spies' insurrection as well as Korach's rebellion. And then there would be the bitter grumblings and grievances at the subsequent stations of Taveirah, Masah and Kivrot Ha'Taavah.

Being "wise of heart," Moses "prepared the remedy even before the onset of the illness," and made sure to have Joseph's coffin near him at all times. The proximity of the coffin enabled him to calm his people and steer them towards greater unity, harmony and brotherhood, towards a "closing of the ranks."

Every time a fight broke out, Moses could point to Joseph's coffin and ask: "Do you know what this contains? Yes, it is Joseph's remains. And do you know how and why he came down to Egypt in the first place, and why we all had to follow in his footsteps? It all started because his own brothers sold him into slavery!"

Indeed, the inescapable conclusion to be drawn from contemplating Joseph's remains is that all the evil decrees, all the suffering, all the slavery and oppression of the Jewish people are the result of internal strife, of discord, dissension and conflict amongst the Jews themselves!

Not in vain did Moshe deserve the title *לב חכם* —"the wise of heart." It was because he embodied the fusion of mind and heart, the unique blend of logic and emotion. This is an important lesson for all subsequent generations, including our own.

I conclude with my blessing to my dear friend, Rabbi Yossy Goldman *שליט"א*, that he carry on his work with vigor and sanctify the name of Hashem. *ויפוצו מעיינותיו חוצה להגדיל תורה ולהאדירה*—May his wellsprings spread ever outward and add to the greatness and glory of our holy Torah.

In friendship and respect,
Rabbi Israel Meir Lau
Tel Aviv, Israel
ניסן ה'תשע"ב / April 2012

Frankly, I never dreamt that I would become a congregational rabbi. Delivering sermons from a pulpit was never on my wish list. My passion was teaching Torah and sharing the Jewish way of life with as many of my fellow Jews as I could possibly reach out to.

It was for this purpose that my wife Rochel and I came to South Africa with our two small children back in March, 1976. We were sent by the Lubavitcher Rebbe, Rabbi Menachem Mendel Schneersohn, of sainted memory, as his *Shluchim* (Emissaries) to strengthen Judaism and Jewish communal life down in what seemed then to be "darkest Africa."

Rabbi Mendel Lipskar, head of the Lubavitch Foundation and its chairman, Rabbi Koppel Bacher, invited me to establish the very first Chabad House in South Africa back in the old Jewish neighbourhood of Yeoville. I devoted ten years of service there, during which time I was privileged to establish many of the core activities and programs of Chabad in Johannesburg, including *The Jewish Sound* radio program, which I would produce and host for some 24 years every Sunday night.

In 1983, I also went on to become the founding rabbi of the Torah Academy Shul. After three years there, in 1986, I was "headhunted" by the chairman of Sydenham Highlands North Hebrew Congregation, Harold Novick. As it was the largest Shul in Johannesburg, I consulted my mentor and teacher, the Rebbe, as he had sent us to South Africa in the first place. With the Rebbe's guidance and blessing I went on to accept this prestigious position, and my *shlichut* changed course into full-time congregational rabbinics.

Sydenham Shul has now been my home for the past 26 years. Our children have grown up here, and Rochel and I have formed many deep and special relationships with so many wonderful people. I am grateful to Harold (who, remarkably, is still the Chairman), the President Stanley Seeff, Gaboim, council members, and congregants (past and present—many precious souls are no longer with us), for their support and friendship and for giving me such a receptive audience every Shabbos and Yom Tov. Like all teachers of Torah, I have learned most from my students.

Long before I knew what the Internet was, a young rabbi named Yosef Yitzchak Kazen would often ask me to send him my synagogue sermons so he could post them on the "World Wide Web." At that stage, I honestly had no idea what he was talking about and dismissed his aspirations as unrealistic idealism and wistful daydreaming. By the time he passed away in 1998 at the young age of 44, "YY" had become acknowledged as the "Father of the Jewish Internet," and his pioneering work created what is now known as chabad.org, one of the world's best and busiest Jewish websites.

Rabbi YY Kazen was my brother-in-law (my wife Rochel is his sister), and I truly regret not taking him up on his invitation all those years ago. If I did, I might have had many more books published by now.

So this book began with YY's gentle nudging to put my synagogue speeches into writing so they could be published on the Internet. My first word of appreciation is, therefore, to him. May his *neshama* bask in the radiance of G-d, and may his huge contribution to the electronic dissemination of Torah stand him in good stead On High and be a blessing for his dear mother (my esteemed mother-in-law, Rebbetzin Shula Kazen), his wife, children, and family.

Eventually, I decided to take up YY's suggestion and spoke to Rabbi Yanki Tauber, the editor-in-chief at chabad.og. I have always loved his writing and was flattered that he liked mine. Reb Yanki got me to commit to a Weekly Sermonette which was published on their website over a period of some three years. And that is how I became a "Parsha Columnist." I am indebted to chabad.org for the opportunity of such a distinguished and popular forum and to Rabbi Tauber, personally, for his occasional editorial suggestions and also for some very creative, catchy titles.

It has been most humbling to see these writings so well received. The original Weekly Sermonettes are today used by rabbis and lay people alike, Jews of all persuasions and many non-Jews too. They are used in pulpits and in printed community newsletters. I myself have used them for many broadcasts on television and radio. At this time, through the international network of chabad.org, they are being translated into a variety of languages including Hebrew, Spanish, Russian, French, and German. I receive appreciative comments from readers in all these languages, so, clearly, it is resonating with people from all walks of life. Indeed, it is a source of deep personal gratification to know that my words are reaching and teaching people around the world. Please G-d, may it continue to be shared and inspire people for many years to come.

I will venture to suggest that the reason for their popularity is that these ideas, which may vary in their degree of depth, are always put across in a style which is simple and straightforward. They are also relevant ideas that speak to people in the real world. They have been tried and tested on my congregation over the years and include some of my most successful efforts. My synagogue, too, represents a very broad spectrum of the community, from fully observant to secular people. And, as Rabbi David Hollander *ע"ה* taught me, *לא המדרש עיקר אלא המעשה'לע*—the story or joke is all-important to the success of a speech—so there is usually a personal anecdote or something humorous to entertain as it educates. That's why the material is eminently usable for everything from a rabbi's sermon to a "vort" at your Shabbos table.

I must also issue a disclaimer. Though some of the content in this book is original, most is not. I freely confess to being a *melaket,* a collector. Over the years I have read, studied, and listened to many an idea that I later took and developed into a sermon or an essay. They come from a variety of sources. Where I have remembered the source, I have happily shared it. Many times I could not remember where I read or heard an idea and was, regretfully, unable to give credit. For this, I beg the authors' forgiveness. Having said that, it is still only the original, core idea that I may have borrowed. But those kernels of truth still needed to be expanded and expounded upon through illustrations, analogies, or anecdotes to give the idea body and substance and transform it into a full speech, sermon or essay.

I express my eternal thanksgiving to Hashem for guiding me through life, for blessing the work of my hands, and for now helping me see the publication of these humble offerings.

I continue to be forever grateful to my saintly mentor and teacher, the Lubavitcher Rebbe, of righteous memory, for his teachings, many of which will be found in these pages. In fact, when I say "The Rebbe" it refers to him, of whose waters I continue to drink. I was privileged to listen to many of the Rebbe's addresses at Farbrengens in my youth, and his writings and dozens of published works continue to be an inexhaustible source of deep wisdom and powerful, life-changing inspiration for myself as for so many around the world.

I also learned much from many teachers and senior colleagues around the world and here in South Africa who inspired me along the way. Some of the most influential were my late Rosh Yeshiva in Montreal, Rav Aizik Schwei ע״ה, my *Mashpia* Reb Itche Meir Gurary שיחי׳ Rabbi Yirmiye Aloy, Rabbi NM Bernhard, and Rabbi Dovid Hollander עליהם השלום and יבדלו לחיים Rabbi Mendel Lipskar שיחי׳, may he be well.

I thank Bernie Sharfstein of KTAV Publishing House for believing in me. His experience in the world of Jewish publishing is unparalleled. Bernie is also a nice guy and a great conversationalist whose company I have enjoyed.

Chief Rabbi Israel Meir Lau שליט״א of Israel became a beloved friend over the years from his visits to South Africa and ours to Israel. I am deeply indebted to him for so kindly gracing me with his Foreword. Thank you, too, to the prominent rabbis, national leaders, and editors who have so graciously shared their kind words of testimonial for me and my writings. I am very appreciative of your kindness.

My son, Rabbi Shmuly Goldman, helped me very much with the editing. My son, Yisroel, (or as he is known professionally, *Izzinizm*) is personally responsible for the graphic design of the beautiful cover. Rabbi Chaim Shaul Brook of New York assisted with the Hebrew verses. Rabbi Alter Eliyahu Friedman of Tzefat translated Chief Rabbi Lau's Foreword. Thank you all.

Last, but most beloved, is my family. My dear parents, Reb Shimon and Esther Goldman of Crown Heights, New York have taught me so much, mostly by example. May they be well together for long, happy lives.

My wife and woman of valor, Rochel, a dynamic activist and role model in our community in her own right, has been at my side encouraging and supporting me throughout. She gets the lion's share of the credit for raising our children. She and the children were often compromised by my commitment to my *shlichut* and life's mission. Whether in the evenings or on weekends, so much of a rabbi's communal work often comes at the expense of family life. I beg their forgiveness and pray that, in the end, the Almighty will compensate them as only He can. You all make me so proud, and I cannot thank you enough for your unconditional love and support, now and always.

With sincere prayers for an end to human suffering and the Jewish People's exile. *In Nissan were we redeemed and in Nissan are we destined to be redeemed again.*

Rabbi Yossy Goldman
Johannesburg, South Africa
Nissan 5772 / April 2012

1

Sefer Bereshit
The Book of Genesis

וַיֹּאמֶר אֱלֹקִים יְהִי אוֹר

And the L-rd said, "Let there be light." (1:3)

Let There Be Light

"And the L-rd said, 'Let there be light' and there was light."

Light has always been the most favored metaphor for all forms of revelation. The "G-dly light," "Divine light," a "new light." Do you still walk in darkness or have you "seen the light?"

Why light?

The mystics teach that light is an obvious choice to illustrate the spiritual because it is the least material of all physical entities. The ray of light that streams into your bedroom window in the morning is ever so subtle, intangible, yet it is a very real, illuminating presence.

As physical light brightens our path so we don't stumble over potholes, so the light of G-dliness, our spiritual awareness, helps us avoid the pitfalls on the journey of life.

Indeed, light is so much more than a mere bulb or fluorescent fixture. Light represents truth, values, and principles that are eternal, the spiritual which transcends the mundane, the monetary, and the momentary.

The story is told of a wealthy man who had three sons. As he was uncertain as to which son he should entrust with the management of his business, he devised a test. Thus, he hoped to soon know who was the wisest son, who would be a true man of vision. He took his three sons to a room which was absolutely empty and he said to each of them, "Fill this room as best as you are able."

The first son got to work immediately. He called in the bulldozers, the earth-moving equipment, and workmen with shovels and wheelbarrows,

1

and they got mightily busy. By the end of the day the room was filled, floor to ceiling, wall to wall, with earth.

Then the room was cleared and the second son was given his chance to fill the room as best he could. He was more of an accountant type so he had no shortage of paper. Boxes, files, archives, records, that had been standing and accumulating dust for years and years suddenly found a new purpose. (You know hoarders like that too? People who never throw anything away just in case they might find a use for it in ten years' time?) At any rate, it didn't take long, and the room was absolutely filled from floor to ceiling, wall to wall, with paper.

Again the room was cleared and the third son was given his turn. He seemed very relaxed and didn't appear to be gathering or collecting anything at all with which to fill the room. He waited until nightfall and then invited his father and the family to join him at the room. Slowly, he opened the door. The room was absolutely pitch black, engulfed in darkness. He took something out of his pocket. It was a candle. He lit the candle and suddenly the room was filled with light.

He got the job.

Some people fill their homes with earthiness, with material things—lots of physical objects and possessions that clutter their closets but leave their homes empty. Our cars and clothes, our treasures and toys, all lose their attractiveness with time. If all we seek satisfaction from is the material, we are left with a gaping void in our lives.

Others are into paper. Money, stocks, bonds, share portfolios. But there is little in the way of real relationships. Family doesn't exist or is relegated to third place at best. On paper, he might be a multi-millionaire, but is he happy? Is his life rich or poor? Is it filled with family and friends, or is it a lonely life, bereft of true joy and contentment?

The truly wise son understands how to fill a vacuum. The intelligent man knows that the emptiness of life needs light. Torah is light. Shabbos candles illuminate and make Jewish homes radiant with light. G-dly truths and the eternal values of our heritage fill our homes and families with the guiding light to help us to our destinations safely and securely.

As we begin a new Jewish year, may we all be blessed to take the candle of G-d and with it fill our lives and illuminate our homes with that which is good, kind, holy, and honorable. Amen.

છળાલ

The Psychology of Sin

If we are all descended from Adam and Eve, then it stands to reason that our characteristics—both positive and negative, fine points and foibles—can all somehow be traced back to our earliest ancestors.

If one studies the accounts of the first man's first sin in the Talmud and Midrash, one is struck by a most remarkable observation. The commandment not to eat from the Tree of Knowledge was given to Adam and Eve only after most of Friday (the sixth day, when they were created) had passed. Furthermore, the prohibition was only until that Shabbos. And it's not as if there was nothing to eat. I mean, there was a whole Garden of Eden with fruit trees galore. Could they not have started with a perfect pear, or a magnificent mango? Did they absolutely have to eat from the one and only tree that was forbidden to them?

The problem is further compounded when one considers that Adam and Eve were not just a couple of homeless hobos. They were hand-made by G-d, formed and fashioned personally by the Creator! Surely such august creatures could have waited a few hours and occupied themselves with the other fruit first. Why did it have to be *that* fruit?

We all know the answer, don't we? Forbidden fruit is always sweeter, isn't it? We play mind games. We imagine that the one forbidden fruit in a paradise island with dozens of other exotic options has simply got to be the most deliciously delectable fruit on the planet. And we just *have* to get our hands on it—and it has got to be now.

We do the same thing as Adam and Eve. But when it comes to our own choices we rationalize, whereas their sin seems ridiculous, foolish and unforgivable. The truth is that it's always the same story all over again. It has been since the beginning of time. It is simply the psychology of sin. It doesn't matter how difficult something is. It might be the easiest commandment, but once we have to do it, it becomes difficult in our minds.

Is it really so hard to be a Jew? Are our traditions so onerous? Is the Torah so demanding and burdensome? Are all those who do keep it such otherworldly saints? Of course not. It's all in the mind.

Is playing golf on Saturday so much more fun than on Sunday? Why can we walk and jog for miles all week long but to walk a mile to Shul on Shabbos is not even up for discussion? Are non-Jewish girls really more beautiful than Jewish girls? If we are honest and objective, we will recognize the truth.

The psychology of sin is that we imagine things to be more difficult than they really are, just as Adam imagined the forbidden fruit to be sweeter than all the others. He had one mitzvah of a few hours duration, and he still blew it. No doubt, it would be the same for us even if the entire Judaism were reduced to one easy commandment. We would still complain and find it too hard.

The sooner we realize it's a mind game, the sooner we will be able to win the game. Good luck.

ഔറ

It's a Brand New World

Let's talk a little philosophy. From the first verse of the Torah it seems that once upon a "time" there was nothing. Then the Creator brought the universe into existence. According to Rabbi Schneur Zalman of Liadi, seeing as the world didn't always exist, it isn't quite "natural" for it to be. Therefore, the creative force of G-d, which brought the world into existence initially, must constantly be present to fuel its continued state of being. Remove that Divine energy from the world, and it simply ceases to exist. It would be like pulling the plug on creation.

This concept is known as the law of "continuous creation." Indeed, in our daily morning prayers, we describe G-d as the One who "in His goodness renews each day the work of creation." The mystics would understand this to mean not only each day but also each moment.

I suppose we could understand this idea from the simple analogy of a baseball pitcher. When he throws a ball up in the air, his strength will determine how high the ball will fly. The stronger his arm, the higher it will fly and the longer it will defy the natural law of gravity. But as soon as the power of his pitch is spent, the ball can no longer defy nature and comes hurtling down again.

Likewise, if we want the initial or "natural" state of the world—which was non-existence—to be defied, then we need to keep fueling that same initial thrust of creative energy into the world that brought it into existence in the first place. Otherwise, the universe simply reverts to its initial state of nothingness and non-existence. Just like the ball that runs out of steam and falls back to earth.

Now let's move from the philosophical to the practical: we discover a beautiful message of hope and inspiration in this concept. We are often burdened by the past, weighed down by our personal history and experiences. Our mistakes and failures still haunt us and prevent us from moving on.

Here then is a stirring message for all who would be hampered by past disappointments. It's a brand new world. Every day, every minute, every second G-d is recreating the world anew. Forget about the past. "What was, was." Today is a new world, a new present filled with exciting new opportunities. At any given moment we can begin again.

Especially in the week of B'rieshit, where we read the Torah from the very beginning, it is a most opportune time for each of us to make a fresh start and a new beginning. New beginnings aren't always easy. But this idea of "continuous creation" offers powerful inspiration to give ourselves a new chance filled with new opportunities. As we start a new Jewish year, let us embrace this promise and be encouraged to begin again.

ℰℭℛ

Noah

My Kind of Hero

The world loves a hero. Every season, Hollywood has to invent new heroes and superheroes to fill the box office coffers. And it works. Why? Well, that's for another sermon. Today, I choose to talk about who is a hero and, more specifically, who is my kind of hero. Superheroes are fantastic. But you've got to admit, they're over the top, rather otherworldly, and, realistically speaking, out of touch and out of reach. We can fantasize about flying through the skies in our capes, climbing skyscrapers with our webs, or rescuing damsels in distress, but at the end of the day, it is nothing more than wistful daydreaming. What bearing does it have on me and my life, me and my problems? The answer is, not much.

That's why Noah always appealed to me. He comes across as a real live hero, real in the sense of being human rather than superhuman and, therefore, realistically possible to emulate. Rashi describes Noah as a man of small faith who had doubts whether the flood would actually happen. In fact, according to the great commentator's understanding, he didn't enter the ark until the rains actually started and the floodwaters pushed him in. That explains why many people look down on Noah, especially when they compare him to other Biblical superheroes, people of the stature of Abraham or Moses.

Personally, this is precisely what makes Noah my kind of hero. He's real. He's human. He has doubts, just like you and me. I know we are supposed to say, "When will my actions match those of the great patriarchs of old?" but I confess for me that is a very tall order. Noah, on the other hand, is a regular guy. He is plagued by doubts and struggles with his faith, which is precisely what makes him a hero. Because the fact is that, at the end of the day, his personal uncertainties notwithstanding, Noah does the job. He builds the ark, *shleps* in all the animals, saves civilization, and goes on to rebuild a shattered world. Doubts, shmouts— he did what had to be done.

There is an old Yiddish proverb that *fun a kasha shtarbt men nit.* Nobody died from a question. It's not the end of the world if you didn't get an answer to all your questions. We can live with unanswered questions. The main thing is not to allow ourselves to become paralyzed by our doubts. We can still do what has to be done, despite our doubts. Of course, I'd love to be able to answer every question every single one of my congregants ever has. But the chances are that I will not be able to solve every single person's doubts or dilemmas. And, frankly speaking, I am less concerned about their doubts than about their deeds. From a question nobody ever died. It's how we behave that matters most.

Noah, the ordinary hero, could easily be the guy next door. He is one of us. His greatness is, therefore, achievable. It's not "pie in the sky." His heroism can be emulated. If Abraham and Moses seem the superhero types, too far-fetched for us ordinary mortals to see as practical role models, then Noah resonates with realism. After all, he had his doubts too, just like you and me. So Noah, the reluctant hero, reminds us that you don't have to be fearless to get involved. You don't have to be a *tzaddik* to do a *mitzvah*. You don't have to be holy to keep kosher, nor do you have to be a professor to come to a *shiur*. His faith may have been shaky. Perhaps he was a bit wobbly in the knees. But the bottom line is, he got the job done. My hero.

৪১৩

The Survivor

Everybody makes jokes about Noah and his ark. Bill Cosby has a whole routine on the subject, which I must confess is uncannily faithful to our commentaries' understanding. Then there's the one about Noah being the first stock market manipulator in history—he floated a company while the whole world was in liquidation!

The Lubavitcher Rebbe saw Noah in a far more serious light. Noah was a survivor. Noah was saved from the deluge of destruction that engulfed his world, and his greatest contribution is that he set out to rebuild that world. We don't read about him sitting down and crying or wringing his hands in despair, although I'm sure he had his moments.

The critical thing the Bible records is that after Noah emerged from his floating bunker, he began the task of rebuilding a shattered world from scratch. He got busy and picked up the pieces and, slowly but surely, society was regenerated.

Only one generation ago a great flood swept over our world. The Nazi plan was for a Final Solution. Every Jew on earth was earmarked for destruction, and the Nazis were already planning their Museum of the Extinct Jewish Race. Not one Jew was meant to survive. So even those of us born after the war are also survivors. Even a Jewish child born this morning is a survivor—because according to Hitler's plan, which tragically, nearly succeeded, he or she was not meant to live. This means that each of us, like Noah, has a moral duty to rebuild the Jewish world.

When I was growing up in Brooklyn I *daavened* in a small *shul* in Crown Heights where every other man at the morning *minyan* bore a holy number on his arm. They were concentration camp inmates, and the Germans tattooed those numbers onto their arms. Sadly, today, the ranks of those individuals have been greatly diminished. Every time one of them would roll up his shirt sleeve to put on *Tefillin*, the number was revealed. It seemed to me as if to them it was nothing special. But to me they were heroes. Not only for surviving the hells of Auschwitz or Dachau but for keeping their faith intact, for still coming to *shul*, praying to G-d, wearing His *Tefillin*.

Today as I am older and more sensitive to the feelings of fathers and children, of family and friends, those men have gone up much more in my estimation. They have become superheroes. After all they went through, to be able to live normal lives again, to marry or remarry, to bring children into this world, to carry on life, businesses, relationships, are mind-boggling achievements. My own father was not in the camps, but he is the only survivor of his entire family from Poland. Some years ago, he recorded his story, and recently it was published in book form—*From Shedlitz to Safety—A Young Jew's Journey of Survival*. We, his children, never knew half of what he went through. When I imagine him sitting as a teenage refugee in Shanghai, China and discovering that his entire family was wiped out and that he was left all alone in the world, I go numb. How did he continue? How did he stay sane? How did he keep his faith?

Thank G-d he did and started a family all over again; otherwise, I wouldn't be here to write these lines. My own father has become a super-hero to me. Says the *Rebbe*, we all have that same responsibility—because we are all survivors. Who will bring Jewish children into the world if not you? Who will study Torah if not you? Who will keep *Shabbos*? Who will keep the Jewish school afloat? Who will rebuild the Jewish world if not you and I and each and every one of us?

In the smaller country communities of South Africa, where I make my home, there are still small bands of dedicated Jews, who come together in someone's home to make a *minyan*, or who serve as an ad hoc *chevra kadisha* to bury the Jewish dead according to our tradition. These are not rabbis, *chazonim*, or *cheder* teachers. They are ordinary people. In the big city they would probably not be anywhere that involved, but in their small town they know that if they don't do it, nobody will.

We need that same conviction wherever we are. Thank G-d for His mercies in that our world is, to a large degree, being rebuilt. Miraculously, the great centers of Jewish learning are flourishing today once more, but far too many of our brothers and sisters are still outside the circle. Every one of us needs to participate. We are all Noahs. Let us rebuild our world.

₿€

נח איש צדיק ... בדורותיו
Noah was a righteous man...in his generation. (6:9)

The Problem with Preaching

Do sermons really work? Can the words of any one individual really have an effect on the way people live their lives? Is anyone out there actually listening? (Reading?) Rabbis are probably unrealistic when they anticipate dramatic results from their sermons. But it's not as bad as the cynics would have us believe, either. The late Rabbi Sydney Katz of Pretoria once compared the chances of a sermon succeeding to the odds of a man standing on top of the Empire State Building and throwing down an aspirin that would be caught by a man on the street below who just happened to have a headache at the time! But we still try.

The Prophet Isaiah called the great flood of this week's parsha, "Waters of Noah." According to commentary, this is because Noah bore a degree of responsibility for the devastating deluge. But why was it his fault? Wasn't he the righteous man of his time? Apparently, because Noah may not have tried hard enough to turn around the corrupt lifestyle of his generation, the waters are named after him. Yes, he built his ark, but did he reach out to those who never saw his ark? Did he shout out to his contemporaries that Doomsday was really coming?

Ever since Noah, this is the mission of anyone charged with the task of being a spiritual leader. What is a rabbi? An "official" to preside over our rites of passage? Sure, that is a very important part of the job, but is that all it is? A functionary? The essence of a rabbi is to be a teacher, a guide for life, a moral barometer, and the conscience of the community. The word *rabbi*—or in Hebrew, *Rabi*—means "my teacher," to teach Torah and to teach right from wrong based on the G-dly value system enshrined in the Torah. So occasionally it becomes necessary for rabbi to play preacher and point out the error of a community's ways. No, it's not the most popular thing a rabbi can do but to quote late Chief Rabbi L. I. Rabinowitz, "I am not prepared to sacrifice my principles on the altar of popularity." That's why the Talmud states, "When you see a rabbi who is beloved by the entire community it is not because he is so good but rather because he does not rebuke them in matters of faith" (Ketubot 105). Speaking for myself, I am not a loner. I'm not anti-social. I like people and would love to be loved by everyone without exception. But there are times when one cannot shirk the moral responsibility to say what is right—and, sometimes, what is wrong.

This brings us back to Noah. Commentary is divided on the extent of Noah's righteousness. Yes, the Bible calls him a *Tzaddik*, a righteous man. But the title is qualified when it adds the word "in his generations." Was he objectively righteous or only in comparison to his evil generation? How would he have rated when compared to a really saintly man like Abraham? As always, both these perspectives are Torah and therefore true. The full picture can only be ascertained when we look at a thing with both eyes. Are we products of our environment? Is it impossible to resist societal pressures? If so, then any good we manage to do is an incredible achievement and deserving of praise. Or do we have the power to triumph over any and every obstacle in our paths? Look at Abraham, who came from a pagan family, discovered G-d, and changed the world. Judged by that standard, anything less than greatness is a failure. Which perspective will it be?

I am not unmindful of the wonderful growth in Jewish communities around the world and, indeed, in my own congregation. Who knows better than me of the inspiring new commitments made by so many, especially over *Yom Tov*. Hundreds of good resolutions for *Mitzvahs—Shul* attendance, *Tefillin, Mezuzahs, Shabbos, Kashrus*, Torah study, *Tzedakah, Chesed-Kindness* and more. In a world gone mad, we are doing fantastic. But from time to time we need to look from the other perspective as well. How are we doing compared to Abraham? Compared to what we could be?

The philosopher Herman Cohen was once asked why his lectures were so deep and over the heads of most of his audience. He answered, "I aim where their heads should be." Well, I aim where your hearts should be, where your souls should be. I fully appreciate where my people are at, but I refuse to lose sight of where they should be going. That is my purpose, my sacred responsibility, and my dream. I dream about the Neshama, the G-dly soul within each of you. You say, "Rabbi, we are ordinary guys." I say no Jew is ordinary.

Every Jew is special. I know what you are doing, and I am proud of you for it. But I also know what you are capable of, so don't sell yourself short. Please, don't shatter the dream. If we stop dreaming, we stop hoping, and we stop living. Every Jew is wonderful. Every Jew is a good Jew. But for me the definition of a good Jew has always been "one who is trying to be a better Jew." As good as we may be, let us try to be better still.

ഇരു

Lech Lecha

לֶךְ לְךָ מֵאַרְצְךָ
Go from your land. (12:1)

Leaving Home — for Good

The story is told of an encounter between two famous rabbis of yester-year—the Vilna Gaon and the Dubner Magid. Apparently, the Magid, or Preacher of Dubna, once visited Vilna and went to pay a courtesy call on the great Sage, Rabbi Elijah of Vilna. The Gaon asked the Dubner Magid to preach to him, as was his specialty. "Give me *mussar* (words of rebuke). Chastise me," said the Gaon. "G-d forbid that I should have the chutzpah to chastise the great Gaon of Vilna," replied the Magid, quite horrified at the suggestion. "No matter, that is your forte, and I want to hear *mussar* from you," insisted the Gaon. So the Dubner Magid thought a while and then, most reluctantly, acceded to the wishes of his illustrious host. Said the Magid (with a fair degree of trepidation, I imagine), "Is it a great achievement to be a Gaon sitting in Vilna in your little secluded *kloiz* (small study)? Why don't you go out into the world, mix with the people, and *then* let us see what kind of Gaon you will be."

Indeed, it is much easier to be scholarly and pious in our sequestered ghettoes than it is in the outside world, so often oblivious—or even hostile—to Torah and its values. This, in fact, was more or less the test of Abraham in this week's parsha. "Go from your land, from your birthplace, from your father's house to the land I will show you." And it was there—far from his natural environment and immediate comfort zones—that Abraham accomplished G-d's mission of monotheism. He spread the name of the One G-d to a pagan world and, in the process, his own name and reputation was established for eternity. It was only after leaving home that Abraham became the Founding Father of the Jewish People.

A hundred years ago, a generation of Yiddish-speaking, observant Jews migrated from Europe. They came to America, the golden land of opportunity, to escape pogroms and persecution. With blood, sweat, and tears they transformed themselves from rags to riches and soon came to personify the American dream, an amazing and inspirational success story. But the fact is that for the most part, as their businesses succeeded their religious lives failed. Unquestionably, Judaism took a severe body blow. Most were unable to sustain their old-world values in new world America. The transition from *shtetl* to suburbia proved too formidable, and children and grandchildren grew up blissfully unaware of their own sacred traditions. And the same story repeated itself in England, Australia, South Africa, and wherever we wandered.

Today, we see this phenomenon playing out on a lesser scale when families emigrate or move from city to city. Displaced from their spiritual support systems, they flounder. The bulk of their efforts are directed at just resettling and reorganizing their lives. Putting religious infrastructures in place often comes last—at great cost in the long run. And on a more subtle level, the very same tests of conscience face us when we take our annual vacations. Away from home and our ingrained norms of behavior, we are challenged to maintain the code of conduct we are committed to all year long. It's like the story of the *shadchan*, the old fashioned matchmaker, who suggested a young lady to a fellow and absolutely raved about her. After their first date, the fellow calls up the *shadchan* and gives him a piece of his mind. "How dare you introduce me to such a girl! Didn't you know she limps?!" Quite unflustered, the *shadchan* retorts, "But what's the problem? It's only when she walks!"

It is when we walk away from our comfortable cocoons and spiritual safety nets into the wider society that we may find ourselves limping somewhat, losing our Jewish equilibrium. It is then that our faith, our values, our morals and beliefs are truly challenged. Please G-d, the children of Abraham will emulate their forefather who left his land and remained strong in faith and family, going on to achieve remarkable success, both spiritually and materially.

ෂාඥ

תן לי הנפש והרכוש קח לך
Give me the people, and take
the possessions for yourself. (14:21)

Give Me the Soul!

The weekly parsha is enlivened these days with the arrival of Abraham on the Biblical scene. Our founding father brings new life to the world as he spreads the message of monotheism in a hitherto pagan society. He also shows his prowess as a fearless fighter for justice and puts his own life on the line to save his nephew, Lot, when he was taken captive in the world war of the day. It was after rescuing his nephew that the King of Sodom thanks Abraham for liberating his prisoners of war at the same time. He offers Abraham the spoils of war and asks only to have his men back. *Ten li hanefesh,* he says: *Give me the people, and take the possessions for yourself.*

Back in 1980, I heard a powerful and passionate call by my saintly mentor, the *Rebbe* of blessed memory. It was Simchas Torah, the *Yom Tov* when we celebrate the gift of Torah in a spirit of boundless joy. He had appealed for *Tzedokah* to be given in the same heightened spirit, that is, beyond normal limitations or the usual budgetary considerations. Later, he explained his call to have been one of *Ten li hanefesh,* which, literally, means *give me the soul.* It was a special moment, and what he was demanding of his followers was a genuine outpouring of soul, a sincere act of pure faith, beyond reason or issues of affordability. The *Rebbe* had called for a total, unconditional commitment.

The call of *Ten li hanefesh—Give me the soul* still reverberates. And it applies to everything we do. We are all composites of body and soul. But more often than not, our physical selves get all the attention while our spiritual side is neglected. How many times do we hear Jews, especially young Jews, complaining that Judaism lacks spirituality; that their synagogues and temples are devoid of any real feeling or atmosphere of sanctity? And then we bemoan them trekking off to the Himalayas to find purpose, depth, and all the spirituality we never gave them. How many *Bar Mitzvahs* and weddings have been reduced to empty shells of materialistic one-upmanship with friends and neighbors compelled to outdo each other in garish extravaganzas that miss the whole point of what the celebration is about? And G-d calls out *give me the soul.* Give me back what is mine. Put some spirit back into Judaism. Enough with the Mickey Mouse routines and rituals, the song and dance gimmicks. Get beyond the external and the plastic. Give me some soul!

When our faith is superficial, we look as foolish as the pathetic thief described in the Talmud (Berachot 63b). *Ganva apum machtarta Rachmono karye—*the thief, at the mouth of the tunnel, calls out to G-d. Here is a *goniff,* a lowly criminal, about to enter the tunnel he has dug to rob a bank, but before he goes in, he prays to G-d for success. What a *chutzpa*! He is about to violate G-d's express command not to steal and has the audacity to still ask G-d to help him do the job?! But such is the effect of superficiality. He has faith, our Talmudic thief. It just hasn't penetrated. Because this shallow pseudo-religiosity hasn't permeated his inner being, he is blissfully unaware of the hypocrisy of his actions. So he sees no incompatibility between stealing and praying at the same time.

The truth is that we all believe, even the thieves among us. The challenge is for the penny to drop; for that faith to reach into our core, to touch our souls. Let us heed the call, *ten li hanefesh—*give me the soul. Let us move beyond superficial Judaism to something deeper, profound and real which will touch our own souls and inspire our children.

ഇരുണ

Airport Story

Every rabbi has an airport story. In fact, some rabbis tell so many incredible stories of providential encounters on airplanes and in airports that I sometimes wonder if it is physically possible for them to have traveled on as many airplanes as they have stories! Why am I going on about airplanes? Because this is the week of *Lech Lecha*, when our father Abraham was instructed by G-d to leave his birthplace and journey to a foreign land that would, one day, be promised to his children. Ever since then, the Jews have been a nation of wanderers. Our ancestors' travels shaped our future destiny. Their journeys became our journeys. And the geographical upheavals the Jewish People have been subjected to over the centuries are mirror images of the footsteps of our forebears.

Anyway, here is an airplane story of my own. Some years back, I was traveling from Johannesburg to Cape Town to join then-President Nelson Mandela at a Banquet honoring South Africa's late Chief Rabbi C. K. Harris and also to deliver a few lectures there at various synagogues. They say "getting there is half the fun," but on this occasion nothing could have been further from the truth. First there was a system malfunction on the aircraft and with it a 30-minute delay. Then there was a missing passenger who delayed takeoff for a further three hours until he was discovered in the airport pub somewhat uncertain of where exactly he was going. Eventually, we landed after 10 PM, and I missed the synagogue lecture that I was scheduled to give at 8 PM earlier that evening.

And why might you be interested in my story? Because I found it fascinating to watch the reactions of the different passengers on the plane while we were waiting impatiently to take off. Some people got very angry. They were screaming and shouting and giving the poor flight attendants a very hard time. Others simply sulked in silence. I couldn't help thinking what a lesson this was on the subject of Divine Providence and who really runs the world. I had given myself ample time to get to my 8 PM lecture punctually. But clearly, G-d had other plans.

So who is actually in control? The best laid plans of mice and men don't necessarily get us to our destinations on time—even if we get to the airport early. I could have become angry myself. Actually, I was very upset. It was quite a disappointment to have missed my lecture. Such a thing had never happened to me before. But my conscience was clear. I had left more than enough time to make it. The fact that I did not was not in my hands. I mean, who runs the world? The answer is, the One Above. If, for some reason known only to Him, He wants me not to give the 8 o'clock lecture, then no amount of huffing and puffing on my part will make one bit of difference.

While pondering on this philosophical perspective, I found myself becoming more relaxed and actually quite serene about the whole frustrating experience. Yes, we must do our share; we must give it our best shot. But beyond that, it's G-d's department. If we can develop this attitude—and, believe me, I also need to develop it further—we will all be better able to cope with the disappointments we so often face in life, and even with real *tzorres* we may sadly encounter. It's all in His hands. If he decided the plane would be delayed, then there must be a good reason.

So there really isn't any major drama in my airplane story. Did I bump into a Jewish passenger and change his life forever? Sorry to disappoint you, but I did not. What I did experience was a personal confirmation of something that I had, of course, always believed theologically. From my little episode on the airplane a basic premise of Jewish belief was rein-forced in my own mind and heart. So even if nothing amazing occurred, I became far more aware that G-d, and not I, is the controller of this uni-verse. I may still have no idea why this delay was part of His vast eternal plan, but I do know that there was a reason. I may never discover what that reason was, but that there was a reason I am convinced.

When we understand this, we will have learned the art of acceptance. When we learn acceptance, we lead calmer, more tranquil lives, without all the unnecessary anxiety we create in our own minds. And I must ad-mit, it is a conviction that has helped me through many disappointments in my own life, from the small stuff to the more serious. I think the famous Serenity Prayer is quite in keeping with Jewish tradition: "G-d, grant me the serenity to accept the things I cannot change, the courage to change the things I can, and the wisdom to know the difference." May all your journeys be safe and successful, and may you get to your destinations on time. And even if you don't, don't sweat. He is in charge.

ഇൗൽ

Vayera

ואברהם שב למקומו
And Abraham went back to his place. (18:33)

A Jew's Gotta Do What a Jew's Gotta Do

Is it a sin to argue with G-d? Is it sacrilegious to question the Divine? Well, Abraham did it. Not for himself, but on behalf of the people of Sodom, whom G-d had decided to destroy because of their wickedness. Abraham was the paragon of *chesed,* the personification of kindness and compassion. He grappled with the Almighty, attempting to negotiate a stay of execution for the inhabitants of the notorious cities of Sodom and Gomorrah.

"Will you destroy the righteous with the wicked?" he asks G-d. "Will the judge of all the earth not do justice?" "If there are 50 righteous men, will you spare them? 45 ... 40 ... 30 ... 20 ... 10?" In the end, Abraham cannot find even a *minyan* of righteous men in the cities and he gives up. And the verse reads *V'Avraham shov l'mkomo—and Abraham went back to his place.* Having failed in his valiant attempt at salvation, he acknowledges defeat and retreats to his corner.

But there is also an alternative interpretation to those last words. *And Abraham went back to his place* can also be understood to mean that he went back to his ways, to his custom. And what custom is that? To defend the underdog, to look out for the needy and to help those in trouble, even if they are not the most righteous of people. Abraham refused to become disillusioned in defeat. He went right back to his ways, even though this particular attempt did not meet with success. He may have lost this particular battle, but he was still in the war.

What happens when we lose? We hurt, we sulk, and we give up. It didn't work, it's no use. All my efforts were in vain. It's futile, why bother? Just throw in the towel.

Not Abraham. Abraham stuck to his principles. He may have experienced a setback, but he would still champion the cause of justice. He would still speak out for those in danger. And he would still take his case to the highest authority in the universe, G-d Almighty Himself.

Abraham teaches us not to lose faith, not to deviate from our chosen path or our sincerely held convictions. If we believe it is the right thing to do, then it is right, even if there is no reward in sight. If it is right, then stick to it, no matter the outcome.

One of my favorite cartoon characters is good old Charlie Brown in *Peanuts.* And one strip that sticks in my memory is where there is a storm raging outside and Charlie Brown is determined to go out to fly his kite. His friends tell him he must be crazy to attempt flying a kite in this weather, it'll be destroyed by the wind in no time. But in the last frame we see Charlie, resolutely marching out the door, his kite firmly tucked under his arm, and the caption reads, "A man's gotta do what a man's gotta do."

Do we believe in our principles of faith because of expediency? Are we virtuous because we believe it is the way to the good life? Are we looking for "brownie points," are we waiting for the big payoff for our good behavior? What happens when we don't see it? Do we become frustrated, disillusioned, and angry at G-d?

Some people become religious for the wrong reasons. They are looking for some magical solution to their problems in life. And when the problems don't disappear as quickly or as miraculously as they expected, they give up their religious lifestyle. It didn't work. *I'm outta here.*

Virtue is its own reward. Sleeping better at night because our conscience is clear is also part of the deal. Or, in the words of the Sages, "The reward for a mitzvah is the mitzvah itself."

Our founding father reminds us that *a Jew's gotta do what a Jew's gotta do,* regardless of the outcome. Whether we see the fruits of our labors or not, if it's the right thing to do, then carry on doing it.

May we all be true children of Abraham.

℠)℣

ותשלך את הילד תחת אחד השיחים

And she cast off the boy beneath one of the bushes. (21:15)

The Boy or the Bottle?

How we spend our money is usually a pretty good barometer of where our priorities lie. And it applies equally whether it is plentiful or scarce.

After the birth of Isaac, his half brother Ishmael behaves threateningly towards him and Sarah finds it necessary to ask Abraham to banish Ishmael from the family home. Together with his mother, Hagar, they wander in the desert. Soon they run out of water.

And the water in the leather flask was finished and she cast off the boy beneath one of the bushes (Genesis 21, 15). So let me ask you what would be called a typical *klotz kasha,* or a seemingly obvious but, nonetheless, stupid question. If the flask is empty, why throw away the child? Throw away the empty flask!

It would appear, then, that when our food supply is depleted and finance is in short supply, the first ones to suffer may be our children. The bank balance is low? How can we even think of a Jewish Day School education? The tuition fees are so expensive. Instead of denying ourselves creature comforts we deem non-negotiable, we sacrifice our children's Jewish upbringing in the name of economics.

It's like the old story of the Jewish mother who came from Eastern Europe to join her son in America and was horrified to see he had shaved of his beard and cast off his *yarmulke.* "What happened to you, my Yankele?" she asked. "Mama, America is not the *shtetl.*" And when she saw him going to work on Shabbos, again he told her America was different. And when she opened the fridge and discovered all kinds of creepy things she never saw in a Jewish kitchen, again he explained that America was not the same as "back home." Eventually, when it was all getting too much, she asked him, "Yankele, tell your old mother the truth. Are you still circumcised?"

It's not only an old *shtetl* story. It's happening right now. We know of too many who left the community they were raised in to make a better life for their children. But emigrating is expensive, and with limited resources one must make choices and prioritize. Many chose to do without Jewish schooling. The rest is history. Bad history. Without a Jewish education young people wander about wondering why they should not be doing what their contemporaries are doing. And the money we saved in school fees is now going to doctors, psychologists, or G-d forbid, drug rehab centers.

Even in Israel, we have to be discriminating when choosing a community. If the other kids on the block are riding their bikes on Yom Kippur, why shouldn't your child? And if you insist and they feel denied, they may opt out altogether.

Kids need stability and an environment with a healthy value system. No matter how tempting or secure other seemingly greener pastures may be, before making a move we ought to consider the spiritual security system our children will need to survive and thrive—as Jews.

Just because the bottle may be empty, don't throw away the child.

Ⅴ⅘

The Acid Test

Last week Abraham received his marching orders from G-d. "Lecha lecha—go from your land, your birthplace, your father's house to the land I will show you." Hashem told him to leave all his familiar comfort zones and travel to a yet-unknown destination. Eventually, it would become known as Israel, and Abraham was the original one it was promised to. At the time, though, Abraham probably had no idea as to where exactly he was going. But orders are orders, and so he went faithfully.

In the end, Abraham's great trek would be the fulfillment of his calling as the father of monotheism. He would take on the whole pagan world of the time and succeed beyond his own wildest dreams. By the way, I think we take our Biblical giants too much for granted. We fail to appreciate the enormity of Abraham's contribution to civilization. What he did was nothing less than single-handedly change the mindset of the world! Believing in one, invisible Creator was culture shock to the idol-worshippers of the day. This achievement made Abraham not only the founding father of the Jewish People but also the father of all the monotheistic faiths of the world. No wonder a statistical study of history's "100 Most Influential People" ranked Abraham way on top, far above other faith founders and even way ahead of all the celebrities and pop icons of the day.

According to Maimonides, this journey to the unknown was the first of ten tests of faith the Almighty would impose upon Abraham. Yet, the final test, which we read about on Rosh Hashana and again in this week's parsha, is considered the supreme test. The Akeda, the binding of Isaac, the near sacrifice of the son he waited a century to have, generates far more coverage in Torah, in our prayers, and in the writings of commentary.

Why should this be the case? The first test of Lech Lecha had a universal impact while the binding of Isaac was just between a father, his son and G-d. Somewhere on a secluded mountaintop, far removed from public scrutiny, a personal drama was played out. The journey of Lech Lecha, however, had an almost global audience. Is it not strange that this universal test should not be considered much more important than the personal test of father and son?

May I suggest that a possible answer might be that before we can undertake a universal mission to humankind, we must first understand our personal mission to G-d. Or, to put it simply, before you can change the world, you have to know who *you* are. If you don't know yourself, if you don't recognize your own personal spiritual mission, how can you hope to influence the broader society?

The rabbis taught, "Perfect yourself before you seek to perfect others." Obviously, this is not to say that we should not try and teach others until we are perfect ourselves (so who is perfect?). What it does suggest is that if we hope to have an impact on others, our call must resonate as authentic and genuine. How can we make an impression on others if we are not credible individuals ourselves? A good salesperson really believes in his product. (Even if he may have talked himself into believing it, sincerity sells.)

The legendary Hillel in Pirkei Avot tells us, "Do not judge your fellow until you have reached his position," and an interesting alternative interpretation understands him to mean that in order to judge any person accurately, one should first establish what kind of reputation that individual enjoys in his own *makom,* in his own city and home. Is there not some truth in Jackie Mason's jesting about the Jewish husband who is a big mover and shaker all over town, but as soon as he walks through the door of his own house becomes a henpecked *shlemiel?*!

Years ago I came across a one-liner that had a profound impact on me personally. "Every rabbi has only one sermon—the way he lives his life." It's all too true. We can preach from today until next Yom Kippur, but if we don't "walk the talk" and live the game we purport to play, we will leave our audiences unmoved. The most eloquent orators will fail to make an impression if their listeners know that their message is hollow and isn't backed up by genuine personal commitment.

So while the story of Abraham's journey and universal mission appears in the Torah and comes chronologically before the final test, in essence, the *Akedah* reigns supreme—not only because it was the most difficult, but because our personal commitment and integrity always form the moral basis for our mission to the world. At the end of the day, only these validate the man and his message. And that is the acid test for all of us.

೫೦೧

Chaye Sarah

ויביאה יצחק האהלה שרה אמו
And Isaac brought her to the tent of Sarah his mother. (24:67)

"G-d Helps Those Who Help Themselves"

Is this statement heresy? Does it deny the hand of G-d in our successes? I recall a conversation with a self-proclaimed atheist who used the expression very cynically, suggesting that his considerable achievements were entirely his own and that G-d had nothing to do with it.

I beg to differ. To my mind, "G-d helps those who help themselves" is a perfectly religious statement. What it means is absolutely consistent with traditional Jewish thinking. G-d does indeed help us to accomplish things, but He requires us to help ourselves first. If we just sit back and wait for miracles to happen, we may be disappointed.

And Hashem your G-d will bless you in all that you do (Deuteronomy 15, 18) makes it very clear. Our blessings come from Hashem, but we must do something about it, too. He helps, but we must *do*. Of course, we believe in miracles—but we mustn't rely on them. The combination of our own hard work and efforts coupled with Hashem's blessing is the ideal road to success.

The classic case is the farmer. He can plough and plant, sow and *shvitz* from today until tomorrow, but if the rains don't come, nothing will grow. Conversely, all the rains in the world will not cause anything to grow if we haven't planted first. After the farmer has done his work and the rains come from above, there will be a plentiful crop. And it is the same story whether we are farmers or shopkeepers, professionals or artisans, employers or employees.

There are religious ideologies that frown upon medical intervention when someone is ill. They see it as a lack of faith in the great Healer of all flesh. In fact, in my own community, there was once a court case because a hospital gave a blood transfusion to a child who was critically ill, but it was against the wishes of the parents, who objected on the grounds of their religious beliefs. Judaism, however, maintains that while Hashem is indeed the Great Healer, He chooses to work through the efforts of trustworthy medical practitioners.

This week's Parsha tells of Isaac taking Rebecca as his wife. *And Isaac brought her to the tent of Sarah his mother.* Rashi, quoting the Midrash, explains this to mean more than the obvious. When she entered the tent, it was as if she was Sarah, Isaac's mother. Because Sarah was of such saintly character, she was granted three special miracles. Her Shabbos candles burned the entire week, her dough was particularly blessed, and a heavenly cloud attached to her tent. When Sarah died, these blessings disappeared. When Rebecca arrived on the scene, they resumed immediately. In fact, this was a clear sign to Isaac that Rebecca was indeed his soul mate and that the *shidduch* was *bashert*.

Each of those three miracles, however, required some form of human input first. A candle and fire had to be found, the dough had to be prepared and a tent had to be pitched before G-d would intervene and make those miracles happen. In other words, He does help us, but we must help ourselves first.

It's a little like the fellow who would make a fervent prayer to G-d every week that he win the lottery. After many months and no jackpot in sight, he lost his faith and patience. In anguished disappointment, he vented his frustration with the Almighty. "Oh, G-d! For months I've been praying to you. Why haven't you helped me win the lottery all this time?" Whereupon a heavenly voice was heard saying, "Because you haven't bought a ticket, dummy!"

I wish it were that simple to win lotteries. But the fact is that it is the same in all our endeavors. G-d helps those who help themselves. May we all do our part. Please G-d, He will do His.

છ૭૧૩

ותהי לו לאשה ויאהבה
She became his wife and he loved her. (24:67)

Love at Second Sight

Why are so many marriages failures? And why do so many fail so soon after the wedding?

This week we read about the first *shidduch* in history. Abraham sends his trusted servant, Eliezer, to find a wife for his son Isaac. He returns with Rebeccah, and they live happily ever after. The verse tells us, "And (Isaac) took Rebeccah, she became his wife, and he loved her." So, it would appear that in the Biblical scenario, true love comes after marriage, not before. Before a marriage can take place, there has to be a commonality between two people, shared values, mutual aspirations and, yes, certainly a degree of chemistry between them. But true love has to be nurtured over time.

Without doubt, a primary cause of many marital breakdowns today is the unrealistic expectations that people have going into marriage. Our generation has been fed a constant diet of romantic novels, hit parade love songs, glossy magazine advice, and Hollywood fiction—all of which bear little resemblance to the real world.

"We fell in love!" "It was love at first sight." I confess to being a bit of a romantic myself, but surely "love at first sight" has got to be a contradiction in terms. "Love," by definition, takes years to develop. If you are honest with yourself, the only thing you can feel at first sight is lust. "Love at first sight" is a monumental *bobba meise!*

So we "fall in love" thinking it's real, hoping it will be true and lasting, and then at the slightest disappointment we fall right out of love. Which only proves that it wasn't true love in the first place. True love takes years. True love is the mature conviction that our lives are intertwined and inseparable no matter what—even if my partner goes gray or flabby or loses his money. That kind of love is measured not in romantics but in long-term commitment.

When I officiate at a Chupah ceremony, I make a point of observing not only the bride and groom, but also their parents. A single glance that passes between father and mother under that chupah—radiating *nachas* and feelings of shared satisfaction—tells me that they have had a good marriage. That, to me, is more telling then the mushy swooning of the newlyweds. As exciting as it is, their love may still be in the infatuation stage. Yet untested, it's still early days.

So the first rule is patience. Love takes time. It needs nurturing. Sadly, too many give up too soon.

Second, the Hollywood effect leaves us so naively impressionable that our partners have got to be the proverbial Prince Charming or Princess Grace. But then, at the first sign of imperfection, "Hey, I bought a lemon! I'm outta here!" Remember, nobody is perfect. Not even you, my dear. In the passage of time we do indeed discover the little imperfections of our chosen partners. Some things can be unlearned, with gentle encouragement and, again, patience. Others, we may just have to learn to live with. Acceptance is an art. Weigh up in your mind the relative significance of minor inadequacies against the greater good in the grand scheme of things. You may very well realize that you can actually live with those small, petty irritants. Admittedly, if it's something major, then you may need to go for some serious counseling.

And in making these calculations consider the following: Do I stop loving myself just because I am imperfect? Do I stop loving my children because the teacher told me they were really bad at school? Of course not. Why then do I have difficulty loving my spouse because of a perceived fault?

Marriage is the beginning, not the end. If we can be realistic about our relationships, we can find true love. But it takes time, patience, and the wisdom to overlook the little things that can annoy us. Then, please G-d, with true commitment will come true love, togetherness, a lifetime of sharing and caring and the greatest, most enduring contentment in our personal lives. Amen.

ℰ⃝

Yiddishe Nachas

Once upon a time, a pious Jew was traveling through the countryside in Eastern Europe. He came to a *shtetl* where the local *schochet* (ritual slaughterer) had just taken ill. The town butcher had no one to do the slaughtering and was desperate when he bumped into the visitor. The traveler looked pious and G-d fearing (perhaps he wore a black hat and had a beard) so the butcher asked him if he was, by any chance, a qualified *schochet*. The visitor replied that he was indeed. Overjoyed, the butcher started arranging for the man to begin work in the slaughterhouse immediately. Then the visitor asked the butcher if he would kindly lend him some money as he had just arrived and needed to purchase a few things. "But you're a complete stranger," said the butcher. "I don't know you at all, how can I possibly lend you money?" Whereupon the visitor replied, "You were prepared to trust me with your *kashruth* even though you never laid eyes on me, but as soon as I asked you for a few rubles suddenly you hardly know me?"

This week's Parsha tells the story of the very first *shidduch* in history. Abraham sends his faithful servant, Eliezer, to find a bride for his son Isaac. He hands Eliezer a document ceding his entire wealth to Isaac and makes him take a solemn oath that he will not bring back a Canaanite woman for his son but someone from Abraham's own family, from Mesopotamia.

Amazing Abraham! He writes over his entire fortune to his son to help him find the right *shidduch.* Is there even a mention that Abraham demanded some security from Eliezer for the wealth that he was entrusted with? On what did Abraham ask Eliezer to take an oath? Not on the wealth, but on the woman! There is not a word about Abraham insisting on any guarantees, promises, or even a handshake when it came to the money. However, when it came to the nature of the woman, the character of the person his son would be marrying, Abraham demanded nothing less than a solemn oath.

What an incredible lesson for our own priority system in life. What is most important to us? What do we truly value? When it comes to our money, everything must be under lock and key, safe and sound, with iron-clad securities. Are we as careful with our children? Are we as particular about whom they go out with, where they go, and what they get up to?

There was a time when Jewish parents actually took responsibility for their children's social well-being and even their matchmaking. Okay, times have changed and children don't appreciate parental interference in their romantic endeavors. Even Tevye the Fiddler had daughters who insisted on marrying for love. But even if we can't "arrange" things, we can still try to "facilitate" an introduction behind the scenes. Or, at the very least, we could take an interest.

Today's young people might be horrified at the thought of a *shadchan* assisting them to find a marriage partner. Still, surely parents should be talking about marriage to their children when they come of age. Surely, the importance of getting married ought to be conveyed to our kids before they turn 35! And wouldn't it be a good idea for parents to sit down with their kids at some stage to discuss what to look for in a marriage partner?

Abraham was worried about the wrong woman having a bad influence on his son. How much more should we be concerned about our children who are rather less pious than Isaac was. And children might want to take their parents' advice a little more seriously. After all, the experience of history indicates that parents often do see things that children—blinded by "love"—do not.

The "singles" phenomenon is arguably the single biggest social problem in the Jewish world today. People are marrying older or not marrying at all. Often, the biological clock runs out before a family can get off the ground. Too often, desperate people make choices born out of desperation, only to regret it in time.

Abraham teaches us that it is our responsibility as parents to ensure that our children mix in the right circles and are not exposed to the wrong influences. Please G-d, all our children will find suitable marriage partners sooner than later and raise strong Jewish families that we will all be proud of.

ଞ୍ଚେ

Toldot

ואלה תולדות יצחק בן אברהם

And these are the generations of Isaac, son of Abraham. (25:19)

Generations

The subject matter of this week's Parsha is indeed rather dramatic, and its significance goes to the heart of Jewish continuity.

These are the generations of Isaac, son of Abraham, begins the reading. We learn of the birth of Jacob and Esau, how they go their different ways, and how, rather circuitously, Isaac bestows the all-important blessings on Jacob. The commentaries explain that this was not merely a blessing but the symbolic handing over of the Jewish legacy to the next generation. Isaac was passing the baton of destiny on to Jacob. (Can you imagine if Esau received those critical blessings and would have become one of our founding fathers?)

Long ago, the Talmudic sage Rabbi Chanina said that he had learned much from his teachers, more from his colleagues but the most from his pupils. I can go along with that. Some time back, a man for whom I had great respect came to see me to discuss certain issues he wanted his rabbi to clarify. This was a gentleman who had reached the apex of his profession, a highly intelligent and sensitive human being—and among other things, he said he had a confession to make. Now we rabbis have no experience at taking confessions—we refer people directly to G-d for that sort of thing. But this man voluntarily wanted to share his most personal disappointment in life with me, and I was profoundly flattered to have been found deserving of his trust.

This was his story. He came home from the wedding of his eldest daughter and, inexplicably, found himself crying. His wife said, "Why are you crying? You should be bubbling with joy." He answered, "I'm crying because I have just given away a daughter I don't know to a man I don't know." It had suddenly struck him with the force of a ton of bricks that he'd spent years and years building up his business, but he had neglected his family. And suddenly the daughter he didn't really know was leaving the family home forever.

Thank G-d, he resolved to rectify the situation and went on to succeed most admirably. But his story made a deep impression on me.

It is not only from a family point of view, but also from a Jewish faith perspective that we need to know our children well. We tend to mistakenly assume that whatever positive feelings of faith, morals, and *Yiddishkeit* we imbibed as children from our parents will somehow automatically be transmitted to our own children. Wrong! It does not happen genetically. It takes lots of hard work and years of intimate, personal guidance by dedicated parents.

It's a new generation, folks. The influences on our kids' lives today are dramatic, powerful, and not always pleasant. Internet, television, movies, computer games, and even cell phones are making our children more sophisticated and grown-up at increasingly younger ages. If once upon a time young people were spared the test of assimilation by staying in a secure social circle, today one can get chatted up by anyone in the whole wide world right in the family study on the computer through the Internet.

Tragically, children from the finest homes have gone terribly astray. If we don't transmit a healthy value system to the next generation, the vacuum will very likely be filled with other willing teachers, many of whom we may not approve of.

The good news is that our kids actually do want our guidance. As autonomous as they may appear, they actually crave direction in life. And at the end of the day, what they learn at home will make a far more lasting impression than what they pick up at school, or dare I say, even at Shul.

Let my friend's story serve notice. Don't wait until after the wedding. Jewish continuity and future generations depend on it. G-d bless you with success and lots of Yiddishe nachas.

ഇൽ

וימכור את בכורתו ליעקב
And he sold his birthright to Jacob. (25:33)

Beans and Birthrights

Children grow up and go their separate ways. Even brothers.

This week we read of the birth of twins to Isaac and Rebecca. Jacob and Esau are very different from the moment they leave the womb. As they grow older, their disparate personality traits become increasingly obvious. Jacob is the "dweller of tents," a diligent Torah scholar, while Esau is "a skilled hunter" and a violent man.

One day when Esau returns from the hunt, exhausted and starving, he finds Jacob cooking a pot of lentils. Esau offers Jacob a deal—give me your lentils and in return you may have my birthright. As the first born twin, Esau would have been the *bechor*, and at that stage in history the first born were chosen to minister in G-d's temple. Jacob accepts the offer, and the deal is done. Both parties agree, and it is a valid transaction.

Yet, when we get to the Book of Exodus (4, 22) when G-d sends Moses to Pharaoh to redeem His people, He describes them as "Bni Bechori

Yisrael"—"My son, My first born, Israel" and Rashi, quoting the Midrash, comments, "Here the Holy One Blessed is He affixed His seal to the sale of the birthright which Jacob purchased from Esau."

Here? Four generations later? It took G-d so long to put His stamp of approval on a deal that was entered into hundreds of years earlier? Why only now?

The late Israeli Rosh Yeshiva, Rav MZ Neriya answered: *You can sell your birthright for beans but you can't buy a birthright for beans.* To throw away one's holy heritage is easy, but to claim it takes years of effort and much hard work.

He used the analogy of a war hero who earned a row of medals for bravery and courage under fire. Sadly, in his old age he was forced to sell his medals in order to survive. So someone else walks into the pawnbroker and finds these war medals for sale, buys them, and pins them to his chest. He might walk down the street, proud as a peacock. But does it have any meaning? Is there any validity whatsoever to this shameless fraud? We all know that this man is no hero. In fact, he is nothing more than a pathetic fool.

To wear the esteemed badge of honor of My Firstborn Israel, the Jewish People had to be worthy of the honor. It wasn't enough that their father Jacob had purchased the birthright from an unworthy but willing seller. The children of Jacob needed to demonstrate that they understood what it meant to be Children of Israel.

When Jacob bought the birthright from Esau, it was a legal deal. One wanted the beans, one wanted the birthright. Fair and square. But did Jacob earn that hallowed title, or was he just being a clever businessman? Was he buying it like the fellow who bought the war medals? But generations later, when his children went through the iron furnace of the Egyptian bondage and still, with amazing faith and tenacity, kept their heritage, then they were deemed worthy of the honor of the birthright. Now, after the trial by fire, after the blood, sweat, and tears of slavery does the great Notary on High, the heavenly Commissioner of Oaths, take out that ancient document, the yellowed parchment deed of sale cracking with age that had been waiting for generations and puts His official stamp and the wax seal on that document. And He says, "Now I am ready to affix my sacred seal. Now you are worthy of the birthright. Today you are My Son, My Firstborn, Israel."

There's a famous graffiti exchange that has much truth in it. Someone not too partial to our faith had scrawled "How odd of G-d, to choose the Jews." And one of our own responded, "No, not odd, the Jews chose G-d."

Being Jewish is indeed the birthright of every Jew. But it's not enough that G-d chose us; we must choose G-d. We need to earn our birthright by living as Jews. Chosenness is not license to snicker or condescend to others. It is far more responsibility than privilege.

It's not good enough that our parents and grandparents were good Jews, or that my Zayde was a rabbi or a Schochet and my Bobba made the world's best blintzes. What are we doing to earn our stripes?

Indeed, you can sell your birthright for beans, but you can't buy a birthright for beans.

——

הַקֹּל קוֹל יַעֲקֹב וְהַיָּדַיִם יְדֵי עֵשָׂו

The voice is the voice of Jacob but the hands are the hands of Esau. (27:22)

The Book or the Blade?

Who are we? Who were we? Who will we be?

The Jewish People are called the Children of Israel; the name derives from the original Israel, third of our patriarchs, our father Jacob. In this week's Parsha, we read how Jacob impersonated his brother Esau in order to be blessed by his father Isaac. He wore the goatskin garments of Esau, prompting the blind Isaac to exclaim in wonderment, *the voice is the voice of Jacob but the hands are the hands of Esau!*

Our tradition has always understood these immortal words to have meaning far beyond the literal story of Jacob's charade. The *voice of Jacob* means the voice of Torah study, the sound of prayer and, generally, refers to the gentle, spiritual sound of the peace-loving People of the Book. The *hands of Esau,* on the other hand, represent the fist, fighting—war and violence, physical might and brute force.

And the question today is whether we are perhaps not forgetting who we are: what we are meant to symbolize as a nation?

Let's face it. Our society is an Esau society. Our children are constantly bombarded by the box, by television, movies, video games, and a media madness that glorifies the physical and, yes, even violence. Never mind the news, which is bad enough. How many thousands upon thousands of murders will the average child witness in all their gory details before his Bar Mitzvah? Parents need to think twice and three times before allowing themselves the luxury of such an electronic babysitter.

Today we see the results. Just watch how kids play, even in nursery school. To tell you the truth, I myself am lucky to be alive. I remember going to do a house call for a family and being attacked by their young son who had an AK-47 and, as I walked through the door, peppered me with bullets. Thank G-d, it was only a toy. How I cringed when his mom said, "Stop it Ryan, you mustn't shoot the rabbi!" Once upon a time kids played Cowboys and Indians. If you were a good shot, one Indian would get knocked off his horse. Today, one victim is nothing. Thanks to modern technology and computer games we can decimate entire armies. Battleships, spaceships, whole planets are being smashed into smithereens by a seven-year-old on his playstation.

A few years ago, I was on a plane where the in-flight program offered the following enlightening choices of entertainment—*Terminator 3, Planet of the Apes, Return of the Mummies*, and a martial arts film in a foreign language. So much for our cerebral society.

The same people who decry *shechita,* the traditional Jewish method of slaughtering animals, say nothing about hunting for sport. In England it might even be the sport of kings. Esau is described in the Bible as *one who knows hunting, a man of the field,* but Jacob is the *sincere man and dweller of tents*—a reference to the tents of Torah. Jacob was the quiet scholar while Esau was the wild hunter. Jews kill for food; for Esau it is a sport.

How about boxing? Whoever beats the other guy to a pulp gets the coveted prize and is crowned world champion. Human guerillas, sometimes convicted criminals and rapists, become international celebrities. Listen to this logic. If someone pinches your parking space and you kill him in an act of road rage, you are a murderer. But if you kill him inside a ring with 25,000 witnesses cheering you on, you are a hero, and the millions come pouring in! I won't even mention the bizarre and barbaric world of "entertainment" wrestling!

This is the sad reality of our world. When it comes to making a buck, there is no conscience and no morality. If your child wants to buy a gun, it is guaranteed there will be someone to manufacture it. There might be some form of quality control to make sure it won't hurt his hand, but unfortunately, it will still harm his soul. All the above social phenomena are deadening our sensitivities and threatening to wipe out our refined Jacob character, spawning a generation of crude and coarse Esaus.

The Talmud says, *When there is a book there is no sword, but when there is a sword there is no book.* We cannot be a nation of thoughtful, intelligent, noble scholars or Nobel Prize winners if we are playing with the sword. We have always been the People of the Book. Jews should want their children to pick up the book and drop the sword.

Do you know who made the following statement? *A violently active, dominating, brutal youth—that is what I am after.* It was a fellow named Adolf Hitler! That is what he wanted for his children. We want our kids to be like Moses, or at least Einstein. When Moses saw two Jews quarreling he said, *Rasha, wicked one, why should you strike your fellow?* At that stage the man had only raised his hand. He hadn't yet made contact, but already in Moses' mind, he was behaving like a *Rasha,* a wicked person.

If young Jews are being threatened by anti-Semites or if Israel is in mortal danger from murderous neighbors, then obviously we need to be able to defend ourselves. Self-defense classes are kosher and the Israel Defense Force protects us from another Holocaust, G-d forbid. But let's not turn brute force into a new value or an ideal to aspire to. We must teach our children Torah and the pursuit of Jewish wisdom. When the *voice is the voice of Jacob,* then no *hands of Esau* will harm us. Please G-d, we will continue to be a wise and sensitive nation of character, secure in our inner strength, and proud of whom we were and will, hopefully, always be.

࠾ৡ

Vayetze

ויצא יעקב מבאר שבע וילך חרנה,
And Jacob left Beer-Sheba and went to Haran. (28:10)

The Pressure Principle

Do we need security and comfort to do well in life? Do we achieve more when we are relaxed and comfortable or when we are challenged and provoked?

And Jacob left Beer-Sheba and went to Haran. Beer-Sheba represented peace and tranquility. Haran stood for violence and immorality. It was the hub of tumult and turmoil, home of Laban the swindler and sheep-thief of note. Yet, ironically, it was there in Haran where Jacob raised his family. There in Haran were the twelve tribes of Israel born and bred.

Abraham had a wonderful son named Isaac, but he also fathered Ishmael. Isaac bore the pious Jacob but also had a ruffian named Esau. Only Jacob is described as "select of the forefathers" because his children were all righteous, his "progeny was perfect."

Would not Beer-Sheba have made a better place for Jacob to have raised his children? Would not Beer-Sheba have been the ideal hot house for the future Jewish People to be conceived and nurtured? Why, of all places, in Haran?

The answer is that the olive yields its best oil when pulverized. To produce gold we need a fiery furnace where the intense heat on the raw metal leaves it purified and precious. Jacob did not have an easy life, but it made him a better man, and it made his children better children.

Many years ago, I met a young man who had just come out of military service in the South African army. I greeted him with a platitude: "So, Joe, did the army make you a man?" He said, "No rabbi, the army made me a Jew!" Apparently he had encountered more than a fair share of anti-Semitism in the military, and it actually strengthened his resolve to live a Jewish life. Today he is the proud father and grandfather of a lovely, committed Jewish family.

Life isn't always smooth sailing. But it appears that the creator in his vast eternal plan intended for us to experience difficulties in life. Evidently, we grow from our discomfort and challenges to emerge better, stronger, wiser, and more productive people. There is always a purpose to pain. As the physiotherapists tell us (with such compassion that I want to hit them!) *No pain, no gain.* It would seem that, like the olive, we too yield our very best when we are under pressure. I don't know about you, but I need to see a deadline staring me in the face to really get myself motivated. The simple fact is that we produce best under pressure.

In fact, one of the reasons we use a hard boiled egg on the Seder Plate over Pesach is to remind us of the festival offering brought on Yom Tov. But the truth is that any cooked food would do, so why an egg?

One of my favorite answers is that Jews are like eggs. *The more they boil us, the harder we get.* We have been punished and persecuted enough but it has only strengthened us, given us courage, faith, and hope. And no matter where in history it has happened, we have always emerged from the *tzorres* of the time stronger, tenacious, and more determined than ever.

Jacob raised a beautiful family in less than ideal conditions. Please G-d, we should emulate his example. Wherever we may be living and in whatever circumstances, may we rise to the challenge and live successful lives and raise happy, healthy Jewish children who will build the future tribes of Israel.

I end with a little poem I wrote many years ago:

> *The tragedy of pain*
> *is we overlook its aim*
> *of leaving us humble and wise*
>
> *Oh how shallow*
> *of man to wallow*
> *in misery and never realize*
>
> *That gold, so pure, is in fire proved*
> *and oil from olive by crushing removed*
> *'tis so with all things of worth*

So differ from the rest
be strong in life's test
and make of ordeal, rebirth

৪০০৪

והנה מלאכי אלקים עולים ויורדים בו
And behold the angels of G-d were ascending
and descending on it. (28:12)

The Ladder

So what's the best way to get to heaven? Walk across a busy highway? Perform some amazing act of faith? Save a thousand lives? Well, a pretty good answer may be found in this week's Parsha.

We read the story of Jacob's dream and the famous ladder with its feet on the ground and head in the heavens. "And behold the angels of G-d were ascending and descending on it."

Let me ask you what they might call in Yiddish, *a klotz kashe* (a simplistic question). Do angels need a ladder? Everyone knows angels have wings, not feet. So, if you have wings, why would you need a ladder?

There is a beautiful message here.

In climbing heavenward one does not necessarily need wings. Dispense with the dramatic. Forget about fancy leaps and bounds. There is a ladder, a spiritual route clearly mapped out for us; a route that needs to be traversed step-by-step, one rung at a time. The pathway to Heaven is gradual, methodical, and eminently manageable.

Many people are discouraged from even beginning a spiritual journey because they think it needs that huge leap of faith. They cannot see themselves reaching a degree of religious commitment which to them seems otherworldly. And yet, with the gradual step by step approach, one finds that the journey can be embarked upon and that the destination aspired to is actually not in outer space.

When I was growing up in Brooklyn, I would pass a very big building on my way to school every morning. It was the King's County Savings Bank. All these years later I still remember the Chinese proverb that was engraved over the large portals at the entrance to the bank. "A journey of a thousand miles begins with but a single step." Now that's not only Chinese wisdom, we Jews agree. And it's not limited to starting a savings plan. It is a simple yet powerful idea that it need not be "all or nothing."

Rabbis today are encouraging Jewish families to take one small step and then another and then a third so that eventually positive change is achieved.

What do you think is a rabbi's fantasy? A guy walking into my office and saying, "Rabbi, I want to become *frum,* now tell me what I must do." Is that what I lie awake dreaming of? And if it did happen, do you think I would throw the book at him and insist he did every single mitzvah from that moment on? Never! Why not? Because "easy come, easy go." Here today, gone tomorrow. The correct and most successful method of achieving our Jewish objectives is the slow and steady approach. Gradual, yet consistent. As soon as one has become comfortable with one mitzvah, it is time to start the next and so on and so forth. Then, through constant growth, slowly but surely we become knowledgeable, committed, fulfilled, and happy in our faith. I'm afraid I haven't had such wonderful experiences with the "instant Jew" types.

When my father was in Yeshiva, his teacher once asked the following question: "If two people are on a ladder, one at the top and one on the bottom, who is higher?" The class thought it was a pretty dumb question—until the wise teacher explained that they were not really capable of judging who was higher or lower, until they first ascertained in which direction each was headed.

If the fellow on top was going down, but the guy on the bottom was going up, then conceptually, the one on the bottom was actually higher.

And so my friends, it doesn't really matter what your starting point is or where you are at on the ladder of religious life. As long as you are moving in the right direction, as long as you are going up, you will, please G-d, succeed in climbing the heavenly heights.

Wishing you a safe and successful journey.

ℴℴ

וַיִּשָּׂא יַעֲקֹב רַגְלָיו וַיֵּלֶךְ
And Jacob lifted his feet and went. (29:1)

Stuck in Circumstance?

Philosophers have long struggled with the great question of our freedom of choice on the one hand and our belief in a higher destiny on the other. Is life determined by fate, or do we enjoy genuine freedom?

Generally, Judaism would seem to subscribe to personal freedom in matters of morality, faith, and the ethical choices we make in life. But when it comes to things like life and death and even health and wealth, much as we would like to think we are in the driver's seat, we do seem to be subject to forces beyond our control. Where we live, how long we will live, how comfortably we will live—these are all in G-d's hands. Where we can and must choose is what *kind* of life we will lead. Whether it will be a G-dly, righteous, upstanding, decent, and honest life—this is up to us and us alone. G-d steps back to grant us the freedom to determine how good, how kind, and how Jewish we will, or will not, be.

And Jacob lifted his feet and went on his way. (Genesis 29, 1) This verse from our Parsha tells of Jacob's journey in his escape from the wrath of Esau. He was on route to Haran where he would eventually establish his family and lay the foundations for the Jewish People. But why the strange language *And Jacob lifted his feet?* Does the Torah really need to tell us that in order to move we have to lift our feet first? Was he stuck in a swamp or something?

So many of us look at our circumstances and shrug our shoulders, *Nu, what can you do?* If we were born into poverty or raised in a less than privileged environment, we resign ourselves to being doomed to failure. So many people have told me that they were part of the "lost generation" of Jews who had no Jewish education or upbringing. Their immigrant parents were so busy surviving in a new world that they had no time or headspace to raise their children with the Jewish value system they themselves had back in Europe. Tragically, these individuals felt that, Jewishly, they were lost forever.

Chief Rabbi Lord Jonathan Sacks tells the story of how, as a young philosophy student at Cambridge, he traveled the world visiting great leaders. When he came to see the Lubavitcher Rebbe, the Rebbe asked him what he was doing for the Jewish students at Cambridge. He began by saying that "In the circumstances I currently find myself . . ." whereupon the Rebbe interrupted him and said, "No one *finds himself* in circumstances. We create our own circumstances."

Of course, there are times when we will find ourselves in circumstances beyond our control. But throughout life we will find ample scope and opportunities to improve our own circumstances. G-d gives each of us our own unique qualities, talents, and potential, and it is up to us to use and develop these gifts. Life is full of inspiring examples of individuals who have overcome disabilities and disadvantages of one kind or another. In the Jewish world, many have risen to prominence from the humblest beginnings. The Torah is the birthright of every Jew. We just have to go out and claim it.

So, the words of our Parsha are quite deliberate and well chosen after all. *Jacob lifted his feet and went on his way.* Some people follow their feet wherever they will take them. No matter the direction, they simply coast along allowing their feet to lead them.

Not so Jacob. He was master of his feet and master of his circumstances. He set his feet on the right road and became master of his destiny. May we all be inspired to lift ourselves beyond our circumstances.

ഇരു

Vayishlach

עם לבן גרתי

I have sojourned with Laban. (32:5)

Jacob's Lament

This week the dreaded encounter between Jacob and Esau finally materializes. After two decades, the twin brothers, who are anything but identical, square up. Jacob, who fled the wrath of Esau as a young man, is returning home with a large family and much wealth. Esau is fast approaching with four hundred armed desperados armed to the teeth. Will it be all-out war or will they make peace? Jacob prepares for all eventualities and also sends a message to his hostile brother.

Im lavan garti—"I have sojourned with Lavan." Rashi interprets the message of Jacob to mean that though he lived with a notorious trickster for all this time, he "had not learned from his evil ways" and remained a righteous Jew committed to the G-dly way of life. This is indicated by the *gematria* (numerology) of the Hebrew word *garti* which equals *taryag*, 613, the number of Mitzvot in the Torah.

But wasn't this rather boastful of Jacob? The same man who will soon be praying for deliverance and saying *kotointi,* claiming that he has been humbled by all G-d's kindnesses to him, now seems to be pointing proudly to his piety, telling Esau how religious he has been?

The Chofetz Chaim offers a novel interpretation. He explains that Jacob's words should not be understood as a boast but rather as a lament. "I sojourned with Lavan but did not learn from his evil ways" means that Jacob did not learn from the way Lavan did evil. How did Lavan do evil? Enthusiastically! With vim and vigor. His wicked ways were undertaken with a passion and energy and Jacob bemoans the fact that his own *good* deeds were not performed as passionately as Lavan's evil deeds.

If the good guys were as incentivized as the bad guys, crime would be dramatically down. If the security forces were as passionate as the terrorists, the world would be a safer place. If the police and justice systems of the world operated with the same commitment and drive as the drug lords, the pirates and the hijacking syndicates we would all be better off. The trouble is that the forces of evil are enthusiastic and highly motivated, while the forces of good often depend on civil servants who are overworked and underpaid.

Soviet leader Nikita Khrushchev (of United Nations shoe-banging fame) was once addressing a large public meeting in Russia during the anti-Stalinist period. He was blasting Stalin's cruel and unforgivable atrocities when a voice in the crowd suddenly spoke up and asked, "If Stalin was such a villain, why didn't *you* do anything about it then?"

"Who said that?!" thundered Khrushchev. There was absolute silence in the hall. Not a sound, not a movement. People froze in fear.

"Now you understand why I didn't do anything," was Khrushchev's convincing answer.

This interesting interpretation of Jacob's lament reminds us that the voice of morality must be at least as loud as the voice of evil. Too often the voice of justice is soft and still while the voice of corruption and degeneracy is loud and bombastic.

Who will amplify the sweet, silent sound of goodness?

Let us strive to become as passionate and assertive for the cause of G-d-liness and goodness as the other side is for evil and injustice. The world will be better balanced, much nicer, and a lot safer.

ഇരു

כי שרית עם אלקים ועם אנשים ותוכל
For you have fought with the Divine and with
man and you have overcome. (32:29)

Fight or Flight?

Of all the things we Jews observe in order to remember events in our historic past, surely one of the strangest must be what we read in this week's Parsha. Jacob wrestles with the angel (Esau's guardian angel), and in the course of the struggle, his hip-socket is dislocated. *Therefore, to this day, the Children of Israel are not to eat the sciatic nerve (of an animal) by the hip joint because he struck Jacob's hip-socket at the sciatic nerve.*

This is why most Kashrut authorities the world over forbid us using the hindquarter of the animal, and we only get to enjoy the cuts from the forequarter. So if it has always bothered you that you never tasted a good rump steak, you can blame it on father Jacob and his wrestling match with the angel of Esau. (Apparently because of the shortage of meat in Israel, authorities there do allow special *treibering* of the hindquarter, and the offending sinews and nerves are removed.)

So, tell me, just because 4,000 years ago one of my ancestors had a hip dislocated must I curb my culinary cravings? Is this fair; is it logical? Why remember; what's the point?

Enter the twelfth century French sage, Rabbi Shmuel ben Meir (Rashbam), a grandson of Rashi and a Biblical and Talmudic commentator of note. The story of Jacob and the Angel occurred just prior to his impending encounter with his estranged twin brother. Esau was coming with four hundred armed men, and Jacob was actually planning to flee from Esau. That was when the angel attacked him. According to *Rashbam*, the reason for the angel wrestling with Jacob was so that he would be forced to stand his ground and not escape via a back route. Destiny itself was compelling Jacob to confront the enemy and overcome him. Only then would he witness the fulfillment of G-d's promise to protect him from harm.

It seemed as if Jacob was coming dangerously close to developing a pattern of escapism. He fled Beer-Sheba when Esau threatened to kill him. He fled from Laban in Haran in middle of the night when he worried that Laban wouldn't give his blessings to his departure. And now he was preparing to flee from Esau yet again. He didn't protest too loudly when Laban cheated him of Rachel and a hundred other times in their livestock business. And any moment now there would be another nocturnal escape.

Apparently, G-d wanted Jacob to learn that a philosophy of escapism is not the Jewish way. So the angel dislocated his hip, preventing him from running away. Now Jacob had no choice but to stand his ground and fight. In the end, he defeated the angel and was blessed with the name Israel, signifying a superior stature, victory, and nobility. *No longer shall it be said that your name is Jacob, but Israel, for you have fought with the Divine and with man and you have overcome.*

Every son and daughter of Jacob must learn this lesson. Every one of us must become a child of Israel. The qualities of fearlessness and courage, of strength and sacrifice, these are the hallmarks of Israel. When we stop running away from our problems and face up to them with guts and fortitude, we enter that higher state of consciousness. We move up from the Jacob Jew who is still struggling to the Israel mode where we finally emerge triumphant. When we are prepared to take up the challenge and go for the fight rather than flight, we move from being wrestlers to becoming winners, from humble Jacob to dominant Israel.

Of course, it's never easy. Escape is usually the path of least resistance. Nor am I suggesting that we go looking for a fight. But the fact is that there will be times when we know that we really need to have that confrontation. We need to square up to a particular problem—or individual—in order to deal with our situation effectively. We shouldn't be confrontational people. But often we know in our heart of hearts that if we don't engage a problem honestly, it will continue to plague us.

If we can move from meekness to manliness, then the story of Jacob's wrestling match will live on and continue to inspire us to become the stronger personalities we really can be. The dislocated hip joint thus becomes worthy of eternal remembrance because it makes us better people. And the small sacrifices we make in avoiding those unkosher cuts of meat around the animal's hip socket are well worth the effort.

ෂංශ

וירץ עשו לקראתו ... וישקהו
And Esau ran towards him . . . and he kissed him. (33:4)

Kiss or Curse?

Which is the greater test of faith, affluence or poverty? Is it harder to be a good Jew when you're rich or when you're poor, when you're successful or when you're struggling? No doubt, we would all much rather accept upon ourselves the test of affluence, wouldn't we? But let's not be subjective about it. Let us rather take an objective historical approach.

Back in the early nineteenth century, Napoleon was conquering Europe and promising liberty and equality for all. When he squared up against Russia, many Jewish leaders sided with him, hoping he would finally bring an end to Czarist persecution and enable Russian Jewry to enjoy full civil rights. Rabbi Schneur Zalman of Liadi, founder of Chabad, thought differently. He actively opposed Napoleon and even had his Chassidim assist in intelligence gathering for the Russian army.

When his colleagues challenged him and questioned his apparent lack of concern for the well-being of his own people, he argued that while Napoleon might be good for the Jews materially, his victory would result in spiritual disaster. History proved him correct. Minus the Little Emperor, Russian Jews remained staunchly Jewish, while French Jewry virtually vanished. How many Jewish Rothschilds are left in the world? G-d knows we could have used them. Most of French Jewry today hails from North Africa. The originals are few and far between.

There is a fascinating Midrashic interpretation in this week's *parshah* about the dramatic encounter between Jacob and Esau. The Torah says, "And Esau ran towards him (Jacob) and embraced him ... and he kissed him." The Hebrew word for "and he kissed him" is *vayishakayhu*. In the Torah, this word is written with a line of dots above it. Says the Midrash Yalkut Shimoni: these dots are there to indicate that the word should be read differently; not *vayishakayhu*, he kissed him, but rather *vayishachayhu*, he *bit* him!

How can we understand a Midrash which seems to change the entire meaning of the word? A kiss is an expression of love and a bite is the opposite! Says the *Sfat Emet* (Rabbi Yehudah Leib Alter, 1847–1905, the second Rebbe in the Chassidic dynasty of Ger), "When Esau kisses, Jacob is bitten!"

The American experience confirms beyond a shadow of a doubt that freedom, democracy and equal rights, while wonderful blessings for Jews for which we should be eternally grateful, also present a profound challenge to our Jewish identity and way of life. In the melting pot of the United States, Jews have integrated so successfully that they are virtually disappearing! Success and affluence are wonderful gifts of opportunity, but we don't seem to be passing the test of faith with flying colors.

French philosopher Jean Paul Sartre argued that anti-Semitism has been good for the Jews. It has kept Jews Jewish! While no one wants to be oppressed, and we reject anti-Semitism categorically, the man does have a point. When anti-Semitism bites, we intuitively know how to respond. But when the world is in a kissing mood, we don't quite know how to handle it.

I remember as a young rabbi working with university students in Johannesburg in the late 1970s. At that time, they were completely apathetic to Judaism. My colleagues and I were struggling to elicit any meaningful response to Jewish programs on campus. During one particular meeting, we seriously contemplated getting up in the dead of night to spray-paint some swastikas on the Student Union building. Surely, that would get some reaction! Of course, we never did it. But the fact that the thought actually crossed our minds demonstrates how external threats have a way of making Jews bristle with pride and righteous indignation.

May we never again face the test of poverty or persecution. Please G-d, we will be proud and knowledgeable Jews successfully meeting the spiritual challenges of the good life.

৩০৪

Vayeshev

The Child in the Pit

There is high drama in the Bible this week as we read the story of Joseph and his brothers. Technicolor dream coats, sibling rivalry, terrifying pits, and attempted fratricide dominate the Parsha proceedings.

When the brothers plot to actually kill Joseph, Reuben, the eldest, makes a valiant effort to save Joseph's life and suggests that instead they throw him into a pit. That would be sufficient to teach him a lesson, and no blood need be shed. In fact, according to Rashi, the Torah itself testifies that Reuben's intention was to save Joseph from the pit.

But destiny had a different plan.

While Reuben was away, the brothers sold Joseph into slavery. When he returns to rescue him, the boy is gone and he rends his garments in grief.

But where was Reuben when the sale took place? Why wasn't he there with his brothers at the time? Where did he suddenly disappear?

Rashi gives two possible explanations. (1) It was his turn to go and serve his aged father. The brothers had a roster and Reuben's time had come, so he was back at the ranch. (2) Reuben was busy doing Teshuvah (Repentance) with sackcloth and fasting because he had interfered with his father's sleeping arrangements (Genesis 35, 22).

I remember hearing the Rebbe ask about the second opinion. According to the second opinion, Reuben left Joseph in the pit to go and busy himself with "sackcloth and fasting," that is, his own repentance for his sins. So let's take a look and see what happens as a result. Reuben is absent, so Joseph is sold into slavery. He is sold and resold and eventually is taken down to Egypt. There he is imprisoned on false charges and, one day, rises to sudden prominence by successfully interpreting the Pharaoh's dreams. He becomes Viceroy of Egypt, then meets his long lost brothers when they come searching for food during the famine. After revealing his true identity, he brings his father Jacob and the entire family down to Egypt where he supports and sustains them.

And that is precisely how the Jews became slaves in Egypt. It all started with Joseph being taken from the pit and sold to the Egyptians. Why? Because Reuben decided to be busy doing Teshuvah! I remember the Rebbe thundering, "The whole Egyptian exile can be traced to Reuben's ill-timed Teshuvah! When a young Jewish boy is languishing in the pit, that is *not* the time for Teshuvah. That is the time to save a Jewish child!"

Of course, Teshuvah is a wonderful Mitzvah. In a way, it is the greatest mitzvah of all because it can repair the damage done by failing to observe all other mitzvahs. And yet, there is a time to do Teshuvah and a time to save lives. And when a life is in danger, even Teshuvah really must wait.

The analogy of the Jewish child in the pit resonates powerfully today. It is not only about saving lives physically but also spiritually. How many millions of Jewish children are at risk spiritually? And how many Jews, indeed how many rabbis, become preoccupied with their own personal spiritual upliftment while ignoring the plight of young people "in the pits?"

It is a sobering thought and one that demands a response.

છ૭ભ

Image and Influence

How much do our parents and grandparents influence us? Of course, the genes we inherit from them determine lots of important things about us—from our cholesterol levels to when we will go grey. But what about emotionally or spiritually?

I'd like to suggest that they influence us more than we might care to admit. We also tend to underestimate the potential they have in molding the value systems of the next generation.

A powerful case in point is the story in this week's Parsha. Joseph is sold into slavery down in Egypt and winds up in the house of Potiphar. His master's wife casts her lustful gaze on the handsome young man and repeatedly attempts to seduce him. Joseph is consistent in his refusal to even consider her advances. Then one day, the entire household goes to the temple for a special occasion. She feigns illness in order to be home alone with Joseph. He comes to the house *to do his work*. Rashi offers two interpretations: the simple—that he came to work; and another, that he actually came to do his work with her!

Determined as he always was, on this occasion Joseph was beginning to falter. Morale and morality were weakening, and it seemed as if he was about to succumb to the temptress' entreaties.

Then suddenly something happened to help Joseph regain his senses and self-control. What was it? Did they come home early? Did the postman ring the bell? Says Rashi, there appeared before Joseph an image, an image so potent that it restored his composure there and then. What was that image? Quoting the Talmud Sotah, Rashi says it was *the image of the visage of his father*. Joseph suddenly pictured his father Jacob's face, and with that his moral resolve returned.

Was it a miracle, a heavenly message from the Holy Land? According to the simple reading, at that stage Jacob didn't even know that Joseph was alive. He had been missing and presumed dead, devoured by a wild animal. The straightforward understanding of this Talmudic passage is that Joseph remembered his father and his patriarchal face, the classical sage with the long, white beard. And with that image in his mind, Joseph found renewed spiritual stamina to resist temptation.

Some might understand this episode as Joseph not wanting to disappoint his aged father. Others might see the image as a catalyst evoking in Joseph his own latent spiritual resources. Either way, with Jacob's visage in his mind, Joseph wasn't prepared to lose the moral high ground. He couldn't and wouldn't do it to his dad. And, through his father, Joseph remembered who he was—a proud son of Jacob and grandson of Isaac and Abraham.

Such was the effect Jacob had on Joseph and such is the effect every father and mother, grandfather and grandfather, can potentially bring to bear on their offspring. Of course, they would have to be respected by their children as men and women of stature for their image to represent any kind of moral symbolism. If the image of a parent or grandparent would send a signal to the young person to, say, "Go for it, my boy!" then clearly the system will fail.

I can safely say that if not for the image of my own father and grandfather and their subtle influence on me, I would never have become a rabbi. They didn't push me at all, but their influence was profound. Just their image—their character and very being—was enough to guide me in the right direction during my own wavering moments of youthful indecision.

Joseph was nearly lost way down in Egypt land but that one image of his father saved him from sin and helped him go on to achieve greatness. May we all be good role models and may our own images help inspire our children and grandchildren.

₧₧

וישאל ... מדוע פניכם רעים היום
He asked, "Why do you look so bad today?" (40:7)

Hello, How Ya Doin'?

Would you believe that *Hello, how ya doin'?* can be a religious question? And that it even bears Biblical significance?

This week we read the dramatic story of Joseph, the Technicolor dream coat, his sibling rivalries, and ultimately his descent to Egypt, sold into slavery. After being framed by his master's wife for scorning her attempts at seduction, young Joseph finds himself incarcerated in an Egyptian jail. There he meets the Pharaoh's butler and baker and correctly interprets their respective dreams. Later, when Pharaoh himself will be perturbed by his own dreams, the butler will remember Joseph, and he will be brought from the dungeon to the royal court. His dream analysis will satisfy the monarch, and the young Hebrew slave boy will be catapulted to prominence and named Viceroy of Egypt.

But how did it all begin? It began with Joseph in prison noticing that the butler and baker were looking somewhat depressed. *And Joseph came to them in the morning and he saw them and behold they were troubled. He asked Pharaoh's officials ... "Why do you look so bad today?"* They tell him about their disturbing dreams, he interprets them correctly, and the rest is history.

But why did Joseph have to ask them anything at all? Why is it so strange to see people in prison looking sad? Surely in the dungeons depression is the norm. Wouldn't we expect most people in jail to look miserable?

According to the Rebbe, the answer is that Joseph was exhibiting a higher sense of care and concern for his fellow human beings. Torn away from his father and home life, imprisoned in a foreign land, he could have been forgiven for wallowing in his own miseries. Yet, upon seeing his fellow prisoners looking particularly unsettled, he was sensitive enough to take the time to enquire about their well-being. In the end, not only did he help them, but his own salvation came about through that fateful encounter. Had he thought to himself, "Hey, I've got my own problems, why worry about them?" he might have languished in prison indefinitely.

Sometimes, says the Rebbe, a simple *Hello, how ya doin'?* can prove historic!

It's a lesson to all of us to be a little friendlier, to greet people, perhaps even to smile more often.

Some years ago after studying in the Talmud how one of the great sages never allowed anyone else to greet him first but always made a point of initiating the greeting, I made a personal resolution to try and put it into practice. Every Shabbos, I walk quite a few kilometers to and from Shul. I pass by many fellow pedestrians, mostly black people. Rarely had any of them greeted me, but now I am the one to say "good morning" to them. They always respond, though I must confess that some do look rather surprised at the acknowledgment. In a country where for many years they were not acknowledged as full-fledged citizens, a simple hello can become a very humanizing experience. I heartily recommend the practice.

Conversely, while most fellow Jews do say Good Shabbos, I am sometimes unpleasantly surprised when, ironically, a *frum* person will walk right by me without even so much as a nod.

When we meet someone we know and ask, "Hey, how are you doing?" do we wait for the answer? Try this experiment. Next time you are asked how you are doing, answer "Lousy!" See if the other person is listening and responds or just carries on his merry way oblivious to your response.

Besides Joseph's many outstanding qualities, which we ought to try and emulate, in this rather simple passage Joseph reminds us to be genuinely interested in other people's well-being. And that it should not be beneath our dignity—nor should we be inhibited—to make an honest and sincere enquiry as to their condition. Who knows? It may not only change their lives, but ours.

♫♪

Miketz

וַיִּיקָץ פַּרְעֹה
And Pharaoh awoke. (41:4)

Famine in the Land

Long before Dr. Martin Luther King, Jr. was having dreams, we read of the dreams of Pharaoh, King of Egypt. When all the king's men and all the king's soothsayers fail in their attempts at dream analysis, the chief butler remembers Joseph and how the Hebrew prisoner who was his cell mate correctly interpreted his own dreams when they were together in jail. In a flash, young Joseph is hauled out of the dungeons and finds himself standing before the mighty monarch. Pharaoh repeats his two dreams— seven fat cows being devoured by seven lean cows and seven healthy ears of grain being swallowed by seven thin ears.

Immediately, Joseph interprets the dreams to Pharaoh's satisfaction. Seven years of plenty will be followed by seven years of famine. His explanation rings true for the king. But Joseph doesn't stop at the interpretation. He goes on to offer some seemingly unsolicited advice to the powerful ruler of the mightiest superpower of the time. *And now Pharaoh should select a person who is understanding and wise and appoint him over Egypt,* continues young Joseph. Let this man oversee the economic plan for the country to store grain during the seven good years of plenty that are coming in order to sustain the people during the next seven lean years.

Brilliant. But who asked him for any advice? And where does this young man, who a moment ago was languishing in prison, get the temerity to offer *eitzos*—unsolicited advice to none other than the king himself? I know Jews are renowned for their *chutzpah,* but still! You gave your interpretation, fine and well, but did anybody ask you for solutions?

One very acceptable answer is that the advice was actually part and parcel of the interpretation. Why were there two dreams with essentially the same message? Why were the thin cows standing next to the fat cows before they swallowed them? Moreover, why did Pharaoh wake up after the first dream, go back to sleep, and only then experience the second dream? According to Joseph all of this was highly pertinent. The dream was repeated because it will happen soon and therefore no time is to be wasted in preparing for the famine. The two sets of cows stood side by side to indicate that there is an important connection between them and to make the Pharaoh realize that the good years can sustain the people in the lean years. And Pharaoh woke up in between the two dreams because G-d was saying to him, "Wake up before it is too late to save your people!" Thus, the solution was implicit in the dreams, and therefore had he chosen not to share that with Pharaoh, Joseph would have been derelict in his duty by omitting crucial sections of their meaning. Offering the advice was not *chutzpah* at all. Withholding it would have been a job half done.

The Pharaoh is so impressed with this explanation that he immediately appoints Joseph as Viceroy of Egypt and the rest, of course, is history.

Long ago the Prophet Amos said,

Behold, days are coming, says the L-rd, when I will send a famine in the land; not a famine for bread, nor a thirst for water, but for hearing the words of the L-rd. And they shall wander from sea to sea, and from the north even to the east, they shall run to and fro to seek the word of G-d and they shall not find it. In that day shall the fair virgins and the young men faint from thirst.

Is this not a prophecy of our own day and age? Are we not witnessing a hunger for truth and authenticity in a corrupt and plastic world? Do our own young people from America and even Israel not go wandering across the far corners of the earth desperately seeking spirituality and some deeper meaning to their lives? And what is our response when many of our youngest and brightest get lost in the East? Do we appreciate the tragedy when they despair of finding fulfillment in the faith of their fathers? Do we mimic the Pharaoh and turn over on the other side going back to sleep even when we seem to be getting heavenly signals and messages that something momentous is about? Or do we seek out the guidance of a "wise and understanding man" who can guide our young people towards the path of what, for them, must be the only truth, the Torah?

In the end, Pharaoh took Joseph's advice, acted responsibly, and spared his nation the famine that engulfed the world. Will we today feed those spiritually starved souls and give them the nourishment they crave? Many among us are trying to do just that. I pray we will all join in.

ഇരു

Wake-Up Calls (and a Chanukah Connection)

Not everyone is lucky enough to get a wake-up call in life. Some people get theirs just in time. Others get it but don't hear it. Still others hear it loud and clear but refuse to take any notice.

Pharaoh got his in this week's Parsha when Joseph interpreted his dreams and advised him to appoint *a wise and discerning man* who would oversee a macroeconomic plan for the country. Joseph explained to the King of Egypt that because he experienced two dreams and woke up in between, it was a sign from heaven to wake up and act immediately as the matter was of the utmost urgency. Pharaoh took the message to heart and the rest is history.

On the health and well-being level, a little cholesterol, climbing blood pressure or recurring bronchitis might be the not-so-subtle signs that it's time for a change of lifestyle. These are the medical wake up calls we receive in life. Do we really have to wait for a heart attack, G-d forbid, to stop smoking, or start eating less and exercising more? That's what wake-up calls are for, to help us get the message before it's too late.

Then there are the spiritual signs.

I will never forget a friend who shared with me the story of his own red lights flashing and how a changed spiritual lifestyle literally saved his life. He was a workaholic driving himself to the brink. Had he carried on indefinitely, he simply could not have survived. Then he decided to give Shabbos a try. What he had never previously appreciated about Shabbos was that it is a spiritually invigorating day of rest and spiritual serenity. And in discovering Shabbos, he rediscovered his humanity. (He also discovered he could play golf on Sundays instead of Saturdays.)

A short trigger film I once used on a Shabbaton program depicted a series of professionals and artisans at work. As they became engrossed and immersed in their respective roles, they each became so identified with their work that they lost their own identities. Monday through Friday, the carpenter's face dissolved into a hammer, the doctor's face took on the surface of a stethoscope and the accountant's head started looking exactly like a calculator. Then on Shabbos as they closed their offices and came home to celebrate the day of rest with their families, slowly but surely, their faces were reshaped and remolded from their professions to their personalities. Total immersion in their work had dehumanized them. They had become machines. Now, thanks to Shabbos, they were human again. That short video left a lasting impression.

It's not easy to change ingrained habits. But Chanukah, which usually falls during this week's Parsha, carries with it a relevant message in this regard. Take one day at a time. One doesn't have to do it all at once. One light at a time is all it takes. On the first night, we kindle a single Chanukah light; on the second night, two; and on the third night, three. We add a little light each day and before long the Menorah is complete, and all eight Chanukah lights are burning bright.

It's okay to take one day at a time. It's not okay to go back to sleep after you get a wake-up call. Whether it's your medical well-being or your spiritual health, the occasional wake-up call is a valuable sign from Above that it may be time to adjust our attitudes, lifestyles, or priorities. Please G-d, each of us in our own lives will hear the call and act on the alarm bells with alacrity.

⁝

והם לא הכירודו

And they did not recognize him. (42:8)

Of Shepherds and Statesmen

Is isolationism the only way to live as faithful Jews, or can we scale the ghetto walls and still remain devout? This is, of course, an ongoing debate among different schools of thought in our community. Some look down on those who insist on insulating themselves as being too tentative, too insecure in their own Jewish identity. Otherwise, why should they fear the outside world? Whereas those who have opted to shelter themselves inside the ghetto would argue that engaging a hedonistic, morally corrupt society is nothing less than spiritual suicide.

And then there are those who took the risk and lived to tell the tale.

Our Parsha recounts the dramatic episode of Joseph and his brothers. The young boy sold into slavery has since catapulted to prominence and is now Viceroy of Egypt. The brothers come down from Canaan seeking sustenance during a famine. They encounter the Viceroy face to face but do not realize that it is their own long-lost brother.

And Joseph recognized his brothers but they did not recognize him (Genesis 42, 8). Rashi explains that when they had last seen each other the brothers, being older, were mature and bearded while Joseph was still young and without a beard. Thus, it was easier for him to recognize them than vice versa.

Applying a more homiletic interpretation, the mystics understand the brothers' lack of recognition not on the facial level but on the spiritual. The brothers were shepherds. It suited their spiritual lifestyle to be alone in the meadows, surrounded by nature and unchallenged by a society that might be hostile to their beliefs. The sheep they tended to didn't give them a hard time on religious issues. That Joseph could remain a devoted son of Jacob, faithful to his father's way of life while working in the hub of the mightiest superpower on earth was totally beyond their comprehension. They could not fathom or *recognize* such a thing. Indeed, later we will read how Jacob himself is deeply gratified to learn that the son he had given up for dead was not only alive but that he was *my son,* that is, faithful to Jacob's traditions, in spite of his high office in Egyptian society.

There is no question that it is easier to be Jewish among your own. Without a shadow of a doubt, it is much tougher and far more testing to practice your faith as a minority. Nobody enjoys sticking out like a sore thumb. So sequestering yourself in your own little comfort zone makes perfect sense.

Unless, of course, you believe that you have a responsibility to the world around you.

When you believe that G-d expects nothing less from you than to change the world, then simply treading water is not enough. Then you have no option but to go out and take on the world, engage it, and make that very world a more G-dly place.

All Jacob's sons were righteous men. But Joseph was the greatest. He is known as *Yosef HaTzadik,* Joseph the Righteous. Because it is one thing to be righteous in the fields and the forests. It is another to be righteous among men, especially men and women steeped in moral depravity, as were the Egyptians.

The Viceroy of Egypt then must be roughly equivalent to the President of the United States, or at least the Secretary of State, today. Imagine that the person holding such high office is a committed, practicing Jew. He is successful in the fulfillment of his governmental duties and brings stature to the position, while at the very same time living the life of a devout Jew. Quite mind-boggling. But Joseph achieved it. And it was in this spirit that he raised his children, Ephraim and Menashe.

That's why Joseph is an important role model for our generation. Most of us find ourselves in a socially integrated society. We mix in many different circles. We live in a wall-less, even wireless community. Will we maintain our Jewishness with dignity and integrity despite the challenges thrust upon us by a wide open society? This is the question that Joseph answers. It may not be easy, but it can be done.

So whether we are head honchos in the corporate hierarchy or diplomats in high office, let the Viceroy of Egypt, Joseph the faithful son of Jacob the Jew, inspire us by his example.

₡₠

Vayigash

The Seventieth Soul?

How many Jews came down to Egypt?

Though at the time of the Exodus we left with 600,000 men of military age (and, according to all estimates, a total of a few million people), the number who originally went down to Egypt in the days of Joseph were only "seventy souls." But if one goes through the Torah text, Jacob's sons and their children—even including Joseph and his sons who were already there—only amount to a total of 69. Commentary offers a number of explanations. The Torah rounds off the number to the nearest ten. Or, Yocheved was born to Levi as they were entering Egypt. Or, Jacob himself is counted as number 70.

But, for me, the most touching one of all comes from the Midrash.

> *What did the Holy One Blessed is He do? He Himself entered into the count and thus it totaled 70, to fulfill his promise made earlier to Jacob (Genesis 46, 3–4), "Have no fear of going down to Egypt, for I shall establish you as a great nation there. **I shall descend with you to Egypt and I shall also surely bring you up . . .**"*

How inspiring! How magnificently encouraging. Hashem is with us in Egypt. Amidst the bondage, the pain and persecution, He is with us. And in all our wanderings and dispersions, He is there. As He assures us in Psalm 91, *Imo Onochi Btzoroh, I am with him in his affliction.* In all our anguish, in all our *tzorres*, He is right there with us!

It was this conviction of the invisible but tangible Divine Presence being with us in the Galut and in the ghettoes that sustained our people throughout a torturous history. This was the promise that inspired us with an inexhaustible fountain of faith, courage, and strength to survive our enemies and to flourish again long after they were gone.

Many continue to ask, "Where was G-d during the Holocaust?" I could never even attempt to debate this question with an embittered survivor who had lost his faith. And who are we to criticize those holy tormented souls? But my father and many like him, who survived with their faith intact, could. How did they maintain their beliefs in spite of their suffering? One answer they might offer is this. "How did I survive? Do you understand how many miracles it took to get me out of Poland? Or out of the camps? And how about escaping Lithuania, Russia, Japan, or Shanghai? How can I deny the hand of G-d that plucked me from danger again and again?"

Surely, the greatest miracle of our generation is that after Auschwitz Jews still wanted to be Jewish. That our people rebounded and rebuilt their families, their communities, and their homeland. For many, the certainty that a higher power was guiding them to survival is what sustained them in their darkest moments and what gave them the confidence to regroup and regenerate.

Soon, we will observe the Fast of Tevet, commemorating the siege of Jerusalem by the Babylonians. So who is having the last laugh? Do you know any grandchildren of Nebuchadnezzar, King of Babylon? Today's Iraquis are not. All that is left of his mighty empire are a few statues. All our enemies, down to the Third Reich, have come and gone. The Jews are here, alive and well, still doing their thing three thousand years later.

G-d's promise to Jacob that *I will go down with you* has kept us going. And the conclusion of the verse assures us all of a happy conclusion. *And I shall surely also bring you up*—from Egypt and from our own exile. May it be speedily in our day.

⁁⁃

ויפול (יוסף) על צוארי בנימין אחיו ויבך ובנימין בכה על צואריו
And he (Joseph) fell on his brother Benjamin's neck and cried,
and Benjamin cried on his neck. (45:14)

No Time to Weep

The wisest of men said there is a time to weep, which implies that there will be occasions when weeping is inappropriate. Though King Solomon's exact words were *there is a time to weep and a time to laugh*, obviously there are times when other responses are called for. Clearly, life is not simply about crying or laughing.

This week's Parsha relates the story of Joseph's dramatic reunion with his brothers. Though he embraces them all, he reserves his deepest emotions for his only full brother, Benjamin. Joseph left him when Benjamin was a mere child, and he was the only one who was not involved in the plot against him. Theirs is, therefore, an exceptional embrace.

And he (Joseph) fell on his brother Benjamin's neck and cried, and Benjamin cried on his neck (Genesis 45, 14).

Rashi, quoting the Talmud (Megilla 16b), explains that for both brothers, beyond the powerful feelings of the moment, their cries were nothing short of prophetic. Joseph cried over the two Temples of Jerusalem, destined for destruction, which were in the land apportioned to the tribe of

Benjamin. And Benjamin cried over the sanctuary at Shilo, located in the land apportioned to the tribe of Joseph, which too would be destroyed.

The question is why are they each crying over the other's *churban?* Why do they not cry over their own destructions?

Perhaps the answer is that when it comes to someone else's problem, we may be able to help but we cannot always solve them. Even good friends can only do so much. We can offer generous assistance, support, and the best advice in the world, but the rest is up to him. No matter how strenuous our efforts, there can be no guarantee that they will be successful. As hard as we may try to help, the individual alone holds the key to sort out his own situation.

So, if we are convinced that we have done our absolute best for the other person and have still failed to bring about a satisfactory resolution, the only thing we can do is shed a tear. We can pray for them, we can be sympathetic. Beyond that, there is really nothing else we can do. When we have tried and failed, all we can do is cry.

But when it comes to our own problems and challenges, our own *churban,* there we dare not settle for a good cry. We cannot afford the luxury of giving up and weeping. If it is our problem, then it is our duty to confront it again and again until we make it right. For others we can cry, but for ourselves we must act.

After the Holocaust, the great spiritual leaders of Europe were counting their losses—in the millions! The great Chassidic courts of Poland, the prestigious Yeshivas of Lithuania—all were destroyed by the Nazi hordes. What did these righteous men do? Did they sit down and cry? Of course there were tears and mourning and indescribable grief, but the emphasis quickly shifted to rebuilding. And today, thank G-d, those same institutions are alive and well, thriving and pulsating with spirit and energy in Israel and the United States with many offshoots around the world. The leadership focused on the future. And painstakingly, over time, they were able to resuscitate and rejuvenate their decimated communities.

Those leaders cried bitter tears for their fallen comrades, but for themselves they did not sit and weep. They set about the task of rebuilding— and succeeded in a most inspiring, miraculous way.

When we have problems (and who doesn't?), so many of us simply moan and groan and heave a good old-fashioned *yiddishe krechtz.* How many times have we sighed, *Vos ken men ton?—What can I do?* And what are we left with? Moaning and groaning and nothing else. In the words of Rabbi Sholom Ber of Lubavitch (1860–1920), *One good deed is worth more than a thousand sighs.*

Leave the *krechtzing* and *kvetching* for others. If it's your problem, confront it, deal with it, work at it. You'll be surprised by the results.

ഇറ

Wandering Too Far?

What toll have the wanderings of the Jews taken on our national psyche? What consequences have there been to our spiritual and cultural identities as a result of centuries of globetrotting, usually out of urgent necessity rather than choice? Clearly, there must have been many dramatic and discernible effects. Today, amidst our own freely chosen migrations and relocations it behooves us to learn the lessons of our history.

This week's Parsha tells the story of Joseph's reunion with his family after some two decades away from them. He is now Viceroy of Egypt and sends for his father Jacob and the rest of the family, promising to support them all during the days of famine that were then gripping the region. Old father Jacob agrees to go down to Egypt but needs some Divine reassurance. G-d provides such encouragement, telling Jacob to have no fear of descending to the land of the Pharaohs.

Why was Jacob fearful, and what did he do to deal with his anxieties?

Commentaries offer a variety of answers. He was reluctant to leave the Holy Land and its special heavenly presence. Egypt was infamous as a morally depraved society. He was afraid of losing his children to an alien culture. He was already old and did not want to be buried in Egypt. Concerning all the above, G-d reassured Jacob. And so he went down, and the rest is history.

But there was something particularly significant that he did before leaving. He sent Judah to establish the first Jewish Day School for the children. Jacob took what he considered to be a vital precaution to prevent any assimilation in Egypt. How best could he guarantee Jewish continuity and the spiritual and moral protection of his grandchildren? There could be no better way, no more effective tool than Jewish education. And so Judah formed the advance guard on the way down to the challenging cultural melting pot of Egypt.

How many of our grandparents declined invitations to leave Eastern Europe in the last century because America was a *treifene medina* (let me be kind and translate that as *an unkosher country*)? A great many, I can tell you. My own Zayde, Reb Yochonon Gordon, of blessed memory, refused to consider moving to the United States back in the 1930s even though he already had three brothers there practicing as *shochtim* (ritual slaughterers) in New York. It wasn't until the Previous Lubavitcher Rebbe, Rabbi JI Schneerson, promised him that his children would remain faithful to Torah and the Chassidic way of life and would even study in the Rebbe's Yeshiva (a fanciful daydream at the time), that he agreed to put in his immigration papers. Thankfully, the dream was fulfilled when the Rebbe came to New York in 1940 and immediately founded a yeshiva where, indeed, my uncles were among the first students.

Sadly, we know of too many children of pious European parents whose children did not fare well Jewishly in America. As religiously committed as their parents may have been, young people born and/or bred in the America of the early to mid-twentieth century were all too often swept away by the dominant culture of the great melting pot. They were quickly Americanized and in the process jettisoned their parental values to embrace the popular culture of a tantalizing new world. It was the exceptional parent who was able to offer any meaningful resistance to this powerful societal trend. Few were creative enough to successfully communicate old world values in the context of the new social order.

Socially, professionally, and economically, those young people did very well indeed and in one generation became educated and successful though their parents were illiterate greenhorn immigrants. But Jewishly? Not too many managed the transition that well. Those who remained faithful to their forefathers' way of life were generally those whose parents worried enough to do something about it. Who survived Jewishly in the end? Only those whose parents ensured a meaningful Jewish upbringing for their children, both in school and at home. It wasn't easy, but there were the moral heroes and heroines who stood out at the risk of ridicule by the majority.

Jacob worried in Egypt, my grandfather worried in Europe, and we need to worry today. Because history has shown that unless we are concerned enough to translate our anxieties into action, the Children of Israel may become disenchanted and mesmerized by prevailing civilizations. May we all have the strength to put work into the aspirations we have for our children, and may we enjoy *yiddishe nachas* now and always.

છબ

Vayechi

וַיְחִי יַעֲקֹב
And Jacob lived. (47:28)

Live — for Life! (and a Touch of Chazak)

A title usually reflects the theme of the subject matter. "Genesis" is about the beginning of the world, "Exodus" is about the Jews leaving Egypt. Whether it is a book or a film, the title should convey some idea of the content under discussion.

Which is why the title of this week's Parsha seems highly inappropriate. *Vayechi—And Jacob lived* (in the land of Egypt seventeen years) is the opening line of the very Parsha which goes on to tell us, not about Jacob's life, but rather about his death. And his last will and testament, and his funeral, and his subsequent interment in Hebron in the Holy Land.

Why would a Parsha that focuses on a person's last days on earth, his deathbed instructions and his burial be entitled *Vayechi—And he lived?*

The answer, say our sages, is that we are not discussing biological organisms, but Jews. And the test of true life for a Jew is whether he lived an authentic, consistent Jewish life—for life. Did he falter before the finish line, or was he faithful to his value system until the end? How do we know that Jacob did indeed live in the fullest sense of the word? That his was a genuine, dedicated G-dly life? When he remained true to those cherished ideals until his dying day. Only then can we say with certainty that his life was really alive; that his was a *Vayechi* existence as it was meant to be. So the fact that Jacob died a righteous man validated his entire being and endowed his life with its richest blessing—true life, genuine, alive, and real from beginning to end.

There are individuals who have their eight minutes of fame, who shine briefly and impress the world, only to fade away and leave us disappointed, watching so much unfulfilled potential dissipate into thin air. Others are longer lasting but don't quite go all the way. Like the *Kohen Gadol* Yochonon who served as high priest for 80 years and then went off the rails. Very scary stuff! No wonder Hillel, in Pirkei Avot, warns us not to trust ourselves morally until the day we die.

Complacency is dangerous. There are no guarantees. One must constantly "live," that is, grow and attempt to improve oneself lest we falter before we finish the game.

I will never forget my experience with a very fine man who was remarkably loyal to the company he worked for. For 45 years he was with the same group, totally and absolutely dedicated. Then he reached the age of compulsory retirement. Suddenly he took ill. The doctors had no real diagnosis. But he got sicker and sicker until he became incapacitated and eventually died. To this day, nobody knows what he died from. But those who knew him well understood that once he left the workplace to which he had devoted his entire adult life, he had nothing left to live for. Sadly, he had few other interests. His work was his life, and without work there was no life left.

It is psychologically sound to take up a hobby, learn to play golf or develop other interests outside of work. A Jew, though, should ideally start studying Torah. Go to classes, read a stimulating book. Studying and sharpening the mind are good for the brain. Recent medical research confirms that it can even delay the onset of Alzheimer's. Most importantly, a person must have something to live for. Find new areas of stimulation. Discover, dream, aspire higher. Life must be lived with purpose and vigor.

That's why at the end of this week's Parsha, which also concludes the Book of Genesis, the congregation and Torah reader will exclaim *Chazak, Chazak V'Nitchazek—Be strong, be strong, and we will all be strengthened.* Because the tendency when we finish a book is to take a breather before we pick up the next one. Even if it's not *War and Peace* but a trashy novel, such is human nature. But a book of the Torah is not just any book. G-d's wisdom is not a cheap read. Torah is not just history or biography. Torah is our source of life, and we dare not ever take a breather from life. *Chazak* energizes us to carry on immediately. And so we do. The very same afternoon we open the Book of Exodus and continue the learning cycle without interruption.

Truth is consistent, from beginning to end. May our lives be blessed to be truly alive—with authenticity, faithfulness and eternal fulfillment. Amen.

₨ℓ₧

יְשִׂימְךָ אֱלֹקִים כְּאֶפְרַיִם וְכִמְנַשֶּׁה

May G-d make you like Ephraim and Menashe. (48:20)

Born in the USA

There is a tradition when we conclude a book of Torah or Talmud that we hold a *Siyum*, a celebration marking what is an admirable achievement, the successful conclusion of an entire section of Torah study. At such occasions it is customary for the student/celebrant to deliver a talk where he or she connects the beginning of the book with the end, thus revealing a golden thematic thread that runs through the whole work.

This week's Parsha, *Vayechi*, concludes the entire Book of Genesis.

What connection can we find between the beginning and end of the Book of *Breishit?* The first part of the book tells the story of Creation, while the end deals with the passing of Jacob and the Children of Israel down in Egypt.

Well, let's think about it. What is Creation? Not just a Big Bang or even Intelligent Design but an expression of a much higher and deeper purpose. The mystics teach that G-d was not content to have angels in heaven singing His praises. He wanted earthly beings, men and women of flesh and blood with earthly passions and temperaments living physical lives and still being able to rise above the moment to experience the spiritual purpose of it all. He desired human beings who would be exposed to all the human distractions associated with the physical condition—from beach holidays to summer sales—and still remain focused on the spiritual.

When we endow our material lives with spiritual value, with a sense of higher purpose, meaning, destiny, and eternity, then we fulfill the Creator's original plan to bring heaven down to earth and build a home for G-d in the physical, often crass, world below.

And therein lies the connection of the beginning of the Book of Genesis with its ending. To be a good Jew in the Holy Land is one thing. To remain holy and heavenly in the fleshpots of Egypt is another. Egypt represented the centre of decadence of the day. For the Children of Israel to go down there and still remain faithful to the G-dly way of life is bringing heaven down to earth big time. To live an upright, moral life in a morally degenerate society is to validate and justify the whole idea of creation and the Creator's decision to bring into existence mortal beings endowed with the freedom to choose how they will live their lives.

Perhaps this is the reason Jacob chose to bless the children of Joseph, Ephraim, and Menashe, with the words, *By you shall Israel bless (their children), saying May G-d make you like Ephraim and Menashe.* Indeed, this is the traditional blessing we give our children to this day, that they grow up to be like Ephraim and Menashe. But why? Why should Jacob promise that for posterity Jews would bless their children to be like Joseph's children? Why not to be like his own children, the twelve tribes of Israel?

Perhaps Jacob knew that in generations to come, Jews would again be wandering through their own Egypts and exiles. He understood that Jewish history was destined to be filled with hostility and challenge. Thus, the role models for young Jews would need to be people like Ephraim and Menashe, who were born and bred in Egypt and yet remained faithful to the traditions of Jacob; who courted with the Pharaoh and still lived righteous Jewish lives.

Twenty-first century kids need heroes they can relate to in order for them to be inspired by their example. Joseph's boys negotiated the tricky turf of Egyptian palace intrigue while never forgetting who they really were. When kids who are "Born in the USA" will still be spiritually connected to the Creator's heavenly way, then we will have made that dwelling place for G-d in the lower realms for which the whole world was created in the first place.

ෆාෆ

ויגוע ויאסף אל עמיו
He expired and was gathered unto his people. (49:33)

Immortality

A book title reflects the theme of the book. Likewise, the titles of our Parshas should be accurate depictions of the subject matter under discussion. Why then does the title of our Parsha, *Vayechi—and he lived*—go on to describe not Jacob's life but the very end of his life and, in fact, his death and funeral?

Let me be faithful to Jewish tradition and try to answer one question with another question. Interestingly, the Torah never actually states that Jacob died. It simply says that *he expired and was gathered unto his people.* This prompted one of the Talmudic sages to expound that *our father Jacob never died.* Whereupon his colleagues challenged him and asked, *did they then bury Jacob for no reason? Did they eulogize him in vain?* And the Talmud answers—*As his descendants live, so does he live* (Taanit 5b).

Life does not end with the grave. The soul never dies, and the good work men and women do on earth continues to live on long after their physical passing. More particularly, if there is regeneration, if children emulate the example of their forbearers, then their parents and teachers live on through them.

When Jacob was about to breathe his last, he called his children to gather round his bedside. Our Parsha recounts what he told each of them. But the Oral Tradition gives us a behind-the-scenes account. Apparently, Jacob was anxious to know whether all his offspring were keeping the faith, and he put this concern to them at that time. They replied, *Shma Yisrael Hashem Elokeinu Hashem Echad—Hear O Israel, the L-rd is our G-d, the L-rd is One.* They were saying that the G-d of Israel their father would always be their G-d too. Jacob was comforted and responded, *Baruch Shem Kevod Malchuto L'olam Vaed—Blessed be the Name of the glory of His Kingdom forever and ever*—or in plain English, *Baruch Hashem!*— *Thank G-d* (Pesachim 56a).

When all of Jacob's children remained faithful to his tradition, that was not only a tribute to Jacob's memory but the ultimate gift of eternal life bestowed upon him. His spirit lives on, his life's work continues to flourish, and he is still present in this world as his soul lives on in the next.

Whenever I have been privileged to attend the International Conference of Chabad-Lubavitch Emissaries in New York, with thousands of rabbis and lay leaders in attendance, one of the most special moments for me in an altogether powerful event is when the Chairman, Rabbi Moshe Kotlarsky, does his now-famous global roll call. While I was proud to rise and represent South Africa when our turn came, an even prouder and profoundly moving moment was when the rabbis were asked to indicate in which decade they went out to their respective communities as Emissaries of the Rebbe on his *Shlichus*. A handful of old men stood for the 1940s, a somewhat larger group of senior rabbis rose for the 1950s, and so it grew by the decade. But when the call was made for those who had gone out to serve communities around the world after 1994, that is, after the passing of the Rebbe, many hundreds of young rabbis rose. At that moment, it was clear to everyone in that huge hall that Jacob never died. Just as his students are alive, carry on his teachings, and still answer his call to go out and change the world, so too does the Rebbe live on. Whether it means moving to Belarus or Bangkok, Sydney or Siberia, Alaska or the bottom of Africa, the Rebbe's mission is still moving people, literally and spiritually.

In following his path, Jacob's children immortalized him. Such a Parsha is aptly entitled *Vayechi—And he lived*. Ultimately, our children make us immortal. And so do our students, our spiritual children. May we each be privileged to raise families and disciples who will be true Children of Israel, faithful to our father Jacob and the G-d of Israel. Amen.

2

Sefer Shemot
The Book of Exodus

Jewish Population Control

This week we open a new book, *Exodus,* second of the Five Books of Moses. The story of our Parsha, *Shemot,* begins with the enslavement and bitter bondage of the Israelites in Egypt. In spite of the back-breaking oppression, hardship, and humiliation, the Jewish People would be forged in this fiery furnace of exile.

Jewish women, in particular, are given much of the credit for our eventual deliverance. *In the merit of the righteous women of that generation was Israel redeemed from Egypt* (Sotah 11b). The most important contribution of the women then was that they were prepared to bring children into the world despite those impossible living conditions. Furthermore, it was they who encouraged the menfolk to raise families during their slavery. The Talmud recounts how the women would soothe their husbands in the fields, charming and gently coaxing them into intimacy. Through their dedication was a generation born.

And today? There is no bondage and little suffering in our lives. Our biggest hardship is paying the mortgage, tuition fees, and fixing the transmission in the second car. Even those among us who struggle financially live far more comfortably than any of our forbears. But we have been so conditioned—make that brainwashed—by a societal value system and media manipulation, that anybody with more than three children is positively primitive and, oh so unsophisticated.

Everyone knows that the very first commandment in the Bible is *Be fruitful and multiply,* and all of us are called upon to build and populate the world. But the argument goes that this only applied in the beginning of time when there was Adam and Eve and a handful of others, but today we suffer from overpopulation, hunger, and poverty. Well, everyone also knows that overpopulation is not a problem in affluent countries and communities. And we also know that hunger could be alleviated if there was an equitable global food distribution program. Having another kid in California isn't really going to cause starvation in Bangladesh.

Certainly from a uniquely Jewish perspective, we Jews are grossly underpopulated. We have still not replaced the one third of our nation wiped out in the Holocaust. By now, we should have been far more numerous. Sure, our numbers are depleting because of assimilation, but also because we are having smaller families. Jews seem to take the two-per-family rule more seriously than most. If anything, we can claim a dispensation from the holy injunction to comply with Zero Population Growth on the grounds that we are still making up our losses. Besides, chances are we won't be turning to the United Nations or the World Bank for their assistance. If necessary, we will help ourselves.

Then there is Israel. Let's face it. A factor which exacerbates our difficulties in the Middle East is that Palestinians have more children than Israelis. If every Israeli family had one more child we wouldn't be so dependent on massive Aliyah numbers from around the world. Isn't it expensive to have a big family? Without doubt, more mouths to feed, clothe, and educate means a bigger family budget. But it is also a question of priorities, allocations, and making choices. A family vehicle instead of a luxury car is only one example of how larger families manage.

At the end of the day, we trust in G-d and really do believe that with every new child comes a new blessing of sustenance from Hashem to help us raise that child. Over the years, on many occasions, I have heard women past menopause say they wish they had had more children. How many famous actresses have been busy with their careers and when they were finally ready to start a family, it wasn't easy. Their own biological clocks ticked away while they were playing other people's lives on screen.

My wife and I have, thank G-d, been blessed with a large family. Over the years, we have been on the receiving end of many jokes and snide remarks. With incredulous, wide eyes people asked my wife, *How many children do you have?!* Her stock answer? *One of each.* I can well appreciate the rabbi who got tired of all the dirty looks at his kids. Wise guys would challenge him with questions like *when are you going to stop?!* His reply? *When I hit six million!* End of discussion.

So, if you're feeling broody, go for it. If you want to bring yourself many beautiful blessings (not to mention grandchildren) for many years to come, have another child. Don't be intimidated by convention, cynics, or even your mother in law! Plan a larger family. It'll make you larger than life and give you much satisfaction and *nachas*—for life.

Our grandmothers in Egypt were heroines. Their faith built a nation. May we do our share and, please G-d, we will be redeemed too.

৯৯

בהוציאך את העם ממצרים תעבדון את האלקים על ההר הזה

*When you take the people out of Egypt,
you will serve G-d on this mountain. (3:12)*

Great Expectations

We never really know why things happen. Do we always deserve every-thing life throws at us, good or bad? Allow me to share a message from this week's Parsha that may shed a little light on the mysteries of life and our higher destinies.

This is the week of the beginning of bondage for the Jewish People in Egypt. Moses experiences his first official Divine revelation at the Burn-ing Bush. There he is charged with the formidable mission to confront the Pharaoh and demand that he *Let my people go*. Moses is full of questions and repeatedly seeks G-d's reassurances.

In one exchange at the Bush, Moses asks, *Who am I that I should go to Pharaoh and that I should take the Children of Israel out of Egypt?* Rashi interprets the first part of the question as Moses doubting his own quali-fications to suddenly become a player in the king's court. In his typical humble way Moses didn't see himself worthy of challenging the mighty monarch of Egypt. The second part of the verse is explained by Rashi to be questioning the worthiness of the Jewish People. What have they actu-ally done to deserve such a miraculous redemption?

To which the Almighty answers, firstly, have no fear and have no doubts; *I will be with you*. And secondly, *this is your sign that I have sent you: when you take the people out of Egypt, you will serve G-d on this mountain.*

Now it's very nice to know that this mountain was, in fact, Mount Sinai and that the Burning Bush encounter occurred on that very same moun-tain. But wherein lies G-d's answer to Moses' second question? He asked *who am I?* So G-d replied to the point and said don't worry: *I will be with you.* But to the question of by what merit did Israel deserve redemp-tion, we don't see any answer. That they *will serve G-d on this mountain* doesn't seem relevant to the discussion at all.

Here it is that we find a fascinating insight into the intriguingly infinite ways of Providence. G-d was saying that it was not necessarily for what they had done in the past that he was ready to redeem the Jewish People but for what He anticipated for them in the future. On this very mountain they would receive His Torah; they would become His chosen messengers to be a light unto the nations; they would be the moral standard bearers for the entire world. Never mind what they did or didn't do in the past. G-d had big plans for this nation, and it would all begin with the impending Exodus.

What a powerful message for all of us. Sometimes, the kindness G-d does for us is not because we've *been* good but rather to enable us to *become* good. It's not for what we have *already* done but for what we still *will* do.

I know a man who in midlife experienced a near-fatal coronary. He collapsed one day while cycling with his friends. Fortunately, his life was saved by the prompt medical intervention of paramedics and surgeons. When I visited him in hospital, he was overwhelmed by one idea: his indebtedness to G-d, the Healer of all flesh. "Rabbi," he said, "I was a goner. What did I do to deserve this gift of life?"

So I shared with him the Rashi mentioned above and told him it might not be something he had done in the past but something he would still do in the future. Perhaps G-d gave him a new lease on life for a reason. Not only to enjoy more years with his family but to do something significant for G-d, for His people, for the world.

The Almighty's confidence proved justified. The man went on to deepen his personal spiritual commitments and also made most meaningful contributions to Jewish life in our community.

So should any of us be the beneficiaries of a special blessing from Above, instead of patting ourselves on the back and concluding that we must have done something wonderful to be thus rewarded, let us rather ask ourselves what G-d might be expecting us to do with this particular blessing in the future. How can we use it to further His work on earth? Special blessings always carry with them special responsibilities.

May each of us successfully develop all the potential G-d sees in us and use it for our own moral development and to somehow better the world around us.

৯৫৫৩

אהי' אשר אהי'
I shall be as I shall be. (3:14)

Who Am I?

This week the "Prince of Egypt" makes a dramatic return to the screens and stages of Jewish life. Moses appears on the Biblical scene. He tries to stop the persecution of his brethren, receives a death sentence for his troubles, and is forced to flee to Midyan, where he marries Tziporah and is tending the flocks of his father-in-law, Jethro. Then, at the burning bush, comes his first divine revelation.

G-d calls upon the young shepherd to go back to Egypt and redeem his people. The mission is nothing less than to face up to the Pharaoh himself and deliver the L-rd's famous stirring message—*Let my people go!*

In characteristic humility, Moses is a most reluctant leader. He seems to be looking for all sorts of reasons why he is unworthy of the task. At one point, he asks the Almighty, *Who shall I say sent me? What is Your name?*

Now we are familiar with many names that G-d goes by, but the one G-d now gives Moses is puzzling and enigmatic, mysterious and mystical—*I shall be as I shall be.* Strange name for a Supreme Being.

Many commentaries expound on the possible interpretations of this most unusual name. Here is one very powerful explanation. The significance of this name is that it is posed in the future tense. *I shall be as I shall be.* Moses was asking the ultimate existential question. How do I call You, G-d? "What is Your name," means how are You to be identified, known, understood? How can finite, mortal man come to know the Infinite Being, was the question Moses was asking.

And G-d's answer was, *I shall be as I shall be*—future tense. You want to know me, Moses? I'm afraid you'll have to wait. You cannot necessarily understand Me by what has happened in the past. Not even in the present. In the here and now, when we stare life and its ambiguities in the face, we experience tremendous difficulty in our vain attempts to grasp the Almighty's vision or perceive His vast eternal plan.

To truly understand the Infinite G-d takes infinite patience. One day, somewhere down the line, in the future, He will make Himself known to us. Only then will we come to really know Him and His inscrutable ways. *I shall be as I shall be.*

Don't we all ask Moses' question at times? Why is there tragedy in the world? Why is there so much human suffering, pain and agony, so much *tzorris* to contend with? How many families have been torn apart literally and figuratively in Israel through war and terrorism? How many individuals do we each know in our own communities, or even our own families, who have experienced personal tragedy in their lives? Why? we cry. Why?

So, we are told that right at the very beginning of Jewish history, the very first time G-d spoke to Moses, he said to him up front—"I know you want to be able to understand Me and My ways; but please accept that it is impossible—for now." *I shall be as I shall be.* One day, you will be able to know Me. Not today, nor tomorrow, nor even the day after—but one day in the future everything will make sense and be understood. Ultimately, in time, all will be grasped and G-d's ways will finally be fathomed.

In the meantime, we live with faith, trust, hope, and a great deal of patience as we see destiny unfolding and we aren't quite sure what to make of it. And we look forward with eager anticipation to that awesome day when the Almighty's great name will be known and understood, and we will see with our own eyes of flesh that G-d is good and His ways are just. May it be speedily in our day. Amen.

છ૭ભ

Vaera

וְהוֹצֵאתִי אֶתְכֶם מִתַּחַת סִבְלֹת מִצְרַיִם
And I shall take you out from under
the burdens of Egypt. (6:6)

Prisoners of Patience

We keep hearing about tolerance. Be accepting of other people, of differences. Diverse cultures need to find ways of coexisting on a planet that keeps getting smaller. But there are times when too much tolerance can be detrimental. Like when the Jews were slaves in Egypt.

And I shall take you out from under the burdens of Egypt is the promise the Almighty told Moses to pass on to the Jewish People in this week's Parsha.

One of my holy ancestors, Rabbi Yitzchak Meir of Gur (widely known by his work Chiddushei HaRim), once reinterpreted the Hebrew word for "burdens"—*sivlos*—to mean *patience*, as in *savlanut* in modern Israeli Hebrew today. What he meant was that before the Children of Israel could be freed from Pharaoh, G-d had to first free them of their own inner bondage. Years of slavery and drudgery had left the Israelites so oppressed and so hopeless that they had sunk into a terrible tolerance, accepting their situation as final and irreversible. Depression had taken its toll on the Jewish psyche, and they were in no position to leave Egypt. They felt so low, so downtrodden, that at that stage freedom was absolutely unimaginable.

Some of us are too tolerant of intolerable situations and so long-suffering that we ourselves become insufferable. Before G-d can take us out of our personal Egypts, we need to banish the "suffering servant" mentality from our own headspace.

Some years ago I was doing marriage counseling for a couple who was having domestic troubles. During one of our sessions, the wife confided that she would never suspect her husband of being unfaithful. When I asked her why, she said, "He's too lazy, listless, and lethargic. He would never have the energy to even attempt an affair. He has no ambition. He never gets angry no matter what I do. I can scream and shout, abuse him, send him to the dog house and he never says Boo! I can feed him bread and jam for dinner every night and he will never complain."

It reminded me of the story of the *shtetl shlemiel* whose wife had her girlfriends over and wanted to demonstrate to them how she was the master of her home. So she called over her husband and started giving him all sorts of little chores around the house. *Shlemiel do this, Shlemiel do that, Shlemiel come here, go there.* The timid little man did everything as commanded. Then for her grand finale, the shrew says, *now Shlemiel, I want you to crawl under the table and stay there until I call for you.* So Shlemiel dutifully obeys. After ten minutes, she calls for him to come out from under the table. At this point our *shlemiel* decides to assert his manhood and defiantly declares *I'm not coming out from under the table just because you told me to. I will stay here as long as I please. I will show you who is the boss in this house!*

I remember when we were busy doing alterations on our house, and I was convinced that the new tiles in one of the rooms didn't look straight. When we had a site meeting with the builder and the architect, I asked the architect to give us his opinion. He said I was right but that, unfortunately, this was the standard of workmanship today, and it was acceptable. I couldn't believe my ears. Why should I have to accept inferior work? It was plain to see that the tiles and the ceiling were not lining up! Sadly, we live in a world of mediocrity, where society—including the very professionals who should be safeguarding those standards—has become tolerant of that mediocrity.

It pains me when I see many Jewish organizations in our community lowering the bar of professionalism and accepting inferior standards on so many levels. We seem to be plagued by a morass of mediocrity. We should always strive for excellence and insist on the highest standards—whether at work or in the synagogue. Patience and tolerance are virtues, but we have become too tolerant.

In order to become truly free we must first remove the shackles of servitude from our own mentality. We must stop being so patient and accepting of all that is oppressive in our lives—whether it be slavery, exile, discrimination, anti-Semitism, or mediocrity in general. We can become masters of our own destiny if we want to. But the first step on the road to our own personal exodus is to lower our threshold for tolerance and break out of the prison of patience.

ॐ

ולא שמעו אל משה מקוצר רוח

*And they did not listen to Moses out of
shortness of breath. (6:9)*

Never Lose the Spirit

"What about the workers?!"

Imagine you have been working on the job for years and years. It is hard manual labor, and you are not simply tired but exhausted, demoralized, drained, and frustrated. And then, one fine day, some new fellow on the floor stands up and promises a whole new world of equality, rewards, and ultimate freedom. Do you believe him or are you beyond hope? Do you dare hold out for a better tomorrow and risk being disillusioned and cast into despair yet again, or do you simply accept your fate and give up dreaming?

So it was with our ancestors in Egypt. They were slaving away all those years when a new face appeared and began making promises. Moses brings a message from G-d that they are about to be redeemed. There is a Promised Land ahead. All is not lost. There is light at the end of the tunnel.

The Jews' response? *And they did not listen to Moses out of shortness of breath and from the hard labor.*

One commentary explains that "shortness of breath" shouldn't be understood only literally. The Hebrew for breath is *ruach,* which can also mean "spirit." In other words, they weren't able to heed Moses' call not only from physical breathlessness but because they lacked the spirit. Having suffered in bondage for so long, they no longer had the faith or hope to believe that freedom was still in the realm of the possible. It was simply beyond them. They had lost the spirit.

In the history of Egypt not a single slave had ever escaped. How could an entire nation ever walk free? Moses was a dreamer, they must have thought. It was just not realistic to hold out such high hopes only to have them dashed yet again. And so the people were utterly despondent and spiritless, and therefore, they could not hear or absorb Moses' message.

It happens all too often. People become so set in their mediocrity that they give up hope of ever achieving the breakthrough. Marriages get stuck in the rut of routine, and the tedious treadmill keeps rolling along until we lose even the desire to dream. And Israel's people, even brave leaders, are so despondent from years of war, attrition, and terror that they clutch at imaginary straws because, basically, if we are honest with ourselves, they have simply lost the resolve.

I have often quoted a wise proverb heard in the name of the legendary Chasid, Reb Mendel Futerfas. "If you lose your money, you've lost nothing. Money comes and money goes. If you lose your health, you've lost half. You are not the person you were before. But if you lose your resolve, you've lost it all." Moses brought new hope to a depressed, dreamless nation. He gave them back the spirit they had lost, and eventually, through the miracles of G-d, the promise was fulfilled and the dream became destiny.

To be out of breath is normal. To be out of spirit is something the Jewish People can never afford. May we never lose the spirit.

₮⃣

Throw Small Stones

Gratitude is an attitude, some wise man must have surely said once upon a time. The Bible in this week's Parsha demonstrates just how far Jewish tradition teaches us to be grateful and to remember our benefactors.

Seven of the ten plagues occur in this week's reading. Moses, messenger of G-d, is busy bringing down these terrifying plagues on Pharaoh's Egypt. Yet, interestingly, he calls upon his brother Aaron to be the agent for the first three plagues—Blood, Frogs, and Lice. Why did Moses not do it himself as he would do the others?

The Midrash, quoted by Rashi, teaches us that because it was through the agency of the waters of the river that Moses was saved as an infant when he was put in the basket. It would have been insensitive and, therefore, inappropriate for him to strike those very life-saving waters in order to bring on the plague. Seeing as the Blood and the Frogs both dealt directly with the water, it was Aaron who struck the water rather than Moses. Similarly with the third plague of Lice. The lice came from out of the ground, and the earth, too, had helped Moses to cover the body of the Egyptian taskmaster he had killed defending the Jewish slave. Therefore, it would have been wrong for Moses to strike the earth and, so, for this plague, too, Aaron was the agent.

What a monumental lesson to each of us on the importance of gratitude. Firstly, do water and earth have feelings? Would they know the difference if they were struck and who was doing the striking? How much more so should we be considerate of human beings who do have feelings when they have done us a kindness. How scrupulous we ought to be not to offend people, especially those who have come to our assistance. Second, Moses was 80 years old at the time of the plagues. The incident with the water occurred when he was a mere infant and with the earth when he was a very young man. Yet, all these years later he is still sensitive not to strike the objects that had helped him. He did not say as so many have after him, "So what have you done for me lately?"

There are a number of theories as to why human beings seem to have this psychological need to tarnish the image of their past benefactors. Perhaps it is because we are inherently uncomfortable with the notion of being eternally indebted to anyone. It cramps our style and diminishes our independence. So if we find fault with those who have helped us previously, we absolve ourselves of any moral indebtedness. Now we're even. I don't owe you anything any more.

The story is told of the Chasam Sofer (Rabbi Moshe Schreiber, 1762–1839) that he once did an enormous favor for someone. Later, the fellow asked him, "Rabbi, what can I ever do to repay you for your kindness?" The Chasam Sofer replied, "One day, when you get upset and angry with me, please remember what I have done for you today, and rather than pelting me with big stones, please throw small stones instead." How sad, but oh so true. In a similar vein, I remember hearing my own Zayde say of someone, "Why does he hate me so much? I never did him any favors!"

This little story of Moshe, which is only an aside to the main body of the Biblical narrative, teaches us to remember the kindnesses that are bestowed, both when they happen and forever. If one who has been good to us in the past does wrong and needs chastising, let someone else volunteer for the job. He may need rebuking but we should not be the ones to do it. Yet again, the Torah teaches us not only religious ritual but how to be better people, more sensitive and, yes, eternally grateful human beings.

Ⅎ⃩Ⅎ

Bo

שלח עמי ויעבדוני

Let my people go, that they may serve Me. (10:3)

Let My People Go

The words ring out again and again. Moses demands of Pharaoh that he finally relent and grant the Jewish People their freedom—*Shalach Ami v'Yaavduni*. "Let my people go that they may serve me" are the precise words G-d told Moses to convey to the stubborn monarch.

It is quite interesting to see how some expressions and phrases become popular, forever memorable, and attract a huge following while others just don't seem to catch on. *Let my people go* became the theme song for the story of Egypt and the Exodus way beyond our own community. It has been used as a catchphrase for a variety of political causes. Sadly, the last Hebrew word of the very same phrase somehow got lost in the shuffle. *V'Yaavduni—that they may serve Me—*never quite made it to the top of the charts. The call to Freedom excites the human spirit. The challenge of service and commitment, however, doesn't seem to elicit as much enthusiasm. We must never forget that the purpose of leaving Egypt was to go to Sinai, receive G-d's Torah and fulfill Jewish destiny.

I remember back in the early '70s when Jews the world over were demonstrating for their oppressed brethren in the then Soviet Union, demanding of the Russian government that they allow Jews the freedom to leave if they wanted to, the rallying cry was "Let my people go." Sadly, they left out the *v'Yaavduni—that they may serve Me.* We were so concerned about political liberties that we forgot a primary purpose of being free, namely to enjoy religious freedom and live fulfilled Jewish lives.

Indeed, for so many of our Russian brethren, obtaining their exit visas and acquiring freedom of movement did little to help them in the service of G-d. 70 years of organized atheism behind the Iron Curtain left its toll. We are delighted that they can live in Israel (or Brighton Beach), but while many organizations dedicated themselves to helping Russian Jews spiritually, the fact remains that far too many are still outside of the Jewish community and its spiritual orbit.

In my own backyard, here in South Africa, this idea has become blatantly obvious. We have now had a democratically elected government since 1994. We have free and fair elections where all citizens have had the opportunity to cast their ballots. It was a long, hard struggle, but political freedom has been achieved. And yet, while confidence levels in our country's future are much improved, millions of people living here are still suffering from the very same hardships they endured under apartheid—ignorance, poverty, and poor health. Nobel Peace Laureate Desmond Tutu even castigated the country's black leaders for allowing a situation where a small number of well-connected blacks have become enriched while the masses remain impoverished. HIV/AIDS is still public enemy number one, and even the sons of some of the most high profile political figures have succumbed to the deadly disease.

It is clear. Political freedom minus spiritual purpose equals disillusionment. Leaving Egypt without the vision of Sinai would be getting all dressed up with nowhere to go. It is not enough to let our people go. We have to take them somewhere. *That they may serve Me* means that we need to use our political freedom to experience the freedom and fulfillment of faith and a life of spiritual purpose dedicated to His service.

ℯᾷ℗

Finding Freedom

Free at last, free at last, thank G-d Almighty we are free at last. Who said these words? No, it wasn't Moses but American civil rights leader, Dr. Martin Luther King, Jr. But it could have been Moses—or for that matter any one of the millions of Jews who were liberated from Egyptian bondage.

This is the week when we read of the great Exodus. *Let my people go that they may serve Me* was the Divine call transmitted by Moses to Pharaoh. Now, if the purpose of leaving Egypt and Pharaoh's whip was to be able to serve G-d, so where is the freedom? We are still slaves, only now we are servants of the Almighty?

Indeed, countless individuals continue to question the merits of religion in general. Who wants to submit to the rigors of religion when we can be free spirits? Religion stifles the imagination, stunts our creative style, forever shouts instructions, and lays down the law. Thou Shalt do this and Thou Shalt better not do that, or else! Dos and don'ts, rules and regulations, are the hallmark of every belief system, but why conform to any system at all? Why not just be me?

Many Jews argue similarly. Mitzvahs cramp my style. Keeping kosher is a serious inconvenience. *Shabbos* really gets in the way of my weekend. And *Pesach* has got to be the biggest headache of the year.

Long ago, the rabbis of the Mishna said it was actually the other way around. *There is no one as free as he who is occupied with the study of Torah.* But how can this possibly be true? Torah is filled with rules of law, ethics, and even expectations and exhortations that we take the high road and behave beyond the call of duty. How can the rabbis say that Torah makes us free? Surely it is inhibiting rather than liberating?

Let me share an answer I once heard on the radio while driving in my car. It was during a BBC interview with Malcolm Muggeridge, the former editor of *Punch,* the satirical British magazine. *Punch* magazine was arguably England's most irreverent publication. It mocked and ridiculed the royal family long before they did it to themselves. In his latter years, Malcolm Muggeridge became religious, and the interviewer was questioning how the sultan of satire, the prince of *Punch* could make such a radical transformation and become religious? How could he stifle such a magnificent free spirit as his?

Muggeridge's answer was a classic, which I still quote regularly. He said he had a friend who was a famous yachtsman, an accomplished navigator of the high seas. A lesson he once gave him in sailing would provide the answer to the BBC man's question. *If you want to enjoy the freedom of the high seas, you must first become a slave to the compass.*

A young novice might challenge the experienced professional's advice. But why should I follow that little gadget? Why can't I go where I please? It's my yacht! But every intelligent person understands that without the navigational fix provided by the compass, we will flounder and sail in circles. Only by following the lead of the compass will the wind catch our sails so we can experience the ecstasy and exhilaration of the high seas. *If you want to enjoy the freedom of the high seas you must first become a slave to the compass.*

The Torah is the compass of life. It provides our navigational fix so we know where to go and how to get there. Without the Torah's guidance and direction we would be lost in the often stormy seas of confusion. Without a spiritual infrastructure we flounder about, wandering aimlessly through life. Just look at our kids when they're on vacation from school and are "free" from the disciplines of the educational system. Unless they have a program of some kind to keep them busy—like a summer camp—they become very frustrated in their "freedom."

Within the Torah lifestyle there is still ample room for spontaneity and freedom of expression. Not all rabbis are clones. To the untrained eye every *yeshiva bochur* looks identical—a black hat, glasses, and a beard. The truth is that every one is distinctively different, an individual with his very own tastes attitudes, personality, and preferences. They may look the same, but they are each unique.

We can be committed to the compass and still be free spirits. Indeed, there are none as free as they who are occupied with Torah.

ജാരു

ולכל בני ישראל הי׳ אור במושבותם
To the Children of Israel there was light in their dwelling.
(10:23)

A Ray of Light

Suffered from any power failures lately? In recent times, there have been some major blackouts of electrical power across vast stretches of the United States. I still remember the essay I wrote in high school on the Great Blackout back in the '60s. In Johannesburg, where I live, we experience localized power failures on a far-too-frequent basis. Sometimes it may even prevent us from enjoying a hot chicken soup or *cholent* on Shabbos.

All these blackouts are but minor inconveniences, though, when compared to the Great Blackout in Egypt before the Exodus. Plague Number Nine was Darkness and from the Biblical account, it would seem to make today's power failures pale into insignificance. *There was thick darkness over the entire land of Egypt for three days. No man could see his brother, nor could any person even rise from his place for three days. And to the Children of Israel there was light in all their dwellings* (Exodus 10, 22–23).

According to the commentaries, it was not merely an absence of light but a tangible fog that got worse with time. The first three days they could not see. The next three days they could not even move. But, miraculously, just down the road in the Jewish neighborhood of Goshen there was light!

This verse, *To the Children of Israel there was light in their dwellings,* prompted the saintly Rabbi Israel of Rizhin to offer the following beautiful homiletic interpretation: *Every Jew is a ray of light. It only depends on their dwellings.* The environment a Jew finds himself in may sometimes cast a shadow over the spirituality and light he possesses innately. In no way, however, does this detract from the G-dly light inside every single Jew. Not every environment is conducive to the light. Sometimes a Jew may be negatively affected by his surroundings but, intrinsically, every Jew is a ray of light.

Do you believe in G-d? Not enough. You have to believe in Jews too. Don't even be cynical about cynical Jews. I know it isn't always easy, even for those of us who, philosophically, identify with this concept. Often I have to argue with members of my Shul's daily Minyan on this point. A fellow comes in to say *Kaddish* after losing a loved one. The Shul regulars sometimes have their little private wagers. Will he stay the course and recite *Kaddish* for the year, or will he disappear after the initial mourning period? Some of the guys are cynical, admittedly from past experience. They quote the old Yiddish adage: *The malach hamoves (Angel of Death) feeds the synagogues.* I often have to play the role not only of defender of the faith but of defender of the flock. Never give up on any Jew, I always tell them. Indeed, many a time we are pleasantly surprised when a Jew for whom the Shul experience was completely foreign goes on to become one of our committed regulars.

I admit there are also times when I have to remind myself never to become cynical and to stand by my own ideological beliefs. One particular incident some years ago stands out in my mind.

We were invited by friends to join them at home to watch a new drama-documentary on the Holocaust. It was a long production, and we were quite a few people. We decided to have an interval. The break also gave us a chance to *daven* Mincha. Among the invitees was an uncle of our hostess. He was a well-known successful diamond merchant. He was also known to be an avowed atheist. When it came time for Mincha, I wasn't sure what to do about him. Should I give him a Siddur or not? Would he consider it a provocation and get upset? In my uncertainty, I left it and decided to do nothing.

Later, when I looked around, he was nowhere to be seen. Sure enough, the next day his niece confirmed my suspicions. He was upset that he was not invited to join the prayers. "Am I not a Jew too?" he asked her. He was justifiably hurt, and I made special efforts in the weeks ahead to pacify him, assuring him that he was as Jewish as I was.

I learned an important lesson from that episode. Never write off a single Jew, not even if he claims to be an atheist. Never be cynical of the cynics. Indeed, every Jew is a ray of light. All we need do is make the environment a little more conducive and the inherent light will shine forth.

 formfeed

החדש הזה לכם ראש חדשים
This month shall be the head of
the months for you. (10:23)

Little Moons

Veteran or novice, whom do you choose? Say you are the coach of a sports team and you have accomplished stars but they may be approaching their sell-by date. Then you have some budding talents waiting on the sidelines to get a shot at proving themselves. Who do you pick for your team? You want to win and are safer sticking with the experienced proven professionals. On the other hand, you want to build a team for the future. So whom do you choose?

In this Parsha we read how G-d commanded Moses and Aaron concerning the Jewish calendar, Rosh Chodesh—the New Moon—and how ours would be a lunar calendar. *This month (Nissan) shall be the head of the months for you.*

According to the Midrash, quoted by Rashi, Moses had a difficulty with the precise definition of *new* moon. So G-d explained it to Moses by showing him exactly what the new moon looked like in the sky. *This month* may thus be understood as *this moon*, that is, this is the type of moon you should sanctify when you proclaim Rosh Chodesh, the new month.

Why, in fact, do we sanctify the moon when it is brand new, a mere speck in the sky? Should we not rather consecrate the moon on the fifteenth of the lunar month when it is full, an impressive, big round ball of celestial proportions? Surely the sanctification of the moon should be when it is majestically full and not when it is still tiny and barely visible?

Indeed, there are two kinds of moons. There is the big, full moon of the middle of the month. But as soon as we go into the second half of the month that moon will start waning and then it will diminish from view until it is completely out of sight. The full moon is one day away from being over the hill, and from there on it's downhill all the way until the end of the month. Whereas the new moon, small as it may be, represents growth. It may be tiny now but it will grow nightly in the sky and will, one day soon, be full and resplendent. And so the Almighty says to Moses, I want you to sanctify the small moon; this little moon is pleasing in my eyes. *This you shall see and sanctify*, the small, new moon that will very soon loom large in your eyes.

Israel is likened to the moon. Ours is a lunar calendar because we are a lunar people. (I did not say lunatics!) The Jewish People, too, have a history of waxing and waning, of ups and downs. And just like the two moons, so are there two types of Jews. There is the full Jew, rich in knowledge and practice but content and complacent, perhaps somewhat fat and lethargic. This Jew is committed to his faith, maybe has been his whole life, but he is on the verge of a decline. He is about to start waning because he is tired and uninspired. He knows it all, he's been there and done it all and like Humpty Dumpty is sitting on top of the wall just waiting for a fall.

And then there is the fledgling Jew, the little new moon that has just emerged from the darkness. He is still tiny but he has just discovered the beauty and truth of Judaism. This Jew is geared for growth, poised for prominence and ready for take-off. He is still very much a novice, his knowledge is still minute; but he is inspired, excited and passionate about his newly found faith.

So which Jew will we count our months by? Who will shape our future? Will it be the old, tired veteran who is too old to change and just about ready to retire? Or will it be the new Jew who, though inexperienced, is still longing to learn and ready for renewal and rebirth?

Personally, I've always been inspired by the new Jew. I get a kick out of seeing that eager, open mind brimming with questions, finding things I took for granted fascinating. To me the new Jew represents hope and optimism, freshness and promise.

G-d told us to count our months by the small new moon. May I humbly suggest that it is the new Jew who will illuminate our world and make G-d count.

ಓ

קַדֵּשׁ לִי כָל בְּכוֹר

Sanctify to me every firstborn. (13, 2)

The Money or the Box?

What? Is the rabbi turning TV quiz show host? Has he become a gambling man? Believe it or not, this rabbi is talking about what all good traditional rabbis talk about—the Parsha. Have no fear; the Bible isn't going to Vegas. The Money or the Box really does relate to the 10th Plague G-d visited upon Egypt prior to the Exodus.

The final, devastating Plague of the First-Born saw the Israelite firstborn spared. Therefore, they are eternally indebted to G-d for their very lives. So ever since then, the firstborn of Israel "belong to G-d." And that's why this Parsha gives us the Mitzvah of Pidyon HaBen, the Redemption of the First-born.

In a tradition that is practiced to this day, when the first-born is a male, the father together with a Kohen—who as minister in the Temple would serve as the Almighty's agent—perform a redemption ceremony after the child has passed his first month of life. This is known as *Pidyon Haben.* (The reason the *Pidyon Haben* is not nearly as well-known as the *Bris* is because it is the exception rather than the rule. It only applies to the first-born and only when the delivery is natural—not by caesarian section—and if either father or mother are of Kohen or Levite families, they are exempt from the procedure.)

In this quaint and curious ceremony, a fascinating dialogue takes place between father and Kohen. The child is brought in, and the father makes the following declaration to the Kohen: "My Israelite wife has borne me this firstborn son." Whereupon the Kohen asks the million dollar question, "Which would you rather have—your first-born son or the five silver shekels you are obligated to give me for his redemption?"

The gathered crowd waits in suspense to hear the father's response. What will he choose? To keep the five silver shekels and give the hassles of newborns, daybreak diaper changes, and future school fees to the Kohen, or will he keep his child and hand over the shekels? Thankfully, Jewish fathers have always made the correct choice, albeit sometimes with a little gentle prodding from their wives.

Now I ask you, is this not ridiculous? "'The money or the child?" This is a serious question? I mean, what normal father is going to willingly give away his child to save a few bucks? What is the point of this discussion? Why engage in ancient, obsolete rituals that have no relevance today?

The answer is that it is very relevant. "The money or the child" means much more than just here and now at the ceremony on Day 31 of this boy's life. The

Kohen is asking the father a very serious question indeed. What he is really asking is this: "Throughout your child's life, what will be most important to you, what will be uppermost in your mind? Will it be money and materialism, acquiring more status symbols than your friends, or will it be your children and your family life? Where will your priorities lie? Will you slave away building up your business and become an absentee dad? And you, Mom, will you wile away the days drinking cappuccino and doing your nails, or will you be personally involved in raising your children, teaching and nurturing them?

That is the Kohen's question. And based on experience, every father should think very carefully before he will answer that question—hopefully, in the affirmative.

So the next time you're invited to attend a *Pidyon Haben* ceremony and you hear that seemingly preposterous question being asked, "Do you prefer the money or the child?" don't laugh and don't snicker. Don't grimace and don't even giggle. Be dead serious. Because a Jewish father is about to decide the future for his family and indeed for our people. Let's hope he makes the right choice.

ℹ℺

Beshalach

ויקח משה את עצמות יוסף עמו

And Moses took the remains of Joseph with him. (13:19)

The Test of Transition

They say *adapt or die*. But must we jettison the old to embrace the new? Is the choice limited to modern or antiquated, or can one be a contemporary traditionalist? Do the past and present ever coexist?

At the beginning of this week's Parsha we read that Moses himself was occupied with a special mission as the Jews were leaving Egypt. *And Moses took the remains of Joseph with him.* Over a hundred years before the great Exodus, Joseph made his descendants swear that they would take him along when they would eventually leave Egypt. As Viceroy, Joseph could not hope to be buried in Israel when he died as his father Jacob was. The Egyptians would never tolerate their political leader being buried in a foreign land. But he did make his brethren give him their solemn promise that when the time would come and all the Israelites would depart, they would exhume his remains and take him along. And so they did. So it was that while everyone else was busy packing up, loading their donkeys, and getting ready for the Great Trek into the Wilderness, Moses himself was busy with this mission, fulfilling the sacred promise made to Joseph generations ago.

Now, according to tradition, Joseph was not the only one to be exhumed and reinterred in the holy land. His brothers, too, were accorded the very same honor and last respects. Yet, it is only Joseph whom the Torah finds it necessary to mention explicitly.

Why?

The answer is that Joseph was unique. While his brothers were simple shepherds tending to their flocks, Joseph was running the affairs of state of the mightiest superpower of the day. To be a practicing Jew while blissfully strolling through the meadows is not that complicated. Alone in the fields, communing with nature and away from the hustle and bustle of city life, one can more easily be a man of faith. But to run a massive government infrastructure as the most high-profile statesman in the land and still remain faithful to one's traditions, this is not only a novelty; this is nothing less than inspirational.

Thrust as he was from the simple life of a young shepherd boy into the hub of the nation's capital to juggle the roles of Viceroy and Jew, Joseph represented tradition amid transition. It was possible, he taught the world, to be a contemporary traditionalist. One could successfully straddle both worlds.

Now as they were about to leave Egypt, the Jews were facing a new world order. Gone were slavery and oppression and in were freedom and liberty. During this time of transition only Joseph could be their role model. Unlike his brothers, he was able to make the transition from meadow to metropolis, from spiritual dreamer to economic strategist. They would need his example to show them the way forward into uncharted territory, the new frontier.

That is why the Torah only mentions Joseph as the one whose remains went along with the people. They needed to take him with them so that, like him, they too would make their own transition successfully.

Ever since leaving Egypt, we've been wandering through our own wildernesses. And every move has brought with it its own challenges. Whether from Poland to America or Lithuania to South Africa, every transition has come with culture shocks to our spiritual psyche. How do you make a living and still keep the Shabbos you kept in the *shtetl* when the factory boss says "Cohen, if you don't come in on Saturday, don't bother coming in on Monday either!?"

It was a test of faith that wasn't at all easy. Many succumbed. But many others stood fast and survived, even flourished. It was the test of transition. And those who modeled themselves on Joseph were able to make that transition while remaining committed to tradition. Democracy and a human rights culture have made that part of Jewish life somewhat easier but challenges abound still.

In all our own transitions today, may we continue to learn from Joseph.

ഇരു

זה א-לי ואנוהו אלקי אבי וארוממנהו
This is my G-d and I will glorify Him, the G-d of my fathers and I will exalt Him. (15:2)

Tradition

How important is *tradition* in Judaism? Obviously, the answer is that it is very important. I mean, they even devoted a major song in *Fiddler on the Roof* to tradition! How strong is the need for tradition in the spiritual consciousness of Jews today?

Despite the effects of secularism, I'd venture to suggest that there is still a need inside us to feel connected to our roots, our heritage, and our sense of belonging to the Jewish People. But for vast numbers of our people, tradition alone has not been enough.

And that applies not only for the rebellious among us who may have cast aside their traditions with impunity, but also for many ordinary, thinking people who decided that to do something just because "that's the way it has always been done" was simply not good enough. So what if my grandfather did it? My grandfather rode around in a horse and buggy! Must I give up my car for a horse just because my Zayde rode a horse? And if my Bobba never got a university degree, why shouldn't I? So, just because my grandparents practiced certain Jewish traditions, why must I? Perhaps those traditions are as obsolete as the horse and buggy?

There are masses of Jews who think this way and who will not be convinced to behave Jewishly just because their grandparents did.

We need to tell them *why* their grandparents did it. They need to understand that their grandparents' traditions were not done just for tradition's sake but that there was a very good reason why their forbears practiced those traditions. And those very same reasons and rationales still hold true today.

Too many young people were put off tradition because some Cheder or Talmud Torah teacher didn't take their questions seriously. They were silenced with a wave of the hand, a pinch of the ear, the classic *when you get older, you'll understand,* or the infamously classic, *just do as you're told.*

There are answers. There have always been answers. We may not have logical explanations for the *tzorris* that befalls so many innocent people, but all our traditions are founded on substance and have intelligible, credible underpinnings. If we seek answers, we will find them in abundance, including layers and layers of meaning, from the simple to the symbolic, the philosophical, and even the mystical.

This week's Parsha features the "Song of the Sea" sung by Moses and the Jewish People following the splitting of the sea and their miraculous deliverance from the Egyptian armies. Early on, we find the verse, *This is my G-d and I will glorify Him, the G-d of my fathers and I will exalt Him.*

The sequence in this passage is highly significant. First comes *My G-d* and only thereafter *the G-d of my fathers.* In the Amidah, the silent devotion which is the apex of our daily prayers, we begin addressing the Almighty as *Our G-d and the G-d of our fathers ... Abraham, Isaac and Jacob.* Again, *our G-d* comes first. So it is clear that while *the G-d of our fathers,* or tradition, most definitely plays a very important role in Judaism, still, an indispensable prerequisite is that we must make G-d ours, personally. Every Jew must develop a personal relationship with G-d. We need to understand the reasons and the significance of our traditions lest they be seen as empty ritual to be discarded by the next generation.

Authentic Judaism has never shied away from questions. Questions have always been encouraged and formed a part of our academic heritage. Every page of the Talmud is filled with questions—and answers. You don't have to wait for the Pesach Seder to ask a question.

When we think, ask, and find answers to our faith, then the traditions of our grandparents become alive, and we understand fully why we should make them ours. Once a tradition has become ours and we then realize that this very same practice has been observed uninterruptedly by our ancestors throughout the millennia of Jewish life, then Tradition becomes a powerful force that can inspire us forever.

ജ⟩ൽ

ויסע משה את ישראל מים סוף
And Moses caused Israel to journey from the Sea. (15:22)

What Does G-d Have to Do with It?

Is it possible to be spiritual and selfish at the same time? Let us have a look at one word in this week's Parsha that sheds important light on this question. *Vayasa Moshe et ha'Am—And Moses caused Israel to journey from the Sea* (Exodus 15, 22). The great miracle happened. The sea had split and the Egyptian army was no more. The word *vayasa* means that Moses had to move his people. But why was it necessary for Moses to have to *cause Israel* to journey? Why wouldn't they move on their own?

According to Rashi, the enemy was so confident of victory against the Israelites that they bedecked their horses and chariots with gold, silver, and precious jewels. These treasures were now being washed up on the seashore, and the Jews were collecting the riches. They were in no mood to move on, but Moses said they had a date with G-d at Mount Sinai. As the nation's leader, he had to compel them to carry on their journey.

The Zohar gives a more spiritual explanation. We are taught that the Divine Revelation at the Splitting of the Sea was quite an extraordinary experience. What a simple maidservant saw at the sea even the great prophets were not privileged to see. According to this mystical view, it was not the material wealth they were obsessed with, but rather the incredible spiritual delights they were experiencing.

Either way, it was up to Moses to move them along to their date with destiny. And the question is this. If it was gold and silver that was delaying their journey to Sinai, we can well understand the need for Moses to hurry them on. But if it was the spiritual experience of inspired revelation, why move at all? Why not stay there as long as possible? Surely, the more G-dly the revelation, the better!

The answer is that G-d Himself was calling. Sinai was beckoning. The whole purpose of the Exodus and all the miracles in Egypt and at the sea was nothing more than to receive the Torah at Sinai. That was the Revelation that would give the Jewish People its unique way of life and its very raison d'être. Sinai represents our mission, our mandate. Sinai made us G-d's messengers on earth. However we may understand the concept of a Chosen People, it was the Sinaitic experience that made us that. Any detours or distractions from the journey to Sinai are therefore out of the question—no matter how lofty or spiritual they might be.

It comes as no great shock to learn that money is not as important as Sinai. But that spirituality, too, must take second place to Sinai is indeed big news. And what exactly is Sinai? Torah. And what is Torah? G-d's will and how He wants us to live our lives. In other words, the bottom line is, what does G-d want? How does He want us to act, to live our lives? So, the big news story here is that even the most amazing spiritual experience, the most extraordinary revelation is not as important as doing what G-d wants us to do.

This is a very important message that emerges from this one word, *Vayasa*. It's not what *we* want that counts, but what *G-d* wants. If we want money and diamonds and He wants to give us His Torah, then we leave the loot and we go to Sinai. And even if it is a spiritual experience we seek and G-d says *Go to Sinai,* we still go to Sinai, and we leave the spiritual inspiration for another time.

It once happened back in the old country (a true story), that late one night, a wagon driver ran into a Yeshiva and cried out to the students to come out and help him. It was urgent, he said. Apparently, his carriage had overturned and his horse was stuck in a ditch and in danger of dying. He needed help to get the carriage upright. It was late at night, and there was no one else he could turn to, so he appealed to the Yeshiva Bochurim to come to his assistance.

At this point, the students' Talmudic training kicked in and a long *halachic* debate ensued. Was it right to leave their Torah study for a horse? After all, is not Torah study equal to all the other Mitzvahs combined? On the other hand, the horse provided this Jew's livelihood. Which takes precedence? The debate raged on and on, and when they finally did decide to go out and help the poor man, it was too late. The horse had died.

Sometimes we can get so caught up in our own spirituality that we become quite selfish. Spiritually selfish, of course, but selfish nonetheless. At the end of the day, it's not whether we are into materialism or monotheism, money or metaphysics. The ultimate question—and, in fact, the only question—is what does G-d want of me at this moment in time? Where should I be, and what should I be doing right now?

So if you find yourself in a quandary or on the horns of a difficult dilemma and you desperately seek clarity, ask yourself this very question, *what would G-d want?* Yes, sometimes it might be helping a horse out of a ditch. But if that is the call of the hour, then so be it. It might not be very spiritual, but it is the right thing to do.

And if it's the right thing to do, that makes it very G-dly.

৪৩৫৪

Yitro

וַיְדַבֵּר אֱלֹקִים אֵת כָּל הַדְּבָרִים הָאֵלֶּה לֵאמֹר

And G-d spoke all these words, to say. (20:1)

But Does It Speak to You?

The locomotive was making its first appearance in the little town of old. No one had ever seen a horseless carriage before. Every one of the townspeople had gathered at the new station to witness history in the making. The gun was fired, and with a flourish of huffing and puffing the locomotive roared down the tracks. Well ... the engine that is. Unfortunately, the *shlemiel* whose job it was had forgotten to hitch the other cars to the engine, and they were left behind in a trail of smoke.

Sometimes the best laid plans of mice and men don't come to fruition: a business strategy, a football game plan, or even—perish the thought—a synagogue resolution made on Yom Kippur!

The introduction to the Ten Commandments we will read in this week's Parsha is, *And G-d spoke all these words, to say ...* in Hebrew, *leimor.* Now, when the Torah uses the word *leimor, to say,* it is usually G-d telling Moses something important that he, in turn, should pass on and tell the Jews. So the word *leimor* makes perfect sense. He said it to him to say it to them. But here we have a problem. You see, every Jew was present at Sinai and, according to the mystics, that includes even the unborn souls of future generations. So there was no need for Moses to pass on anything to anyone. All the Jews heard the Ten Commandments directly from G-d, so why the word *leimor?* To say to whom?

Rabbi Dov Ber, the great Maggid of Mezeritch, explained that here the word *leimor* means *to speak to you.* That these words should not remain mere words but that they should resonate and say something meaningful to you personally. They should be said and heard so that they continue to reverberate forever in your minds, heart, and deeds. The Ten Commandments dare not remain an abstract idea, an unhitched engine, a nice philosophy, or an interesting cultural practice—something akin, say, to the ancient Incas of Peru. The Ten Commandments must be relevant enough to make a difference in our lives; otherwise, whom did G-d say them to and whatever for?

The rabbi was in his study when in walked Berl, the town pickpocket. "Rabbi I was walking down the street and found this wallet lying on the ground. I know that to return a lost article is a Mitzvah of the Torah so I brought it in. Perhaps you can make an announcement in Shul and find the rightful owner."

The rabbi sees there is a fair amount of cash in the wallet. He is so inspired at Berl's change of heart that he embraces him and congratulates him on his reformation. Later, on his way out, the rabbi notices that the gold wristwatch he had in his jacket pocket is missing. He calls Berl and asks him if perchance he may have inadvertently taken his watch. Berl confesses to the crime and the rabbi is rather perplexed. "I don't understand you Berl. You find a wallet full of cash in the street and you return it and then you go and steal my gold watch?"

Berl answers, "Rabbi, returning lost articles is a big mitzvah but when it comes to picking pockets, business is business."

We all believe and we all want to do mitzvahs, big and small. The trick is to translate our inner piety into outer practice. What does my faith do for me? Does it speak to me? How does it transform my behavior, my life? Does it make any tangible difference in my value system? The Torah cannot remain a theory on the drawing board.

The Ten Commandments do indeed speak to us. The question is, are we listening?

⁗

לֹא תַחְמֹד
You shall not covet. (20:14)

The Most Difficult Commandment?

This is the week G-d gives the Torah to the Jewish People. The reading of the great Revelation at Sinai occurs in this Parsha and with it come, of course, the world famous Ten Commandments.

Which would you say is the most difficult of the Big 10 to keep? Would it be the first, the mitzvah to believe in G-d? Faith doesn't come as easily to our generation as it did in the days of our grandparents. Children with aged parents suffering ill health and who require much attention might argue that the fifth commandment, Honor thy Father and Mother, is the most difficult. Still others would say that Number 4, keeping Shabbos, cramps their lifestyle more than any other.

While each has a valid point, personally I would cast my vote for the last commandment, Number 10, Thou Shalt Not Covet. *You shall not covet your friend's house; or his wife, servant, ox, donkey, or anything that belongs to your friend.* Or in simple English, don't desire his beautiful home, stunning wife, super-efficient P.A., nifty sports car, or anything else that is his.

Now it's one thing not to steal the stuff, but not even to desire it? That's got to be the hardest of all. Really now, is G-d not being somewhat unreasonable with this one? Is He being realistic? Surely our Commander-in-Chief doesn't think we are angels!

So allow me do what all good Jews do and try to answer a question ... with another question. Why does the text of this commandment first list a variety of specifics (house, wife, servant, etc.) and then still find it necessary to add the generalization (and all that belongs to your friend)?

One beautiful explanation offered by the rabbis is that it is to teach us a very important lesson for life—a lesson which actually makes this difficult commandment much easier to live with. What the Torah is saying is that if perchance you should cast your envious eye over your neighbor's fence, don't only look at the specifics. Remember to also look at the overall picture.

Most people assume the grass to be greener on the other side. But we don't always consider the full picture, the whole package. So he's got a great business and a very healthy balance sheet. But is *he* healthy? Is his family healthy? The wife looks great at his side when they're out together, but is she such a pleasure to live with at home? And if he should have health and wealth, does he have *nachas* from his children? Is there anybody who has it all?

Every now and then I am reminded of this lesson. A fellow who seemed to be on top of the world suddenly has the carpet pulled out from under his feet and in an instant is himself in need. Another guy who you never really thought that highly of turns out to be an amazing father, raising the most fantastic kids. As the Yiddish proverb goes, everybody has his own *pekkel.* We each carry a knapsack through life, a parcel of problems, our own little bundle of *tzorris.* When you are young, you think difficulties are for "other people." When you get older you realize no one is immune. Nobody has it all.

There is a famous folk story of a group of villagers who formed a circle. Each individual opened his knapsack, revealing the contents for all to see. They walked around the circle of open parcels, and everyone had the opportunity to choose whichever one he liked. Interestingly, in the end, each one chose his own.

I believe it's more than just a case of "better the devil you know." When we actually see with our own eyes what the other fellow's life is all about behind closed doors, what's really inside his knapsack, we feel grateful for our own lot in life and happily choose our very own *pekkel,* with all its inherent problems.

The Almighty is giving us good advice. Be wise enough to realize that you've got to look at the whole picture. When we do, this difficult commandment becomes more easily observable. Not only is it sinful to envy what other people have, it is foolish. Why? Because life is a package deal.

₭)℁

Keep Your Balance

So what is the definition of a well-balanced individual? One who has a chip on both shoulders!

This week we read the Ten Commandments. The great Revelation at Sinai saw Moses come down the mountain bearing the Tablets of stone with the Ten Commandments engraved on them. As we know, the two tablets were divided into two columns—the Mitzvahs between us and G-d and the commandments governing our human relations. The one side was devoted to our responsibilities to G-d, such as Faith and Shabbat, while the other side dealt with our inter-personal duties, such as no murder, adultery, and thievery.

The message that so many seem to forget is that both these areas are sacred, both come directly from G-d, and both form the core of Torah law and what being Jewish is all about. We must be well-balanced Jews. We may not take the liberty of emphasizing one tablet over the other. A healthy, well-rounded Jew lives a balanced, wholesome life and is, as the Yiddish expression goes, *gut tzu G-t un gut tzu leit*—good to G-d and good to people. If you focus on one side of the tablets to the detriment of the other, you walk around like a *hinke'dike,* a handicapped Jew with a bad limp.

A good Jew is a well-balanced Jew. This means that it's not good enough to be *frum* on the ritual side of Judaism and free and easy on the *mentschlichkeit* side. You've got to be honest and decent and live with integrity so people will respect you too. If you are *frum* to G-d but not fair with people, you can become a fanatical fundamentalist blowing up people in the name of G-d! The same G-d who motivates and inspires us to be G-dly and adhere to a religious code also expects us to be a *mentsch.* There is no doubt whatsoever that it is, in fact, a *mitzvah* to be a *mentsch.*

But neither can we neglect the right side of the tablets. A good Jew cannot simply be a democrat, a humanitarian. Otherwise, why did G-d need Jews altogether? It is not enough for a Jew to be a nice guy. Everyone must be nice. All of humankind is expected to behave honestly and honorably. To be good, moral, ethical, and decent is the duty of every human being on the planet. A good Jew must be all of that and then some. He or she must be a good person and also fulfill our specific Jewish responsibilities, the Mitzvahs that are directed to Jews which are uniquely Jewish.

I recently came across an interesting statistic on the Ten Commandments. The right-hand tablet bearing the duties to G-d consists of 146 words. The left-hand tablet listing our human responsibilities only has 26 words. Yet, tradition has it that both tablets were filled with writing. There were no big, blank spaces. So how did 26 words equal the space of 146 words?

Well, anybody who uses a computer or word processor knows the answer. You simply adjust the font size. You can type in 10 point size or 24 point size. Take your pick. So if we apply that same principle to the tablets we have a simple solution. The 26 words on the left, reflecting our moral and ethical human responsibilities were simply a bigger size than the 146 words on the right reflecting our G-dly, religious responsibilities. So, I guess we shouldn't be underestimating the importance of the human relations side of the Ten Commandments.

Then again, just so we don't start limping, the very same G-d who said we should be nice also said we should have faith, keep Shabbos (yes, it is one of the Big 10), kashrut, mikvah, and the rest of it. In fact, when people say to me, "Rabbi, I'm not that religious but I do keep the Ten Commandments," I often wonder whether they are actually aware that keeping Shabbos is Commandment Number 4.

As we read the Ten Commandments this week, let us resolve to keep our Jewish balance, not to limp or become "one-armed bandits." Please G-d, we will live full, wholesome, rich and well-balanced Jewish lives. Amen.

೫ೱ

Mishpatim

Is Religion Still Relevant?

Cyberspace, outer space, inner space. Genome maps, globalization, going to Mars. Smart cards, smart bombs, stem cells, cell phones. There is no denying it. We live in a new age. Science fiction has become scientific fact. And the question is asked: In this new world order, with science and technology changing the way we live, is religion still relevant? Do we still need to subscribe to an ancient and seemingly long obsolete code of laws when we are so further advanced than our ancestors?

This question reminds me of little old Hymie Levy of London who somehow found himself attending a cocktail party in the company of aristocracy. Poor Hymie was completely out of place mingling with the lords and ladies of British royalty and high society. One duchess was so irritated by this ordinary Jew's presence that she confronted him directly. Oozing sarcasm, in her finest elocution, she let on to Hymie, *Did you know that my family traces its lineage back to the very people who were personally present at the signing of the Magna Carta!* Hymie Levy was unfazed. He gave a little shrug of his shoulders and whispered straight into the ear of Her Haughtiness, *Un Mein Zayde Moishe vos poisonally present by de giving of de Tzen Commendments!*

Have the Ten Commandments passed their sell-by date? Are Atheism, Murder, Adultery, Thievery, Lying, and Jealousy out of fashion? Notwithstanding all our marvelous medical and scientific developments, has human nature itself really changed? Are not the very same moral issues that faced our ancestors still challenging our own generation? Whether it's an ox cart or a Mercedes, road rage occurs, and courteous coexistence is still a choice we must make. Looking after aged parents is not a new problem. Whether it was Adam and Eve or Michael and Sheryl, the grass somehow always seems greener on the other side. For some inexplicable reason, the other guy's wife, house, horse, or Porsche still seem more attractive and desirable than our own.

The very same issues dealt with in the Bible—sibling rivalry, jealous partners, and even murder—are still the stuff of newspaper headlines today. So what else is new? Has anything changed? Yes, today we have astronauts and space stations, laser beams and laptops, but the basic issues and choices human beings must face remain identical. Once upon a time the question was *do I hit him with my club or slice him up with my sword?* Today the question is *do I call up the nuclear submarines or send in the guided missiles?* Technology has developed in leaps and bounds. Fantasies of yesterday are reality today. Communication, automation, and globalization have altered our lives dramatically. But the core issues, the basic moral dilemmas, have not changed one iota. We still struggle with knowing the difference between right and wrong, moral or immoral, ethical or sneaky, and not even the most souped-up computer on earth is able to answer those questions for us.

Science and technology can do wonders for humankind. But they can also blow us all to kingdom come faster than Attila the Hun could have ever imagined. Science and technology answer *how* and *what.* They do not address the question of *why.* Why are we here in the first place? Why should I be nice to my neighbor? Why should my life be nobler than my pet Doberman's? Science and technology have unraveled many mysteries that puzzled us for centuries. But they have not answered a single moral question. Only Torah addresses the moral minefield—as it does repeatedly in the civic and social laws contained in this parsha.

And those issues are perhaps more pressing today than ever before in history. Torah is truth, and truth is eternal. Scenarios come and go. Lifestyles change with the geography. The storylines are different but the gut level issues are all too familiar. If we ever needed religion—or in our language, Torah—we need it equally today, and maybe more so.

May we continue to find moral guidance and clarity in the eternal truths of our holy and eternally relevant Torah. Amen.

৵৵ঞ

אם בגפו יבוא בגפו יצא
If he came in alone, he goes out alone. (21:3)

No Deposit, No Return

Once upon a time, Yiddish-speaking Jews coined the phrase *luftmentsh* to describe that incurable dreamer type who is always building castles in the sky. *Luft* means air, and someone who lives in the air with pie-in-the-sky fantasies qualifies for this title of dubious distinction. "If only this deal comes off, I'll be set for life!" "When I win the lottery," etc., etc. The money has been spent before he has even bought the ticket. He's always anticipating the big breakthrough and then, in the end, explaining why it didn't quite happen. This is the life story of our *luftmentsh.*

There is a line in the beginning of this week's parsha, Mishpatim, concerning the Jewish bondsman, which sums up this phenomenon. *Im b'gapo yavo, b'gapo yeitzei—if he came in alone, he goes out alone.* Simply speaking, this tells us that if he entered his period of service unmarried, he must leave unmarried, and his master may not exploit him to father children who would be born into servitude. But this Torah phrase has become a traditional way of expressing one of life's basic home truths: *no deposit, no return.* No effort, no reward. No risk, no profit.

Whether in business, relationships, the social intercourse of communities and nations, or in raising our children, the principle holds true. "The only place success comes before work is in the dictionary." Or, in the words of the Psalmist, "Those who sow in tears will reap with songs of joy."

There is the old story told of Shmerel, a poor man who once walked by the home of the richest man in the *shtetl*. There was an aroma wafting out of the dining room where the wealthy man was enjoying his favorite dish, cheese blintzes. Shmerel took one whiff and was overcome with temptation. He just had to taste those blintzes. As soon as he comes home, he begs his good wife, Chasha, to make him some of those blintzes. Chasha says, "I'd love to make you blintzes, Shmerel, but I have no cheese." "*Nu,* my dear, so make it without the cheese." "But we've got no eggs either." "Chasha," says Shmerel, "you are a woman of great ingenuity. I'm sure you can make a plan." So Chasha sets out to do the very best she can under the circumstances. Her work done, she sets the plate of blintzes in front of her dear husband. Shmerel takes one taste, crooks his nose and says, "You know Chasha, for the life of me, I cannot understand what those rich people see in blintzes."

Clearly, you cannot make good blintzes without using the right ingredients. Just as clearly, we cannot have *nachas* from our children without putting in the necessary ingredients of a good Jewish education, a solid upbringing at home, quality family time, and above all, by setting a good example.

Too many parents assume that *nachas* is a democratic right, almost a genetic certainty. If parents are good, successful people and committed Jews, then surely their children will turn out the same. But there are no such guarantees, especially in today's complex, confusing and very troubled society.

A hundred years ago Rabbi Sholom Ber of Lubavitch said, "Just as it is a Biblical commandment to put on *tefillin* every day, so is it obligatory to spend a half hour daily thinking about our children and to do whatever possible to ensure that they follow the path in which they are being guided."

So don't be a *luftmentsh*. Put in the effort, and please G-d, you will see the rewards. Whether it's our work or our children, may we enjoy the fruit of our labors.

ℴℴ

לא אגרשנו מפניך בשנה אחת ... מעט מעט
I shall not drive them away from you in a single year ... little by little. (23:29–30)

Not Yet

Everyone knows that Rome wasn't built in a day. There isn't a building site on earth where the contractor hasn't explained away his delays by using that well-worn cliché. But did you know that Jerusalem wasn't built in a day either? Nor was the Holy Land.

In this week's reading, the Almighty tells the Jewish People that they will not inherit the land of Canaan immediately. It will be to their benefit that the conquest of the Promised Land be gradual and deliberate. To settle the land successfully would take time, and they were cautioned up front to be patient. The process would unfold at a slow but steady pace so that there should be a smooth transition.

I shall not drive them away from you in a single year, lest the Land become desolate and the wildlife of the field multiply against you. Little by little shall I drive them away from you until you become fruitful and make the Land your heritage.

Overnight sensations are often just that. They don't necessarily last. Slow and steady, step-by-step, the gradual approach usually enjoys longevity and enduring success.

Every Jew has a share in the Promised Land—not only geographically but spiritually. There is a piece of Jerusalem inside each of us. We all have the capacity for holiness, sanctity, and spirituality. But sometimes we may be discouraged from beginning the journey to our own personal promised land. The road seems too far, the trip too long and arduous. Here G-d is giving us wise words of encouragement. Don't expect overnight miracles. Don't say *I have a whole country to conquer, how will I do it?* Rather, say *Where should I start today?* Don't look at the end of the road; look at the first few steps you need to take right now. Then tomorrow, you will take a few more steps and the next day the same and before long, the whole land will be yours.

If you were just starting your first business venture and I asked you, *are you a millionaire?* would you say *no* or would you say *not yet, I'm working on it?* The optimistic entrepreneur will accept that, having just begun his career, he may not have made it big yet, but being a go-getter, he is convinced that it is only a question of time before success will be his. It should be the same in our Jewish journeys.

Franz Rosenzweig (1886–1929) was a German-Jewish philosopher who as a young man actually considered opting out of Judaism completely. But his intellectual bent compelled him to at least do a proper examination of Judaism first. So he went to Shul and, as it happened, experienced a spiritual transformation. He went on to become a serious student of Judaism. It seems that when Rosenzweig was once asked, *do you put on Tefillin?* his answer was *not yet.* Not *no,* but *not yet*—and there is a critical difference between the two. *No* implies that I am not doing it now nor do I have any plans to do it any time soon. *Not yet* means that while presently I may not be there, I am still open to the suggestion. Hopefully, the time will soon come when I will be ready to make Tefillin part of my daily observance.

The *not yet* approach is a good one. There is no one who does it all. We all have room for growth. We should all want to aspire higher. If we don't practice a particular good deed at the moment, there is no reason why we cannot begin doing it in the near future. Let us never be discouraged by the length of the journey. Let us begin the first steps and keep moving. It may be slow, but as long as there is steady growth, we will get there. *Rome wasn't built in a day* and *a journey of a thousand miles begins with but a single step.*

So if someone asks, *do you put on tefillin,* or *do you keep kosher,* or *do you observe Shabbos,* and you don't, please don't say *no.* Say *not yet.*

೮ನಿ૭

Terumah

תִּקְחוּ אֶת תְּרוּמָתִי

And you shall take for me a contribution. (25:2)

Giving or Getting?

The very first United Jewish Appeal was launched this week. Our Parsha deals with the first fundraising campaign in history. Moses initiated it in order to build the sanctuary in the wilderness as well as to acquire all the materials needed for the special utensils required for the sacred services. This is, therefore, a good time to talk about the art of giving.

The holy Rabbi Israel of Rizhin said that while some people claim, "If you give you are a fool and if you take you are clever," Jewish tradition teaches us that those who give and think they are only giving are, in fact, the fools. But those who give and understand that they are also receiving at the same time are truly wise.

The truth is that in giving, we actually receive more than we give. And not only a slice of heaven in far away paradise but even in the here and now. Certainly, in our relationships—whether family, business or social—our generosity is often reciprocated, and we find the other party responding in kind. But it goes beyond giving in order to get back. The very fact that we have done good, that which is right, noble and just, gives us a sense of satisfaction. "The takers of the world may eat better. But the givers of the world sleep better."

This explains the unusual expression in our Parsha, *V'yikchu li terumah—and you shall* take *for me a contribution.* Why *take?* Surely, *give* would be the more correct term. But because in giving we are also receivers, the word *take* is entirely appropriate.

For the same reason we find that the Hebrew expression for acts of loving-kindness is *Gemilus Chasodim.* It is no mistake that this is in the plural form. Because every time someone performs a single act of kindness, at least two people are benefiting—the receiver and also the giver.

I have seen people over the years who were good people, giving people, who shared and cared for others. Then, after years of being givers, they stopped. Why? They became frustrated at the lack of appreciation for all their hard work. After all, they had done for others, they never even got a simple "thank you." So they were disappointed, disillusioned, and in some instances, even bitter. They resigned from public life and from whatever community services they were involved in.

How sad that they didn't realize that even if human beings are notoriously unappreciative, G-d Almighty takes note of every act of kindness we perform. And He responds with infinite blessings in His own way. In fact, our sages taught that if we express regret over the good that we have done we might well forfeit all the merits we would have otherwise deserved.

The rabbinate is but one example of the helping professions. Anyone involved in a congregational position doesn't only make speeches and teach Torah. One is called upon to serve in a pastoral role—visiting, helping, counseling, comforting. While it can be very taxing and often emotionally draining, it is, without doubt, a source of deep satisfaction, particularly when one is able to make a real difference in people's lives.

There are, of course, many people I have been privileged to help in one way or another over the years. One feels a very profound sense of purpose knowing that you were able to help someone through a crisis, or lift their spirits in a hospital, or give them hope and solace in a time of loss. Sure, I was the giver. But I received so much back in return. My life was rendered so much more meaningful, more worthy, for having helped a person in need.

I shall never forget the look on a young woman's face when I gave her the good news that I had managed to locate her wayward, absentee husband and convinced him to sign on the dotted line to give her the long-awaited *Get,* the Jewish divorce that would finally free her to get on with her life. She was so radiant, absolutely beaming with joy. Whatever efforts I had made on her behalf were well worth it just to see her feel the freedom.

So whenever you think you're a big deal because you did something for a good cause, remember: you are receiving much more than you are giving. Let us all be givers and be blessed for it.

શળ

וְעָשׂוּ לִי מִקְדָּשׁ וְשָׁכַנְתִּי בְּתוֹכָם

They shall make for Me a sanctuary that I may dwell among them. (25:8)

Sinai or Sanctuary?

And in the beginning G-d was homeless and so He asked His People to set Him up with some digs. Where does it say *that*? Well, nowhere, actually. But it does say that G-d instructed Moses to tell the people *They shall make for Me a sanctuary that I may dwell among them.*

Now the question is, was G-d really homeless? Wasn't He already dwelling with the people? Why, it was just the other week that we read of the Revelation at Sinai and the Ten Commandments where G-d came down from heaven to earth? So why suddenly the need for a sanctuary for Him? The answer is that there is a fundamental difference between Sinai and the Sanctuary. Sinai represents a revelation thrust upon the people from above. G-d initiated and activated that encounter. In this experience the Jewish People were somewhat passive. All the thunder and lightning, physically and spiritually, came at them from On High.

The Sanctuary, however, had to be built by the Jews themselves. They had to take the initiative. From the fundraising campaign to raise and collect the raw materials needed for the sanctuary down to the nuts and bolts of construction, the *Mishkan* was a man-made edifice.

At Sinai the heavens opened for the greatest sound and light show on earth leaving a nation mesmerized and awe-inspired. But they themselves were passive recipients of this unique, never to be repeated gift from above.

To build a sanctuary took a whole building campaign. Men and women, young and old, everybody rolled up their sleeves. It took weeks, months of hard labor, meaningful contributions by every individual, planning and programming, designing, and then actually building a holy house for G-d. We made it happen. And thereby, it was the people who brought G-d down to earth.

Apparently it was important for the Jews to appreciate the value G-d attaches to self-help and to DIY projects of a spiritual nature. It is not good enough to sit around waiting for the extraordinary revelations, those once in a lifetime supernal visits the Good L-rd might bestow upon us. It is necessary for us to create the infrastructure, to take the building blocks in our hands and *Make me a Sanctuary.* To put it simply, are we waiting for G-d or is G-d waiting for us? Who makes the next move?

I met a guy not long ago and, as often happens to rabbis, the discussion turned to "Religion." He was pretty blunt about it and said, "Not for me, Rabbi. If G-d wanted me to be *frum,* he'd have made sure I was born in Bnei Brak, or at least into a religious family here." I told him he reminded me of the comedian who had a terrible fear of flying and argued that "If G-d intended man to fly, he'd have given him wings—or at least made it easier to get to the airport!" So he says, "If G-d wanted me to be an angel, he'd have given me wings too."

The fact is, G-d did give us wings. That's what Sinai was all about. He gave us a dose of revelation, of spiritual shock treatment that has saturated us with an eternal capacity to fly high, to touch the divine. But those were just the tools; now we have to learn to fly.

We may have been endowed with the potential to develop our connection to G-dliness, but after Sinai it's up to us to make it happen and to actually bring our innate power to the fore. True revelation is rare. While there certainly are those special moments when we witness the unmistakable presence of G-d in our lives, we cannot wait for lightning to strike. We need to build our personal sanctuaries for G-d in order to embrace Him and bring Him into our homes and families.

The Rebbe of Kotzk was once asked, "Where is G-d?" He answered, "Wherever you let Him in."

৪৩৫৪

Going for Gold

Did you know that, according to the Midrash, gold was only created to beautify the Beit Hamikdash, our holy temple in Jerusalem. That's right. It wasn't created to sit in Fort Knox or to stabilize the world's currencies or even for commodity traders to make the occasional windfall. And it was most definitely not put on this earth to adorn our bathroom sink handles. The rabbis taught that if the community could easily afford it, even the floors of the Beit Hamikdash should be paved with gold!

This week's *parsha* deals with the construction of the first *Mishkan*, the portable temple in the days of Moses, and we read of much attention to detail here. Gold, silver, copper, and other precious metals were donated by the Israelites to create a beautiful dwelling place for the Divine Presence.

Similarly, we are taught to beautify all our *mitzvahs*. A nice Menorah, a handsome Etrog Box, silver crowns for the Torah: these are but some of the ways we show respect for that which is sacred in our lives. Now, obviously, G-d doesn't need our gold and silver. But from our side we ought to make that which is important to us as beautiful as possible. A Shul can be a humble hut, but we need to demonstrate what our values are and where our priorities lie. To give honor and glory by beautifying His Holy House is one way of paying homage to G-d and thereby acknowledging the source of all our blessings.

A former South African Chief Rabbi, L. I. Rabinowitz, once penned an eloquent contrast between the "cathedral" type synagogue over which, ironically, he himself presided and the simple little *chassidic shtibl* of old. Everything was elegant and pristinely clean in the glorious domed Great Synagogue while the unadorned *shtibl* was anything but grand. On the one hand, the residue of the *kichel*, herring, and *schnapps* on the tables at the back didn't exactly inspire reverence for the celestial. And yet, wrote Rabinowitz, there was a certain spirit there that was lacking in the formal synagogue. There one could sense the scent of a sincere genuine prayer, hear a heartfelt *yiddishe krechtz* and be warmed by the special *chaver-schaft* and camaraderie.

Nevertheless, we should be asking ourselves whether we are paying enough attention to the state of our synagogues. Would we accept that our private properties be as poorly maintained as we do for G-d's property? Why is it that in our own homes the bathrooms are not only clean but also Italian tiled while the Shul facilities are often a shameful *schmutz*?

I remember getting a call one day from a wealthy man who had just finished building a stunning new home. He asked whether it was true that all the doorways in the home required a *mezzuzah*. When I answered in the affirmative, he complained bitterly at the high cost of *mezzuzahs*. Frankly, I had little sympathy knowing how many millions he had just spent on the house. Never mind the building costs; for every latest gadget and accessory he had money—but for the *mezzuzahs* suddenly finance was a problem. We go out to posh restaurants and spend lavishly to dine out in style—and then complain bitterly about the price of *kosher* food. We will happily pay fortunes for the Bar Mitzvah or wedding party with all that goes with it and then resent why the Shul charged as much as it did for the *Chupah* or why we were asked for a donation on the *Bimah*. The caterers, florists, musicians, printers, party coordinators, and entertainers all make a living on the *simcha,* and the Shul that was responsible for the main event is an afterthought.

My Shul president once told me that he was seeing congregants before Rosh Hashanah who wanted to book seats for the High Holy Days. One woman asked to be subsidized. When he asked her about her circumstances and why she had fallen on hard times, she replied that she hadn't at all. Why then was she requesting a discount on the normal fees? It turned out that she discovered that her sister-in-law had been subsidized. So if discounts were going, she wanted one too.

I know it is a long-standing Jewish tradition to drive a hard bargain and make sure you get value for money, and why not look for the proverbial *metziya,* a bargain, if you can find one? But that should not apply to our religious, educational, or communal institutions. Especially when it comes to the synagogue, we should remember why gold was created in the first place—to decorate, adorn, and beautify our places of worship.

By all means, live well. Spend on yourself and your family and enjoy. But let us try and give at least equal respect to the house of G-d.

₭₧

Tetzaveh

ואתה תצוה
And you shall command. (27:20)

Missing Moses

A seemingly dubious distinction belongs to this week's Parsha, Tetzaveh. It is the only reading in the Torah where the name of Moses is not mentioned, from the moment he was born until his passing. The opening words are *V'Atah Tetzaveh—and you shall command.* The *You* is Moses and G-d is telling him what to instruct the Jewish People. But the verse only says *You;* no name, no Moses.

Why?

Some explain that Moshe's *yahrtzeit,* 7 Adar, almost always occurs in this week and the absence of his name is an appropriate symbol of his demise. Others suggest that it is as a result of Moshe's own words. Remember the Golden Calf episode? The people had sinned, and G-d was going to wipe them out and start over again with Moses and his own dynasty. Moshe defended his errant flock before the Almighty, arguing for their forgiveness. And if not? Well, Moshe used some very strong words there. *Micheini noh misifrecho—Erase me from Your book that You have written!* Moshe himself said his name should be erased from the Torah if G-d would not forgive his people. So even though He did forgive them, the words of a Tzaddik are eternal and leave an impression. The effect of those words, therefore, was that somewhere in the Book, in Torah, his name would be erased. Moshe would be missing where he normally should have appeared. Thus it is that, in the week when we remember his passing, Moshe's name is gone.

So say a variety of commentaries. But, characteristically, the Chassidic commentaries, reflecting the inner dimension of Torah, go a step further— and deeper. What's in a name, they ask. Who needs a name? Does a person require a name for himself? Not really; he knows who he is. So a name is essentially for other people to be able to attract his attention, so they can call him, address him, and so on. In other words, a name is only an external handle, a vehicle for others to identify or describe him, but it is all outside of himself and peripheral to his own true, inner identity. Names are secondary to the essence of an individual. The essence of every person, who he or she really is, is beyond any name, beyond any superficial title.

So why is Moshe's name not mentioned? Because he said, "Erase me" at the Golden Calf? Because he spoke with *chutzpah* before the Almighty? You think it is a punishment? Not at all, says the Rebbe. On the contrary, this was perhaps the greatest moment in the life of our greatest spiritual leader.

What would we imagine to be Moses' finest hour? Receiving the Torah? Leading the Jews to the Exodus? Splitting the Sea? Would you be shocked if I told you it is none of the above? Indeed, Moshe's finest, most glorious, absolutely greatest moment on earth was when he stood his ground before G-d, pleading for his people, fighting for their forgiveness. His most brilliant, shining hour was when he put his own life and future on the line and said "G-d, if they go, I go! If you refuse to forgive these sinners, then erase my name from your holy Torah!" It was through Moshe's total commitment toward his people that the faithful shepherd saved his flock from extinction. And G-d Himself was pleased with His chosen leader's words and acceded to his request.

Is that something to be ashamed of? Far from it. It is something to be immensely proud of and something that serves as a shining example of what true leadership is all about. It is dedication and sacrifice, not power and honor.

So the absence of Moshe's name this week, far from being a negative, carries with it a profound blessing. It does not say the name Moshe, but *V'Atah*—and *You*. A name is only a name, but here G-d talks to Moshe in the second person directly. *You.* And the *You* represents something far deeper than a mere name; it is the *You* symbolizing the spiritual essence of Moshe. And what is that essence? *Mesiras Nefesh*—his unflinching commitment to his people, come what may—even if it was at his own expense. This is the very soul of Moshe, the faithful shepherd. The *You* that goes beyond the superficial and beyond what any name could possibly encapsulate. It represents the deepest core of his *neshoma,* deeper than any appellation or detailed description could hope to portray.

Moses' name may be missing, but his spiritual presence is felt in a way that no name could ever do justice to. May all our leaders take note and be inspired.

ⓈⓄⒸⓇ

How to be Jewish in a Non-Jewish World

Unlike a generation ago, today the walls of the ghetto no longer sequester us from the rest of society. We fraternize and do business with non-Jews on a daily basis and have become fully adjusted to Western culture. The contemporary question is how do we strike a balance between retaining our Jewish identity while at the same time being citizens of the world, especially when that world may be indifferent or even hostile to our Jewishness?

This week, we read about the pure olive oil necessary for the kindling of the Menorah in the Mishkan, Moses' sanctuary and the forerunner of the Temple in Jerusalem. The Rebbe taught that oil actually holds the secret formula for how to successfully live a proud Jewish life in an environment that may be far from Jewishly conducive.

Oil, you see, is something of a paradox. It contains conflicting characteristics and puzzling properties. On the one hand, it mixes easily and spreads very quickly, seeping through and permeating the material it comes in contact with. Ever try drying the excess oil off a potato *latke?* Good luck. Your napkin will be very oily indeed in no time at all.

On the other hand, when mixed with other liquids, oil stubbornly rises to the surface and refuses to be absorbed by anything else. (I remember in my student days in Yeshiva, one of my roommates had no *menorah* for Chanukah. Rather ingeniously, he collected eight empty bottles, filled them almost to the top with water and then poured some olive oil into the bottles. I was most intrigued to see the oil remain clearly distinguishable from the water as it floated above the water. He then added the wick, lit it, and his makeshift menorah worked like a charm. A modern day Chanukah miracle!)

In other words, like oil, Jews too will often find themselves mixing in a wide variety of circles—social, business, civic, communal or political. And there's nothing necessarily wrong with that. At the very same time, though, we need to remember never to lose our own identity. We should never mix to the point of allowing our own Jewish persona to be swallowed or diluted. When we mix in outside circles, we often feel a strong pressure, whether real or imagined, to conform to the norms around us. Few among us enjoy sticking out like a sore thumb. The fact is, however, that other people respect us more when we respect ourselves. If we are casual and cavalier in our commitment to our own national principles, then our non-Jewish associates might worry whether we might not betray them next.

Just one example: every major city of the world has any number of kosher restaurants filled with Jewish business people entertaining non-Jewish partners, clients, or would-be clients. Some establishments may be more upmarket than others, but everyone seems to manage and the deals get done.

One can be perfectly sociable without giving up one's principles. Most people are quite happy to accommodate individual needs and sensitivities. It seems to me that it is the Jews who complain more about kosher food than the non-Jews. Our apprehensions about stating our religious requirements are often exaggerated and unfounded. Provided we do it honestly, respectfully, and consistently, our adherence to a code of values will impress our associates and inspire them with greater confidence in our character and trustworthiness in all areas of activity.

A friend of mine, Rodney (Refoel) Unterslak, was a young doctor when he was called up for a stint of national military service. He was very obviously religious from his yarmulke and beard. In fact, the beard didn't exactly meet army regulations, and it was only with great difficulty that he managed to obtain special permission to keep it. Far from being a nuisance, he conducted himself with dedication and integrity, and at the end of his tour of duty walked away with the Surgeon General's top award for excellence. That was a *Kiddush Hashem*—a public sanctification of G-d by a proud, practicing Jew who found himself in a decidedly un-Jewish environment.

Compromising our values and principles is a sure way to lose the re-... we crave from the world around us. Dignity, pride, and self-respect the esteem and admiration of others, whether Jews or non-Jews. ...me-tested and well-proven method. Just learn from the oil. By all means, spread around and socialize. But remember your uniqueness. Be distinctive and proud and know where to draw the line.

෭ා౷

Ki Tisa

Picking Up the Pieces

It's too late. I'm too far gone. It'll never be the same. How many times have we heard those words? Or, worse, said them?

This week's Parsha tells the story of the Golden Calf, the worst national sin in the history of the Jewish People. Now, frankly, if I were the editor of the Bible, I'd have left that part out. How humiliating to the Jews! Just weeks after the greatest revelation of all time, when they saw and heard G-d up front and personal, they go and bow down to a cow? How fickle can you get! But the Torah is unflinchingly honest and records this most unflattering moment of ours in all its gory detail.

Why?

Perhaps the very important lessons we need to draw from this embarrassing episode are, first, that people do sin, human beings do make mistakes, and even inspired Jews who saw the divine can mess up—badly. And, second, that even afterwards, there is still hope. No matter what. In the very same Parsha we read how G-d tells Moshe to carve out a second set of tablets to replace the first set he smashed when he came down the mountain and was shocked by what the Jews had gotten up to. (Sort of "You broke them, you fix them." Like the guy who fell asleep during the rabbi's sermon and the rabbi tells the Shamash to go and wake the fellow up. The Shamash says, "Rabbi, you put him to sleep, you wake him up!")

The Torah does not intend to diminish our respect for that generation, but rather to help us understand human frailty, our moral weakness, and the reality of relationships, spiritual or otherwise.

G-d gave us a perfect Torah. The tablets were hand-made by G-d, pure and sacred, and then we messed up. So is it all over? Is there really no hope now? Are we beyond redemption? After all, what could possibly be worse than idolatry? We broke the first two commandments, and the tablets were shattered into smithereens because we were no longer worthy to have them. This was the ultimate infidelity.

So Torah teaches that all is not lost. As bad as it was—and it was bad— it is possible for man to repair the damage. Moshe will make new tablets. They won't be quite the same as G-d's, but there will be tablets nonetheless. We can pick up the pieces of life. Hope springs eternal.

I once heard a good *vort* from a colleague about the significance of breaking the glass under the Chupah. Besides never forgetting Jerusalem and praying for her full restoration, this ceremony teaches a very important lesson about life to a bride and groom who are about to embark on their own new path in life.

What happens immediately after the groom breaks the glass? Everyone shouts Mazel Tov! The message is clear. Something broke? *Nu*, it's not the end of the world. We can even laugh about it and still be happy. *Nisht geferlich. Lo nora.* This too shall pass. A very practical, useful peacekeeping tip for the new couple.

There are most definitely second chances in life. At my Shul we run an adult education programme called CAJE, the College of Adult Jewish Education, and the byline we use in the CAJE logo is *Your Second Chance to Know*. There are second chances and third chances, too. Many Talmud Torah dropouts have passed through our classes and, as adults, learned to read Hebrew from scratch. Today, some of our graduates can even lead the Shul Service, and I am very proud of them and our program.

It is possible to pick up the pieces in life. Whether it's our relationships with G-d, our marriage partners, our kids, our friends or our colleagues, we can make amends and repair the damage. Falling off a horse or a bicycle dare not mean that we never ride again.

If the Jews could recover from the Golden Calf, our own challenges are small indeed.

₧₧

ויקומו לצחק

They arose to revel. (32:6)

Heresy Cloaked in Piety

How did the Jews who had just weeks earlier personally experienced the Revelation at Sinai and the Ten Commandments justify their demand for an idolatrous golden calf?

Well, on the face of it, it did seem as if it might have been a genuine expression of a need for leadership. What was their argument? *Make for us gods who will lead us because this man Moses who took us out of Egypt, we do not know what has become of him* (Exodus 32). Moshe, still up on the mountain, appeared to be late in returning, and they feared he wasn't coming back at all. The people's demand for a visible, tangible leader to replace Moses appeared reasonable. Arguably, it seemed to be a sincere call for religious guidance and for a means of better identifying with the

One G-d. But where did it end? Not only in blatant idolatry but also in adultery and even murder. The verse reads *Vayokumu litzachek—And they arose to revel.* Commentary interprets the word *litzachek—revel—*as depraved merry-making, which included wild orgies of unbridled immorality and even the killing of Hur, son of Miriam, who tried to stop them.

Here we find a profound message as relevant today as in days of old. It sometimes occurs that people make demands cloaked in piety or religious fervor. But, beneath the surface lies a selfish desire and sinister motivations. Often, people ask for G-d when what they really want is sin!

Where was G-d during the Holocaust? This most disturbing question may be asked in a variety of ways. It could be out of a genuine desire to understand the most challenging philosophical issue of the day. On the other hand, it might also be asked almost flippantly as a convenient excuse for one's own religious inadequacies.

A good test of where the question is coming from is this: if I gave you a watertight answer for the question of G-d and the Holocaust (assuming I had one), would you begin living a G-dly life? Would you start putting on Tefillin today? Will you be in Shul tomorrow? If not, then the fact that you don't do so now cannot be attributed to your having a gripe with G-d. Either you weren't raised with that important tradition, or you aren't sure how to do it, or perhaps you just couldn't be bothered and are using the Holocaust as a convenient rationalization.

Do you know how expensive it is to keep Kosher? Again, this may be a passionate cry of religious zeal, or perhaps a real concern to make Kashrut more accessible to the masses. Unfortunately, it might also be a cheap excuse for someone who has no intention of keeping kosher at any price.

I once heard a story from Reb Yisroel Hazdan *olov hasholom* about three Jewish apostates in Russia of old. They met for drinks in the local tavern and were discussing the reasons why each of them left the faith. One says being Christian opened new doors for him in business. The next said he fell in love with the Squire's daughter and had to convert to marry her. The third says he had philosophical difficulties with the Torah and Talmud and was inspired by the theological doctrines of Christianity. Whereupon the other two turned on him and told him in no uncertain terms that he was bluffing. "That story you can tell the Goyim. Us, however, you cannot fool. We want the truth!"

Let us be honest. Why blame our own spiritual shortcomings on a mysteriously inexplicable G-d or on a Judaism we find fault with? Why say we are looking for G-d when we are really looking for the path of least resistance? Let us not abuse that which is holy for purposes of self-justification. Even if we are not prepared to live a holy life, at least let us be honest.

☙❧

הַרְאֵנִי נָא אֶת כְּבֹדֶךָ

Show me please Your glory. (33:18)

Where is G-d?

So you think you're the first guy out there looking for G-d? Sorry, my friend, you didn't discover America. People have been searching for spirituality, exploring the metaphysical, and generally searching for truth for millennia.

Even the greatest prophet of them all, Moses himself, was preoccupied with seeking the Divine. Moses wanted to see G-d in all His glory.

Show me please Your glory, he appeals in Exodus 33. The commentators understand this to mean that he wanted it all, the ultimate revelation. Others see it as a quest for understanding the infinite ways of G-d, like why the righteous seem to be perennial sufferers and the wicked seem to be laughing all the way to the bank.

Whatever the meaning, the Almighty places limits on Moses' understanding. *You will see My back, but My face may not be seen.* Finite earthlings—even a Moses—can only perceive so much and no more. The face of G-d, the ultimate full picture, is beyond human comprehension.

A youngster was being given his first theology lesson and he asked *where is G-d?* The answer he received was *G-d is everywhere. That's the problem,* he said, *I want a G-d who is somewhere!*

Everywhere is abstract, theoretical, and rather intangible. *Somewhere,* on the other hand, is more defined, substantial, and real. Yes, Judaism definitely believes that G-d is everywhere. But even more important is the *somewhere* where G-d is to be found.

In Judaism we find a clearly developed infrastructure of life. There is a list of behaviors that are considered G-dly and another list that may seem a lot more attractive but is deemed to be ungodly. We know exactly what G-d expects of us—and what He does not. The Torah is filled with nitty gritty dos and don'ts. It isn't left to our energy levels on the day or what feels good or bad to us in our highly personal and very subjective mindsets. There are objective rules of right and wrong. Morality and ethics are in the province of G-d and are therefore non-negotiable. Contrary to current thinking, they are not meant to be decided by popular consensus. Oh, we can talk about it and debate the issues all night long, but ultimately, our moral code had better be Divine and absolute, or it will change annually, depending on which way the wind is blowing.

I was once challenged along these lines and had to think really fast. A congregant was appearing in court on a charge of some form of white-collar crime, and I was called to give character testimony for him. At one point during my testimony, the non-Jewish judge asked me, *Rabbi, would you describe the accused as a religious man?* I was taken aback and somewhat flustered for a split second. But I held my composure and said *Yes, your Honor.* Now, in Judaism, there are pretty clear definitions of what constitutes a religious personality. The most obvious one is Shabbos observance. The accused, I knew, was not yet Shomer Shabbos. So how could I have described him as "religious"—especially as I was under oath?

The simple answer is that I was talking to a non-Jewish judge in a non-Jewish court. From his perspective a man who is a believer, comes to synagogue faithfully every week, and does charity work qualifies to be called "religious." The fact that my standards of defining "religious" are different from the judge's didn't deter me from answering his question affirmatively. And I stand by my answer with no apologies to the purists among us.

For me, this was a moment of personal insight. Our Torah has a more demanding benchmark for calling oneself "religious." To be a person of faith, to attend Shul and to help out are all very nice and very important but still not enough to earn that exalted title. They are in the *Everywhere* category. Keeping Shabbos, though, is more in the *Somewhere* department. It is clearly defined and absolute. It goes beyond the surface-level feel good stuff. As Jews, we require a more precise definition before we can really call someone "religious." G-d must be *Somewhere* not just *Everywhere.*

While I myself have argued that we don't really know who is "religious," in the final analysis, it is when we connect to G-d by doing His will that we really see and feel G-d and experience the greatest revelations.

හ)ব্ঃ

Vayakhel

וַיַּקְהֵל מֹשֶׁה אֶת כָּל עֲדַת בְּנֵי יִשְׂרָאֵל

Moses gathered the assembly of the Children of Israel. (35:1)

The Day After

Some years ago, in Johannesburg where I live, the United Nations held the International Summit on Sustainable Development. The Summit was a great success. One wonders, though, whether all the wonderful decisions and resolutions that were adopted were ever implemented. In other words, were they themselves sustainable? Good ideas and worthwhile projects are suggested regularly. The question is, do they get off the drawing board? And if they do, how long do they last? What degree of permanence do they enjoy?

Moses gathered the assembly of the Children of Israel—these are the opening words of Parshat Vayakhel. Rashi tells us that this day of assembly was the day after Yom Kippur. Moses came down from Mount Sinai on Yom Kippur bearing the message of G-d's forgiveness for the sin of the Golden Calf. The next day, he gathered the people and commanded them to build the sanctuary.

Why is it important to know that this was the day after Yom Kippur? Perhaps it is because while on Yom Kippur everyone is holy, the challenge is to be good *after* Yom Kippur. It is relatively easy to be holy on the holiest day of the year. The test of faith is to maintain our good behavior in the days and weeks following the awesome, sacred experience. Will we still be inspired or will our enthusiasm have waned straight after *Neilah?* How many synagogues are filled to capacity on Yom Kippur and struggle for a *minyan* the next morning? A son says Kaddish for his father or mother faithfully—for the week of Shiva. And then? Or perhaps he comes to Shul regularly and recites Kaddish for the full 11 months. And the next day he's gone. And it's not only about Shul; it's about life. What happens after the honeymoon? Or the first anniversary? Do we have the commitment and the staying power to be in for the long haul?

Many people get inspired at one time or another. Over the years, I've seen hundreds of men and women go through a phase of dedicated Jewish living only to see them fall back on old habits and lifestyles. And it wasn't because their commitment faltered, but because they did not implement a sustainable program for that commitment to thrive.

Take Shabbat. A person experiences a real sense of Shabbat for the very first time in his or her life. Then again, and again, until they decide that they really want this for themselves. It's so serene, so spiritual, and so special. So they commit to keeping Shabbos. They start walking to Shul every Saturday. There's only one problem. They live three miles from the Shul that inspired them. Okay, it's not impossible to walk three miles; lots of people do it every day to keep in shape. So, as long as they are still on a spiritual high it works, but the reality is that it is simply not sustainable. If they don't move closer to their favorite Shul, something will snap.

I remember a couple that went so far as to buy an apartment near the Shul and they moved in every weekend. They managed for a while but even that was not sustainable. It became a bothersome *schlep* to have to move out every Friday and move back every Saturday night. It just didn't last.

So this is a call not only to maintain the momentum of our spiritual inspiration but also to take practical steps to do so. To succeed in the long term, we must have a pragmatic plan, a realistic, workable, achievable program to see us through to the end. Otherwise, G-d forbid, our fervent feelings of the moment may turn out a flash in the pan.

Let us be inspired enough to make sure our inspiration lasts.

ജ

ראה קראתי בשם בצלאל בן אורי בן חור למטה יהודה

"See G-d has appointed Betzalel, the son of Uri, the son of Chur of the tribe of Judah. (35:30– 31)

Bar Mitzvahs: Magic or Tragic?

Now Chur, Betzalel's grandfather, was a son of Miriam, Moshe's sister. That would make Betzalel a great grand nephew of Moshe. Indeed, the Talmud (Sanhedrin 69b), records that Betzalel was a mere 13 years old at the time when he was appointed as master architect and designer for the sanctuary. Imagine a little Bar Mitzvah boy telling the great Moshe how to build the Tabernacle! Remarkable—and regrettably all too rare.

Ask any congregational rabbi today, and he will tell you that it is the exceptional young man who experiences a sense of true maturity at the time of his Bar Mitzvah. In fact, it may sound shocking, but the average Bar Mitzvah is a failure. I don't mean that the young man failed his test or didn't perform adequately on the Bimah. And most parties are successful and lots of fun, too.

Bar Mitzvahs are failures because once the gifts have been unwrapped, the cash deposited and the balloons popped, what is left? Is there any lasting value to this year of study, of running to Shul for lessons, of nerves and anxiety? The success of a Bar Mitzvah should really be judged by the sustainability of the experience and by the value added to a young man's life.

Bar Mitzvah is meant to be an initiation into Jewish life, but we've turned it into a graduation. A young man goes through the compulsory 12 months of drudgery and then wipes his brow and with a deep sense of relief quotes Dr. Martin Luther King, Jr., who said, "Free at last, free at last. Thank G-d Almighty I'm free at last."

It's like the old story with the Synagogue that was plagued by mice until the rabbi decided to give all the mice a Bar Mitzvah. They were never seen again. Or, the rabbi who said he finally worked out what happened to the 10 Lost Tribes of Israel. *They never really got lost,* he said. *They just had a Bar Mitzvah!*

A generation ago, the Jewish historian Cecil Roth advocated that the age of Bar Mitzvah should be moved up to 17 or 18 in the hope that we might then be addressing a more mature young man and appealing to his rational mind to better appreciate the Jewish way of life he was being introduced to. After all, just because he's reached puberty and biological maturity—the *halachic* measure of majority—doesn't mean he is emotionally mature. Perhaps an 18-year-old would respond more wisely and actually be inspired by what Judaism has to offer.

While to this day nobody has acted on Roth's suggestion, all agree that something must be done and that throughout most of the twentieth century and now into the twenty-first, the Bar Mitzvah syndrome is one of Judaism's most spectacular educational failures. Do we really think we can prepare 13-year-old boys or 12-year-old girls for the big issues of life? Can we teach Jewish philosophy to this age group? What is the meaning of life? Can one prove the existence of G-d? Why do bad things happen to good people? Where was G-d in Auschwitz? The only answer we're giving them to all these questions is a singsong passage they must learn to parrot by rote. And more often than not, they have no clue what they are singing about either!

The truth is that it's not the young man's fault. Nor is it the teacher's fault. And far be it from me to blame the rabbi! It is the system that is doomed to failure unless an exceptional effort is made by all concerned that this Bar Mitzvah experience will be different. Honestly, do we really expect a boy of 13 to change his lifestyle on his own? Do we expect him to come home and share everything he's learned and change his whole family and their lifestyles? Once in a blue moon it actually happens, but those are few and far between.

The average Bar Mitzvah fails because the average family doesn't really want any dramatic change in their son's life. Nor do they want him to come home from his lessons and start preaching to them. What must happen if Bar Mitzvahs are to enjoy any measure of long-term success is that parents sit down and give some serious thought to what they actually want from their son and for their son. Do they want a nice performance in Shul, a clever speech, and a cool dinner dance? Then that's what they will get. If, however, they sincerely desire a meaningful rite of passage and a mature sense of earnest acceptance of Jewish responsibilities, then they too—and indeed the whole family—will need to prepare themselves for meaningful change.

That is a tall order for most people. Realistically speaking, it might be more practical to aim for one new mitzvah for the young man. A daily commitment to Tefillin by him is a basic traditional resolution. And a new mitzvah for the family—like coming to Shul more regularly—might be a good start for them. Then we can hope that there will be some follow through and lasting value to this Bar Mitzvah.

The truth is, it really must start long before the 12th year of a boy's life, and it certainly cannot end after the party. Synagogues, too, must offer imaginative programming for teens that will captivate them and inspire them to keep coming back to Shul. That way when they are more emotionally mature, they will be there to get those important answers to life's questions.

On the positive side, many good things can come from the Bar Mitzvah experience. Setting goals, achieving them one by one, a schedule of hard work leading to recognizable achievements, and at the end of it all being rewarded for a year-long effort—these are all valuable lessons for life.

Bar Mitzvah is uniquely Jewish. Non-Jews don't have any celebrations at the age of 13. In fact, many non-Jewish kids are clamoring for their own equivalent party. Why should their Jewish friends have all the fun? In other cultures, 13 is actually an unlucky number. Caterers omit table number 13 at functions, hotel elevators mysteriously skip from the 12th floor to the 14th and Friday the 13th is a disaster waiting to happen!

But in Judaism 13 is special, and it is a milestone that can be made special if we address ourselves to it with intelligent forethought, creative programming, and a personalized approach. At the end of the day it is not the frills that will determine the success of our Bar Mitzvahs but the meaningful impression they make on a young man.

My father, in his book, *From Shedlitz to Safety*, recounts the incredible non-event his own Bar Mitzvah was back in pre-war Poland. He was already studying at a Yeshiva boarding school away from home. "Shortly before my 13th birthday, I received a parcel from home. Inside were a pair of Tefillin and a note from my father telling me to make sure I was called to the Torah for an Aliyah for the occasion." That was it. No invitation, no party, no photographs, no cash. But he was given the essential ingredients for a successful Bar Mitzvah—Tefillin to bind himself to G-d and an Aliyah to learn from the Torah how to live. Thank G-d; they stood him in good stead.

Many Jewish Day Schools today are introducing innovative ideas to make the experience meaningful, positive, and more successful in the long term. With imagination, confidence, and effort it can be done.

I end on a positive note with a personal anecdote. Some years ago, on a trip to New York, we paid a visit to a family member whose daughter had gotten married some months back. Since we were unable to attend the wedding and as she had just received delivery of the wedding video, it was assumed that we couldn't wait to watch the whole wedding in the full, three hour unedited version! As you know, these recording can become somewhat tedious, especially at the point where guests at the tables are invited to give greetings on camera. Most people repeat the identical clichéd messages of "Mazel Tov," "Lots of *nachas*," and so on. It really was becoming quite humdrum, and I confess to having begun to fidget uncomfortably.

Suddenly there appeared on the screen an old Jew with a long white beard and not a clue as to how one is meant to use a microphone. Shouting his message in Yiddish was none other than the venerable *chasid,* Reb Berke Chein, a man who had endured much pain and sacrifice in Communist Russia and was only reunited with his family in his later years. He still wore his trademark black Russian cap; his eyes burned with love and zeal; his face was absolutely radiant. He was on a different planet from the one with the tired, hackneyed messages that preceded his on the video.

Said Reb Berke Chein: Change is a very difficult thing. The hardest thing to do in life is for people to change. There are, however, a few rare moments in life when there is a special window of opportunity for positive change. A wedding is one such time. A Bar Mitzvah is another. At these special moments, during these milestones of life, we can find a measure of strength and courage we don't normally possess. Grasp this opportunity, Reb Berke told the bride and groom. For me, that was a rare moment in an otherwise routine wedding video.

His message brings us hope for Bar Mitzvahs too. Betzalel was an extraordinary young man inspired with G-dly talents. While we cannot realistically expect that from every 13 year old, we can look to the occasional successes and draw from their experience. If we apply ourselves, it can provide that special window of opportunity.

Whether today's Bar Mitzvahs will be magic or tragic will depend on the will and determination of parents. Please G-d, with their genuine commitment, coupled with good Shul and school programs as well as inspired teachers, we will make the magic the Jewish People need to build our future.

80CR

Pikudei

The Final Exam

Transparency and accountability—new buzz words for today's standards of corporate governance. No doubt all upright, honorable people welcome every genuine effort to stop corruption and dishonesty in whatever sphere of society—corporate, governmental, or personal. But is this really a new phenomenon? Is ours, in fact, the first generation in history concerned about such issues?

This week in Pikudei we learn that way back in the days of Moses a transparent accounting and detailed audit was conducted over the donations made by the Israelites towards the building campaign for the sanctuary and its sacred vessels. The contributions of gold, silver, and copper were all weighed out and totaled so that no one could cast any aspersions on the integrity of Moshe and his team. In fact, the commentaries derive from this episode that those in charge of communal charity funds should likewise hold themselves accountable. We all need to be "innocent in the eyes of G-d and man." Ethics of the Fathers reminds us to consider that one day we will all face ultimate accountability. Each of us will stand before the heavenly tribunal to give a *din v'cheshbon,* a "full justification and an accounting" for the way we lived our lives.

It is fascinating to note that somehow the Talmud (Shabbos, 31a) was able to get wind of the actual questions we will be asked by that supernal tribunal. (I can't help imagining the scene up in heaven of the tough-guy cop pulling over his suspect and saying, "We'd like to ask you a few questions.")

Know what the very first question is going to be? Surprise, it's not did you believe in G-d, or fast on Yom Kippur. Believe it or not, the first question on this final of final exams is "Did you deal faithfully in business?" Not how religious you were with G-d but how you conducted your business affairs. Were you honest and fair with people?

The second question, however, does go to the heart of our Jewishness. "Did you set aside fixed times for Torah study?" It would appear that familiarizing oneself with Torah and becoming a knowledgeable Jew is the key that opens the doors to everything else in Jewish life.

Is it not an anomaly of our times that many of our most brilliant legal minds—attorneys, advocates, and judges—may have never opened a single page of the Talmud, Judaism's classic encyclopedia of law? Or that some of our finest doctors may be completely unfamiliar with the medical writings of Maimonides, the great twelfth-century physician and scholar? Or that our brightest business magnates remain Jewishly ignorant, even illiterate? How many spiritually enlightened Jews who meditate daily have never been exposed to the teachings of authentic Kabbalah and Jewish Mysticism?

In our day and age, with so many new opportunities for Torah study available, Jewish ignorance just doesn't wash. If the Talmud was once a closed book, today it's available in English—and there are teachers to go with it too. Jewish Studies opportunities abound in every community. And if one is geographically challenged, the Internet with its excellent Judaism sites can work wonders. You can even find yourself a virtual rabbi!

Let's ensure that when they pull us over to ask us a few questions we'll all be able to answer in the affirmative.

3

Sefer Vayikra
The Book of Leviticus

Sacrificial Lamb, Anyone?

"Sacrifice" is not a word one hears very often these days. It seems to pretty much have fallen out of our lexicon. "Sacrifice" has a negative ring to it, like giving up something precious or losing out on something big. Nobody is getting in line to be the "sacrificial lamb." It simply has a bad vibe to the modern ear.

Well, this week we begin reading and studying a book of the Torah, Vayikra-Leviticus, which essentially is a book about sacrifices—specifically the variety offered on the altar of G-d in the Temple in days of old. So let's confront some of our attitudes towards the word.

It's been some decades now that the pursuits of self-fulfilment, personal self-esteem and Looking Out for Number 1 have been taken as necessary givens in our lives. Assertiveness, self-respect, not to allow anyone else to make us their doormat, these are all taken for granted. Although of late martyrdom has become popular in certain cultures, generally Western sophisticates are not looking to be martyrs for anyone, and sacrificial lambs are ancient, antiquated, and decidedly not on today.

Take the case of Jewish mothers. Those loving, selfless souls have long ago been tried, found guilty and convicted of smothering their children. "She demanded medical school or else!" "She force fed me chicken soup—intravenously!" Famous Jewish novelists have made millions denouncing their mothers to the world.

While there may be an element of truth in the notion that Jewish parents can sometimes be overbearing or a little too pushy, I would venture to suggest that the sacrifices our parents, and especially our mothers, have made over the generations are worthy of our respect and eternal gratitude rather than our laying the blame for all our neuroses at their doorstep.

I think if we are objective, we would have to admire and hold up as an icon any human being who puts the welfare and happiness of others

111

above their own. Why is such selflessness and sacrifice admirable in the heroes of nations and freedom movements but disdainful in our mothers? Surely the successes of Jewish sons and daughters must have a lot to do with the people who bore and raised them. It is a modern miracle that a generation of penniless Jewish immigrants is directly responsible for their offspring's smooth integration into the new world and their remarkable achievements in virtually every sphere of contemporary life. It simply could not have happened without major sacrifices and a total commitment by parents to their children.

But that was then. Today, we take a somewhat more enlightened approach. "I should ruin my own life for my kids' sake?" "I need space." "I need my own opportunities for self-expression and personal gratification." All valid needs and worthy goals. But too often we seem to carry it a little too far. Why should a woman who has decided that she wants to be the best mother for her children that she possibly can be made to feel inadequate if she gives up her career or even puts it on hold? If she derives genuine gratification from seeing her children well-nurtured, independent, moral, and proudly Jewish, is that a sin? Does that make her an anachronistic *Bobba?*

Once upon a time husbands and wives did not go out every single Saturday night, but they stood by each other through thick and thin. Once we were taking our kids to extramurals. Today we go to our own extramural activities—gym, golf, bridge, poker, the manicurist and, of course, the therapist.

In fact, it may be that the reason we run to therapists is because we're so darn busy with ourselves and we simply think about ourselves too much. "I'm overweight, I'm unfit, I'm unfulfilled, I'm depressed," and so on. If we spent more time thinking about others and extending ourselves, whether to our own families or the wider community, we might very well be a lot healthier emotionally.

Judaism teaches that sacrifice and selflessness are character traits to respect, admire, and hopefully emulate. The *Yiddishe Momma* of old will be an eternal heroine to our people. Let's stop being so obsessed with ourselves and our own satisfaction and start thinking about what we are needed for in this world. Please G-d, we will be able to keep our social and family balances on an even keel. May the sacrifices we make and the caring and giving we do bring us the blessing of real *nachas* and ultimate personal satisfaction too.

୫୬୯

אָדָם כִּי יַקְרִיב מִכֶּם קָרְבָּן
When a man will bring an offering from among you. (1:2)

Bulls and Lambs

Not only animal rights groups have difficulty with this week's Parsha. Many, if not most people in our modern era, have a problem with the whole concept of animal sacrifice, which is a major theme of the third book of the Torah, Leviticus.

But I have no wish to enter into a rationalization of biblical morality. The second verse in the book lends itself to some interesting homiletic interpretation, which makes it quite clear that the Torah's focus on sacrifice is not so much on the animal on the altar as on the owner who is offering it. *Adam ki yakriv mikem korbon—when a man will bring an offering from among you to G-d, from the animals, from the cattle or from the flock shall you bring your offering.*

Now, clearly, the language here is rather strained. In fact, most translators have edited the text to read more smoothly—*when a man among you will bring an offering,* clearly an improvement in the flow of the verse. Rabbi Schneur Zalman of Liadi, in his classic Likutei Torah, insists, however, that the Torah's syntax is deliberate. *When a man will bring an offering,* that is, he will want to come closer to G-d—the Hebrew word *korbon* has in it the root of *korov* to come close—then he must know that *mikem korbon,* the offering must come from *you,* from the animal within you.

Every one of us possesses animalistic tendencies, and these must be consumed on the altar of G-d. We are obliged to slay our inner animal and humanize ourselves by working on developing our character traits until the beast within us has been neutralized—and better yet—sanctified.

What exactly does this mean? The verse continues, *from the cattle or from the flock shall you bring your offering. Cattle*—some individuals may behave like a raging bull, goring and trampling on everyone and everything in its way. He is the proverbial bull in a china closet, stomping, aggressive, bullying, domineering, and utterly insensitive to people's feelings. Others might be like the *flock*—the meek, little lamb that timidly follows the crowd. She has no opinion of her own; whatever the last person she spoke to said becomes her opinion for the moment. She has no backbone, no sense of self or self-respect. She stays with the flock at all costs lest she be labeled a "black sheep." Still others might be moody and temperamental, changing colors and character traits from day to day. One minute they might be like the raging bull and the next the docile lamb.

So the Torah teaches us to be *Adam,* a human being of human—indeed

G-dly—character. Be a man not an ox, a lady not a lamb. Be a *mentsch,* behave like a mature, refined person not like a *vilde chaya.* Examine your own behavioral tendencies; check out your inner feelings and dispositions. Are you satisfied with yourself as a human being? Are those around you happy, or do you intimidate them with your temper tantrums? Are you mature and mild-mannered or do you suffer from road rage even when you're not in traffic?

Searching our souls and our inner psyches for unacceptable behaviors and then doing something about it is what we mean when we say to bring the animal up on the altar of sacrifice. It is the animal within each of us. The true and ultimate sacrifice is the sacrificing of self.

∞∞

נפש כי תחטא
When a person will sin. (4:2)

Identity Crisis

Amnesia is a frightening illness. Imagine forgetting who you are—no family, no history, and no identity. It can happen to an individual, and it can happen to a people. There have been times in our history when we seemed to forget who we were and where we came from. And all too often, we seem uncertain about where we are going.

In the opening chapters of Leviticus, we read the expression *Nefesh ki techeta—when a person will sin.* The Torah goes on to describe the various atonement offerings necessary to absolve one from their trespasses. The Kabbalistic classic, Zohar, renders this phrase both literally and spiritually. *Nefesh* is interpreted as not merely a *person* but a *soul,* and the verse is punctuated by a question mark. In other words, the Torah is asking *Nefesh ki techeta—shall a soul sin?* Can a Jewish soul, a *yiddishe neshama,* a spark of divinity, really and truly stoop to commit a lowly sin? How is that possible?

Indeed, the only way it can happen is when we forget who we are, when we are no longer in touch with our true spiritual identity, when we start to suffer from spiritual amnesia.

Sadly, it does happen. In fact, it's not really that difficult. After all, we live in a secular society. The old ghetto walls are no longer there to insulate us. We are exposed to the big wide world with all its seemingly tantalizing diversions. Even if we do marry within the faith, we become culturally assimilated. Slowly but surely, then, even a *nefesh*—a Jewish soul—starts forgetting who she is and can fall into the web of sin.

Remember the "wise man" from Chelm and his "problem?" He worried that when he went to the public bathhouse where everyone is unclothed, he wouldn't know who he was. Without his own personal set of clothing to distinguish him from others, he might suffer an identity crisis. So he devised a plan. He tied a red string around his big toe so that even in the bathhouse he would stand out from everyone else. Sadly, when he was in the shower, the water and soapsuds loosened the red string, and it slipped off his big toe. To make matters worse, the red string floated along to the next cubicle and twirled around the big toe of the fellow under the next shower. Suddenly, our *Chelmer Chochom* discovered that his string was gone. He started panicking. This was a serious identity crisis. Then he saw that the fellow next door was sporting his red string. Whereupon, he ran over to him and shouted, "I know who *you* are, but who am *I*?"

Who are you? You are a Jew! You are a son of Abraham, Isaac, and Jacob, a daughter of Sarah, Rebecca, Rachel, and Leah. You are a member of the "kingdom of priests and holy nation." You were freed from Egypt and stood at Sinai. You have survived countless attempts on your life and your faith. You emerged from the ashes of Auschwitz only to live again. And you ask who am I? This is a serious case of national amnesia.

So the holy Zohar reminds us that we are not only "persons who may sin" but we are a soul, and *shall a soul sin? A neshama* is by definition part and parcel of the Divine. And for the G-dly soul within us, distancing ourselves from our very source is absolutely unthinkable.

How then can we explain the phenomenon that after 70 years of Communist atheism, Jews in the Former Soviet Union are today fervently embracing the faith of their forefathers? Or that after decades of apathy, American Jews of all ages are desperately seeking spirituality? Or that the renaissance of Jewish life has become a reality around the globe? Yes, there are good people out there igniting sparks and fanning them into a fiery faith. But the sparks would never take if there was not a burning ember inside every Jewish soul, an ember that remains inextinguishable no matter what.

So if you ever have doubts about who you are, remember the Zohar. You are a soul. And a soul never dies.

ജാ

Tzav

צו את אהרן ואת בניו
Command Aaron and his sons. (6:2)

Staying on Top

Some people are bulldozers. They move mountains, conquer countries, achieve the seemingly impossible. But then when there are no more mountains to climb, they falter. Routines, maintenance, and sustainability are not their strong points. They are bulldozers, driven by the pioneering spirit. The day-to-day grind is not for them. They respond to excitement and challenge, not to the uneventful, monotonous daily slog.

The title word of this week's Parsha, *Tzav*, means "Command." It introduces G-d's call to Moses to instruct the Kohanim about the laws of the burnt offerings in the sanctuary. Rashi points out that the word *Tzav*, "Command"—rather than the more familiar and softer "Speak" or "Tell"—is generally reserved for instructions which require a sense of zealousness. These are things which need to be performed not only immediately but for posterity as well.

Would G-d have doubted the commitment of Aaron and his sons? Was there concern that they would do anything other than what they were instructed to regarding the sacred services? After all, they were the most saintly and dedicated of men. Was there really anything to worry about? Why employ a word implying such urgency?

Says Rashi, it's not only the need for immediacy but also the insistence that the services carry on throughout the generations in the very same way. It is one thing to be committed and excited now when the mitzvah is still fresh and new, but what will happen in future? Will that same commitment still be there down the line, or will the enthusiasm have waned?

In the sporting arena there are athletes, and even teams, who make wonderful starts but then fade before the finish. Others go great guns throughout a contest, but then "choke" at the very end. It is important to be consistent. One cannot achieve greatness by erratic bursts of energy. Concentration and consistency are needed to carry us through until the final moment of the match.

So too in life. People in Hollywood seemingly have no difficulty in finding someone to marry. But how many stay married? And it is no different in Judaism. Lots of Jews are excellent at Yom Kippur. But what happens all year round? Many have moments of inspiration, but they are allowed to become a passing phase.

A fellow came to Shul to observe a Yahrtzeit but, sadly, they were struggling to make a Minyan. He vented his anger at not being able to recite Kaddish. One of the men present was less than sympathetic. "And where were you yesterday when someone else had Yahrtzeit and needed a Minyan?" he retorted.

King David in Psalm 24 asks, "Who may ascend the mountain of G-d and who may stand in His holy place?" In other words, it is one thing to climb the mountain but quite another to be able to stay on the summit.

There are outstanding trailblazers who struggle with the everyday maintenance of the very programs they themselves initiated. In an ideal world, pioneers would do the initiating, and ordinary folk would carry on the routine. But it doesn't always work that way. We cannot necessarily afford the luxury of focusing only on the parts of life we enjoy and are stimulated by. More often than not, life is a grind. Moments of excitement and discovery are rare. Charting new courses are not everyday experiences. Our creations need long term, consistent sustainability; otherwise, they collapse.

The command to the Kohanim echoes down the ages to each of us. If it is important, do it now. And if it is sacred, carry on doing it forever.

ଈୠ

ריח ניחוח לה'
Satisfying aroma to G-d. (6:14)

The Only One

Without going into the whole question of sacrifices, one difficult phrase that appears in this week's reading and throughout the early chapters of *Vayikra* (Leviticus) is *reiach nichoach l'Hashem—a satisfying aroma to G-d*. These few words seem to accentuate an element of appeasing the Deity in the sacrifices. Why the repeated emphasis on satisfying G-d?

Some have suggested that with all the pageantry associated with Temple rites and rituals, people might come to place undue importance on the Kohanim and their ceremonials. The ritual directors might become so prominent in people's eyes that they would forget about the Almighty. It was therefore necessary to remind worshippers to whom they ought to be directing their offerings, thoughts, and prayers.

As a rabbi, I am often called upon to pray for people. This one is in need of a blessing for improved health, the other wants to earn a better living, and so it goes. Of course, there are set times for such prayers in the synagogue service, and I am happy to oblige. But I also suggest to people that they themselves should be in Shul for the prayer too.

Furthermore, there is no more sincere prayer than that of the person in need. Surely their sincerity will be unmatched, even by the most pious of rabbis.

The story is told of a saintly rabbi of yesteryear who was approached by a woman in need of a blessing for her child. The rabbi demanded a large amount for charity in return for his prayer. The woman was apologetic and said she didn't have that amount of money. Could the rabbi reduce the price? But he was adamant. After all her haggling got her nowhere, the woman stormed out in a huff. "I'll pray for myself," she said angrily. "Aha," said the rabbi. "That is exactly what I was hoping to hear. Your prayer will, in fact, be better and more effective than anyone's." The saintly man understood that this woman was placing too much credence in him and forgetting about G-d.

There used to be an unhealthy—and thankfully now largely discredited—attitude among many that one could hire a rabbi to perform all religious duties on their behalf. Let the rabbi keep kosher and let him observe Shabbos and Yom Tov. Let him study the Torah to keep it alive to pass on to the next generation ... of rabbis! Meanwhile, I will live the easy life and pay for the services of a rabbinical professional when I need them. Until then, don't bother me, I'm busy.

I once encouraged someone to try putting on Tefillin in the mornings. His response: "Rabbi, you do it for me." I asked him if I could also eat for him and sleep for him. Rabbis are not meant to be intermediaries between Jews and G-d. Every Jew has a personal and direct relationship with G-d. There are not 612 commandments for ordinary Jews and 614 for rabbis. We all have the same 613 obligations, no more, no less. Rabbis are only teachers, to advise and to guide. The rabbi will be happy to help and do whatever he can, but remember that, ultimately, we have to help ourselves and each of us can turn to the single most important address in the universe and that is G-d.

Rabbis may be very reliable, but don't rely on the rabbis. Kohanim, Levites, rabbis, and teachers all have their important roles to play. But never confuse the messenger with the One who sent him. Long ago, our sages taught (and it has even become a popular Israeli bumper sticker) *We have no one to turn to but our Father in Heaven.*

ℰᏡᏟℛ

Shmini

קָרֵב אֶל הַמִּזְבֵּחַ

Approach the altar. (9:7)

Just Do It!

How do you develop confidence when you don't have it? How does one overcome fear, nerves, and anxieties? Well, without going into major psychological dissertations, let's see if we can find some insight in this week's Parsha.

Everything was set for the inauguration of the sacred service in the sanctuary. The week-long preparations had been completed. Now it was Aaron's turn to approach the altar and begin the service. But Aaron was reluctant. He still felt a sense of shame for his part in the Golden Calf episode. So Moses calls out to Aaron, "Approach the altar and perform the services." Aaron did so and completed all the required tasks correctly.

But what exactly did Moses say to Aaron to assuage his fears? All he said was "Come and do your thing." He never actually dealt with his issues. How did he address his concerns or his feelings of inadequacy?

Well, perhaps, Moses was saying "Come and do" and you will see that all your fears will be put to rest. You lack confidence? Start performing the services, and you will come to realize that it fits you like a glove. You were born to be a High Priest, and that's where you belong.

Moses was telling Aaron that if he would begin performing his chosen role, the rest would follow. As they say in Yiddish, *Apetit kumt mit'n essen.* Even if you're not hungry, if you start eating, your appetite will follow. I suppose that's why the first course in a meal is called an appetizer. (Trust Jews when it comes to food.)

Dr. Moses was dispensing sound psychological advice. The surest way of developing confidence is to begin doing that which you fear. Throwing kids in the deep end to teach them how to swim may not be everybody's cup of tea, but it usually works. Some of the finest public speakers were microphone-shy, even neurotic at first. When we lack self-assurance, confronting our fears and phobias can be the best therapy. We discover that it really wasn't all that bad after all, and we actually manage better than we ever imagined. And from there our self-belief grows until we become quite relaxed about the whole thing.

I remember as a young rabbi just starting out in my career. One morning, the dreaded phone call came. A relatively young woman had passed away. I knew I had to go to the family to comfort them, but what would

I actually tell them? Did I have answers for people who had just been bereaved of their loving wife and mother? Could I play G-d? I was feeling rather paralyzed for a while and fiddled with all sorts of matters of far less importance. And I knew why. Simple. I was stalling. It was a case of plain procrastination because I couldn't face this most unpleasant task that I felt unqualified to deal with.

Eventually, I forced myself to go because I knew I had to. It was my job, and they were waiting for me. And guess what happened? Lo and behold! There were no hysterics, no challenges thrown in my face about where was G-d? I was actually able to deal with the family and their questions. And I discovered then that they didn't really expect me to wave any magic wands or resurrect the dead or answer for G-d. They felt very comforted by my presence and were grateful that I was there for them and with them in their hour of need.

It was for me a very important lesson and a growth point in my rabbinical practice. Experience really is a fantastic teacher.

I would venture to add that it applies to each of us in our Jewish lives. So many people are reluctant to get involved. Too many are intimidated by Shul, and because they are not confident enough about synagogue protocol or their Hebrew literacy, they simply opt out—and lose out. I can attest to hundreds of Jews of every age and stage who have been in that very position and then began coming to Shul. It didn't take them long at all to feel part of the Shul family, and they've never looked back. But this most spiritually gratifying part of their lives would never have been theirs if they didn't take that first brave step.

"Come and do" said Moses to his humble and hesitant brother. Aaron came and did, and the rest is history.

෨ඏ

Siblings in Synch

The Jewish People had been busy inaugurating the Mishkan, the sanctuary in the wilderness and G-d's first official dwelling place on earth. A whole week of consecrations and offerings had taken place, but still there was no sign from Above. Aaron, the High Priest, was bitterly disappointed. In his humility, he assumed it was his fault. After all, hadn't he been an accomplice—albeit unwittingly—to the sin of the golden calf? Surely, the Almighty was displeased with him, and therefore there was no sign of acceptance from heaven.

Moses, his brother, stepped forward and offered a special prayer and immediately the Shechina—the Divine Presence—rested upon Israel. He then blessed the people with the words that would become the concluding verse of Psalm 90, *May the pleasantness of the L-rd our G-d be upon us ... may he establish the work of our hands for us.* Then all the Children of Israel beheld how Aaron was indeed the chosen one, and they were overjoyed that their work was now, finally, blessed by G-d.

It is a beautiful and touching story of filial love. No ego, no one-upmanship, no envy—only a pure untainted love between two brothers.

I once heard Israel's Chief Rabbi Y. M. Lau contrasting this act with previous brotherly encounters in the Bible. With the very first brothers on earth, the world got off to a very bad start after Cain killed Abel in a fit of jealousy. Later, Abraham's sons, Isaac and Ishmael, didn't exactly get on like a house on fire either. Indeed, their enmity continues unabated to this day. The next generation wasn't much better. Jacob and Esau were caught up in sibling rivalry almost all their lives. The saga continued into the next generation with Joseph and his brothers. They nearly killed him and, in the end, "only" sold him into slavery. How refreshingly different, then, that Moses and Aaron were so supportive of one another. How sweet, how beautiful, as the Psalmist says, *Behold how good and how pleasant it is when brothers dwell together in unity* (Psalm 133).

What an important message for us today. Whether it is on the political front in Israel or in our own communal lives, so often we are our own worst enemies. If Israel and all her associated support groups spoke with one voice we would be so much stronger in our international interface. If Jewish organizations could act in concert instead of constantly competing with one another—or worse still, undermining each other—all our communities would be healthier.

Please G-d, we will all take a cue from Moses and Aaron and the Presence of G-d will dwell upon us too.

₧

Why Keep Kosher?

An observant Jew was experiencing a crisis of faith. He decided to sneak into a non-Kosher restaurant and have a fling. He orders "you know what," and is pumping adrenalin big time, full of nervous anticipation of what that forbidden "white meat" really tastes like. Unfortunately for him, his rabbi was walking down the road behind him and saw him enter the restaurant. The rabbi was shocked. He waited outside to see what he would order, and when the waiter duly arrived and removed the tray cover revealing the swine in all its glory, decorated with the customary apple in its mouth, the rabbi rushed in and confronted the Jew. "How could you?!"

he demanded. The shamefaced Jew trying desperately to explain himself out of a corner replies, "Rabbi, this is such a fancy restaurant. All I ordered was an apple and look what a production they make!"

This week's Parsha, Shmini, introduces the Bible's dietary laws. Animals must chew their cud and have split hooves, fish need fins and scales, and a long list of forbidden fowl is enumerated.

To those of us in Jewish education, it is a continuing source of disappointment that so many Jews still believe the Kosher laws to be outdated. After all, they reckon, in the desert our ancestors needed to protect themselves from trichinosis and all sorts of diabolical diseases so some kind of dietary system was needed. But today, they argue, in an age of government inspection and modern hygiene standards, Kashrut is archaic, anachronistic, and quite dispensable.

How sad. The fact is that the Kosher laws were never given to us for health reasons. If they happen to be healthy or provide good hygiene, that is purely a fringe benefit. It may well be one of the perks, but it has never been the reason.

I often joke that if Kashrut was for health, then all the rabbis should look like Mr Universe! And those who don't keep kosher should look sickly. In fact, anecdotal evidence seems to prove the very opposite. Your average religious type looks rather scrawny (or overweight) and the non-kosher guys are the ones with the big biceps. So let it be stated categorically. Kashrut is not for our physical health but for our spiritual health. It is not for our bodies but for our souls. It is a Jewish diet to help Jews remain spiritually sensitive to their innate Jewishness.

While the Torah actually records no official reason for these laws and kashrut is a *chok*, a supra-rational decree, the rabbis and philosophers have speculated on their purpose. They act as a bulwark against assimilation, we are taught. On a simple level, if we keep kosher, inexorably, we will remain close to Jewish communal life. We will shop in the Jewish neighborhood, possibly find it more convenient to live nearby, and generally mix in Jewish company.

A rabbinic friend of mine once asked a very high-profile Jewish businessman why he was about to marry a non-Jewish woman. Couldn't he find a "nice Jewish girl?" His reply was very revealing. "I just don't mix in those circles anymore, Rabbi." There is no doubt that had he still kept Kosher he would have been compelled to mix in Jewish circles, and his life choices may well have been very different.

On a deeper, more spiritual level, keeping kosher keeps our Jewish souls sensitive to things Jewish. This is clearly a mystical concept and completely imperceptible, but according to our sages, it is a fact. Just as too much red meat or fatty foods are bad for your cholesterol, non-kosher foods are bad for your *neshoma.* They clog your spiritual arteries and prevent those warm, healthy Jewish feelings from circulating through your *kishkes* and your consciousness.

It's very important to have a Mezuzah on your door. It identifies your home as Jewish. But what really defines your home as a "Jewish Home"—what your Zayde meant when he said with pride "My children run a Jewish Home"—is the kitchen! A kosher kitchen makes a Jewish home truly Jewish. It also extends a very warm and eloquent invitation to all fellow Jews. *Here you are welcome. Here it is safe to come in and eat. Make yourself at home.*

Your favorite diet may build healthy bodies but a kosher diet builds healthy souls.

ଚ୍ଚର

Tazria

וביום השמיני ימול בשר ערלתו

And on the eighth day the foreskin of his flesh shall be circumcised. (12:3)

The Eternal Covenant

The above verse comes from the opening lines of this week's Parsha and, as they say in the classics, the rest is history. A *Bris* is a covenant, and through the millennia, Jews have kept this *mitzvah* like no other and have thereby maintained their eternal covenant with G-d.

There were times when giving one's son a *bris* was punishable by death. Jewish parents still kept the covenant. My wife's grandfather, Reb Elchonon Shagalov, became a holy martyr for his faith because in Stalin's Russia he dared to practice as a *Mohel* circumcising Jewish children in the town of Homil. One day he was taken by the KGB and never seen again. His wife and children struggled valiantly and eventually made it to the free world where they raised dedicated families of faithful Jews.

Today, so many young—and not so young—Jews throughout the Former Soviet Union are embracing the covenant knowing full well that it would have been far easier at eight days old. And though we now hear voices from so-called enlightened quarters suggesting that circumcision is barbaric and an invasion of an infant's human rights, it still remains the most widely practiced *mitzvah* in the world. And, please G-d, it will retain that distinction forever.

I have no intention of getting into the health debate. I am a rabbi not a doctor. There are enough medical experts who can prove the physiological benefits and certainly justify it even were there no compelling religious motivation. Nor do I intend waxing philosophical here on the underlying symbolisms of circumcision. Simply speaking, from a traditional Jewish point of view, this is the way we connect to G-d. It is an indelible, eternal connection between the Jew and His creator. The fact that it is performed on a newborn child who wasn't asked his opinion only emphasizes the idea that the covenant is not limited by our finite rational mind but transcends the boundaries of human understanding.

Our bond with G-d is not something that can be explained rationally. Were that the case we would have long ago ceased to be. The continuing saga of Jewish survival defies logic. Logically we shouldn't exist. The *bris* symbolizes that transcendence and the Jewish People's never-wavering commitment to the covenant has always been reciprocated by the G-dly miracles that have delivered us time and again.

Some years ago my wife and I were leading a discussion group with young couples. At one point in the evening a young man poured cold water on my arguments by declaring himself an agnostic. I asked him if he had any children. He said yes. I asked did he have a son. Again, he answered affirmatively. "Did you give your son a *Bris*," I asked. At which point he looked at me as if I had just arrived from another planet. "What kind of ridiculous question is that?" he demanded. I explained that if you're really not sure that there is a G-d out there, then why subject your child to unnecessary surgery? Without the religious motivation it might very well be considered barbaric. Through his son's *bris* he realized he wasn't such an agnostic after all.

I am not a Mohel, but as a rabbi have attended hundreds of circumcision ceremonies. Personally, I find it very moving to see parents, including those who are not at all religiously observant, cry with emotion as they experience the continuing link of Jewish Peoplehood being manifested in their very own family dynasty.

I guess most fathers would probably have trouble explaining why they gave their son a *bris*. But I imagine they'd have much more difficulty if they had to explain why they didn't.

ഇന്ദ

When Was Your Last "Spiritual"?

This week we read all about the Kohen examining people to determine whether they were afflicted by *tzora'as*, the leprous curse. It was a physical inspection that had spiritual implications. The person might be pronounced *tahor* or, G-d forbid, *tamei*, all depending on the results of the Kohen's examination.

I couldn't help thinking about going to the doctor for our annual medical examination, or a "physical." We go through the routine check-up—height, weight, blood pressure, cholesterol, and stress tests on the treadmill and up and down the little staircase.

But have you ever thought of going for a "spiritual"?

What's our "height?" Do we walk tall? Are we proud and upright Jews or are we apologetic, stooped and bent over by the burden of an inferiority complex?

What about our "weight?" Are we on a well-balanced diet of Torah, the sustenance of souls, or do we suffer from spiritual malnutrition?

And how is our heart doing? A Jewish heart doesn't only pump blood; it pumps warmth and love. A healthy Jewish heart is the emotional center of the person. It emotes and feels the pain of another. And healthy hearts are inspired by events that point unmistakably to the hand of G-d in the world. If we aren't feeling what we should be, then we might be suffering from blocked arteries.

When the doctor took my blood pressure I immediately made the obvious connection—*Tefillin.* I remembered the story of the simple farmer who went for his first medical check-up. When the doctor checked his pressure he asked what that was all about. The doctor explained patiently that he was checking the heart rate. "But why are you holding my arm if you want to see how my heart is?" "When I check your hand," replied the physician, "I know how your heart is." The hand that gives *Tzedokah,* for example, indicates a healthy Jewish heart.

Then came the stress test—up the stairs and down the stairs, up again and down again, and again and again. How do we handle the ups and downs of life? Are we smug and arrogant when we're up and dejected and depressed when we're down? How do we deal with stress? Do we trust in G-d that everything has a purpose and a positive one at that? Or do we become angry and bitter at life's unkind twists of fate?

Finally, there was the treadmill. I really dislike treadmills. After two minutes I said to the nurse I'd had enough. "The doctor said you must do four minutes," she informed me callously. "Four minutes?" I cried, "This feels like four hours!"

Life can be a tedious treadmill. We find ourselves running and running and getting nowhere fast. The treadmill, the meandering merry-go-round, the grueling rat race where even if you win you're still a rat—all of it leaves us wondering what it's all about and why we are working so hard with no meaningful, consequential reward.

So this year, in addition to going for a *physical,* why not go for a *spiritual?* Find a *Kohen,* a Jewish spiritual healer, who can search your soul for its healthy characteristics as well as your necessary growth points and prescribe a spiritual fitness program tailored for you and your *neshoma*. May we all be healthy, physically and spiritually.

෨෬

Metzora

Speak Nicely, but Clearly

That the Torah speaks in refined language is a principle of Biblical studies. The classic example is back in the story of Noah. There, when G-d tells Noah to take all the animals into the Ark, he speaks of the "clean" animals (*hatehora*) and the "animals which are not clean" (*asher einena tehora*). Although the Torah is generally exceedingly cryptic and sparse on words—every seemingly superfluous letter is expounded upon and interpreted by the Sages—here it uses an additional eight letters to avoid using the word *teme'ah* (literally, defiled or impure). From this, the Talmud teaches that we should never allow a shameful expression to pass our lips. If the Torah deliberately used eight extra letters that could have been avoided simply by saying the word *teme'ah*, then this sends a powerful message to us to watch our language.

And yet, a cursory look at this week's readings reveals the word *tamei* occurring numerous times. Why is it that in the story of Noah the Torah goes out of its way not to use a negative word, and here it uses it repeatedly, almost at whim?

The answer is that where it is a storyline, one can afford to be more subtle and not pronounce a negative word. However, when it comers to *halacha*, to determining Jewish Law, one cannot afford subtleties or flowery language; one must be crystal clear in laying down the law and, yes, we must call a spade a spade. The Law is sacrosanct, and in matters of Law there may be no ambiguities.

Noah and the Flood is essentially a historical narrative, whereas the laws of our parsha deal with dos and don'ts that must be expressed in no uncertain terms. When a rabbi is called upon to answer a *halachic* question, he should not beat around the bush. His response must be clear and unequivocal. And if it is *treif*, then he must pronounce it *treif!*

Now, generally speaking, rabbis should be gentle, nice, and soft-spoken. They should suggest, not demand. The old "fire and brimstone" types don't work that well today. But sometimes rabbis can be too gentle, too subtle, and too undemanding. And not only in *halachic* matters but even in counseling.

Psychologists and social workers will, in principle, never be directive with their clients. It is part of their professional code not to impose their opinions or personal values on those seeking their guidance. They will try to help them "see the wood from the trees" so they can make their own informed decisions. Rabbis, on the other hand, should have no qualms about giving direction. After all, it's their job!

A fellow once came to see me about his therapist. "She doesn't tell me what to do," he complained. I explained that therapists don't work that way. "You want someone to tell you what to do? Go to a rabbi."

If a couple goes for marriage counseling, a counselor is likely to guide them based on their hopes and aspirations. Do they really want to work it out, or are they going through the motions on the way to the divorce lawyer? And if it is the latter, the counselor may very well help them on their way.

A rabbi will not hesitate to explain that marriage is sacred and should be worked on and that divorce is an absolutely last resort when all else has failed. The counselor might ask "would you guys like to stay married?" while the rabbi might say "you must stay married." Then, he may refer them to a professional counselor who is committed to saving marriages.

Remember the kleptomaniac who bumped into an old friend? The friend recalled how guilty he had felt because of his compulsive shoplifting and asked him whether he still had the problem. "No," said the fellow. "I went to a psychiatrist and he helped me solve my problem." "That's great—so you don't shoplift anymore?" asked the friend. "Sure I shoplift. I just don't feel guilty anymore," answered the kleptomaniac.

Please G-d; rabbis will be soft, supportive, friendly, loving, and gentle. Please G-d; they will give clear direction when they have to.

∞

Silver Linings

Does every cloud really have a silver lining? Is there always a blessing in disguise inside every curse? Well, admittedly, it isn't that easy to discern, but we most certainly do believe in the concept.

This week's Torah reading deals with the purification of those afflicted by the strange leprous-like malady known as *tzoraas* (a word uncannily similar to *tzorres!*). The Parsha recounts different types of *tzoraas* manifestations—on a person's body, in his clothes or even in the walls of his house. In the latter case, if after the necessary quarantine period the stain had still not receded, the stones of the affected wall would have to be removed and replaced with new ones.

Now imagine the walls of your house being demolished. Is that a blessing or a curse? No doubt the homeowner in question did not feel himself particularly blessed. But according to Rashi, the previous Canaanite owners would bury their treasures inside the very walls of their homes. The only way an Israelite would ever discover those hidden valuables in his newly acquired home was if the stones of the house would be removed. When this happened, it didn't take long for the poor unfortunate *tzoraas*-afflicted homeowner to be transformed into the wealthy heir of a new found fortune. Suddenly his dark cloud was filled with linings of silver, gold, and all kinds of precious objects. For him, in a moment, the curse became blessing.

Some time ago a friend's business went into liquidation. Naturally, he was absolutely devastated. After a while, he opened a new business which, thank G-d, prospered. He later confessed to me that in retrospect he was able to see how the earlier bankruptcy was truly a blessing. I still remember his words: "Before we were working for the banks; now we are working for our families."

A woman in my congregation was suffering from heart disease, and the doctors said she really needed bypass surgery. But she also had other medical complications that made a heart operation too dangerous to contemplate. Her quality of life was very poor. If she went for a walk, she would have to stop and rest every few minutes. Then, one day, she suffered a heart attack. She was rushed into hospital, and the doctors said her only chance of survival was an emergency bypass operation. There was a 50/50 chance of success, but if they didn't do it she had no chance at all. They performed the surgery and, thank G-d, she made a full recovery, enjoying many years of greatly improved quality of life with *nachas* from children and grandchildren. For years she would joke, "Thank G-d I had a heart attack. I got my bypass!" It was no joke.

It would be naïve to suggest that it always works out this way. Life isn't so simple, I am not that simplistic, and sometimes it takes much longer to see the good that is hidden in the traumas and difficulties of life. But we will continue to believe that G-d is good, that He really does want the best for us, and that, one day, with hindsight we will see how each of our frustrations did somehow serve us well in the long term.

All of us will at one time or another experience disappointments in life. The challenge is to learn from those disappointments and grow from them. Who knows if the wiser, more sensitive person we become is not the silver lining itself?

In general, there are two qualities that form a powerful combination to help us appreciate that there is a hidden goodness inside every misfortune—faith and patience. With faith that there is a higher, better purpose to life, and with patience to bide our time for its revelation, we will be able to persevere and weather the crises of life.

May we all find our silver linings soon.

ಬಿ

Achrei

Moral is Normal

If anyone was bent on convincing us that Torah was old-fashioned, this would be a good Parsha to prove it. Leviticus, Chapter 18, contains the Bible's Immorality Act. Our moral code—the forbidden relationships, who may marry whom and who may not—all come from this week's reading.

We read this same chapter every year on Yom Kippur afternoon. And every year in every Shul around the world someone asks the very same question. "Why on Yom Kippur, Rabbi? Was there no other section of the Torah to choose besides the one about illicit sex? Is this an appropriate choice to read in Shul on the holiest day of the year?"

Fair question. So the rabbis explain that this is, in fact, the ultimate test of our holiness. The most challenging arena of human conduct, the one that really tests the mettle of our morality, is not how we behave in the synagogue but how we behave in our bedrooms. To conduct ourselves appropriately in public is far easier than to be morally consistent in our intimate lives.

Old-fashioned? You bet. In a world of ever-changing, relative morality where everything goes, the Torah does indeed seem rather antiquated. Man-made laws are forever being amended to suit changing times and circumstances. When a new superhighway is built, traffic officials may decide that it is safe to raise the speed limit. Should there be a fuel shortage, these same officials may decide to lower the speed limit in order to conserve the energy supply. Human legislation is constantly adapting to fluctuating realities. But G-d's laws are constant, consistent and eternal. Divine legislation governs moral issues. Values and ethics, right and wrong, these are eternal, never-changing issues.

Humankind has been confronting these problems since time immemorial. From cavemen to Attilla the Hun to nuclear superpowers, the essential issues really have not changed very much. Questions of moral principle, good and evil, have been there from the very beginning. Life choices are made by each of us in every generation. These questions are timeless.

So we read that adultery was forbidden in Moses' day, and it still is in ours. So is incest. But it wouldn't shock me at all if the same forces motivating for new sexual freedoms soon began campaigning for incestuous relationships to become legal. And why not? If it's all about consenting adults, why deny siblings? Given the slippery slope of our moral mountains, nothing is unthinkable any more.

Ultimately, morality cannot be decided by referendum. We desperately need a higher authority to guide us in the often confusing dilemmas of life.

In Egypt and Canaan lots of degenerate behavior was acceptable, even popular. In this week's Parsha, G-d tells His people that He expects us to march to a different beat. We are called upon to be a holy nation, distinctively different in this, the most challenging test of our morality. It doesn't matter what is legal or trendy in Egypt, Canaan, America, or Scandinavia. We have our own moral guide, our own book of books, which requires no editing or revised editions for the new age. Because right is right and wrong is wrong, and so it will always be.

Rabbi Dr Norman Lamm once wrote that we mustn't confuse "normal" with "average." Since there are people out there who, tragically, may have lost a leg, this would mean that the "average" person has something like 1.97 legs. But that isn't quite "normal." A normal person has two legs. When Torah teaches us to be holy and distinctive, it is reminding us to be normal, not average. Average can be rather mediocre. Just be normal and retain your Jewish uniqueness. It may not be easy. It may not be politically correct. You probably will not win any popularity contests. But you will be faithful to the eternal truths of life. And in the long run, you will be right.

ഐവ

Kedoshim

קְדֹשִׁים תִּהְיוּ
You shall Be Holy. (19:2)

Spiritual versus Holy

In a Parsha where we read the golden rule of "Love Thy Neighbor as Thyself" and numerous others, I find it necessary to focus on a commandment that in our own day seems to have been forgotten, much to our own detriment, I fear.

Under the general command to "Be Holy," the Torah instructs us not to engage in sorcery, superstition, and other related activities that were practiced by the heathen nations of old. Elsewhere in Deuteronomy the Torah includes other practices, such as consulting the dead. Jews are told to be "sincere and wholehearted with Hashem," to follow the Torah way of life and, when in doubt, to consult the prophet or the recognized spiritual leaders and Torah authorities of the day. Sorcery, dabbling in the occult, and "crossing over" are serious infractions to be strenuously avoided.

A Jewish grandmother once took her grandson to a séance. After making her magic the crystal ball lady claimed she had made contact with the woman's deceased husband, Chaim. Indeed, they heard a male voice saying how everything was well with him on the other side, and he answered all their questions. Then, little Harry, the grandson, piped up and asked, "Zayde, may I ask you one more question please. When did you learn to speak English so well?"

Whether you believe that those who practice spiritualism are indeed making contact or not makes little difference from the Jewish perspective. Imaginary or real, the Torah forbids it. Even if it is *real*, that doesn't mean it is *right*. Not everything that *can* be done *ought* to be done. Most people seem to be confused by all of this. They become convinced that if it really is able to happen, then this legitimizes it. Often, it is those who have been bereaved, especially under tragic circumstances, who are anxiously seeking answers and grasping for comfort through these unholy sources.

Unholy, you ask? Yes. You see, there is a fundamental difference between *spiritual* and *holy*. Not everything spiritual is necessarily holy and not everything holy need be spiritual.

Balaam was a heathen prophet (Numbers 22–24). He was able to communicate with G-d. But he was very unholy. He tried to put a curse on the Jewish People that would allow their enemies to destroy them completely. They had done him no harm. He was a greedy, lustful anti-Semite, far from a holy man. But he was very, very spiritual. Clearly, not everything spiritual is holy.

On the other hand, take money as an example. Money is very, very physical. But if you use it for holy purposes, like charity, it becomes holy. Clearly, not everything holy need be spiritual.

It may be possible to "cross over." But, in the process, we may be getting ourselves involved with unholy forces. There are forces of darkness out there too. And if we are not dealing with Jewish prophets of old or bona fide holy mystics we may, G-d forbid, get burned. And, who knows if our connections are not seen as interference. We may well be guilty of disturbing the dead, in which case we might actually be doing more harm than good.

My brother-in-law, Rabbi Shabsi Alpern, is the Chabad shliach in Brazil. Many such practices occur in his community. He once asked the Lubavitcher Rebbe what to tell people about this. The Rebbe answered to tell them that every Jew has a direct connection to G-d, and we do not require a medium to connect. In fact, why take the circuitous route if you can go direct?

If we want to help the deceased, Judaism has many worthwhile suggestions. Kaddish, Tzedokah, and any Mitzvah in memory are all good deeds that have positive effects on the soul of a loved one. Torah study, particularly Mishna, is highly recommended.

By all means, we should all deepen our spirituality. Study the esoteric side of Torah with reliable, trustworthy teachers to gain an appreciation into Jewish Mysticism. But at all times, remember to be wholesome with Hashem. Don't dabble in forbidden fields. Be holy—in the way our holy Torah tells us to be.

ജോൽ

Who Is Holy?

Who is holy? Is it the mystic in the mountains, the monk in the monastery, or the guru in the garage? Perhaps it is the lady with the crystal ball or the meditating yogi?

People today have fallen in love with Spirituality, Mysticism and Kabbalah. Great. I've even given a whole series of Kabbalah classes myself. Judaism is certainly rich in spirituality, and the mystical perspective helps us to a deeper understanding of our faith and its practice. But how would Judaism define "holy"? Must one be a mystic to be holy?

The Parshah of Kedoshim (Leviticus 19–20), begins with the injunction you shall be holy. Then it launches into a litany of biblical laws from religious to ethical—respecting parents, elders, charity to the poor, honesty in business, observing the Shabbat, not to dabble in the occult, the famous "Love Thy Neighbor," not to take revenge, the forbidden relationships—all kinds of things that would not necessarily be associated with becoming spiritual.

So it seems clear from our Parshah that while we do most definitely believe in the spiritual component of Judaism, the road to holiness is not so much ethereal or otherworldly but practical and pragmatic. Holiness is to be found more in the ordinary everyday things we do or don't do than in mantras and metaphysics. Self-restraint, discipline, honesty, decency, doing the right thing—these are the things that can lead us to holiness. You don't need a guru with a guitar, séances, incense or even long, flowing robes. You need to be a mentsch, controlling your passions and behaving correctly. And that, as opposed to all the spooky stuff, is what constitutes holiness.

At the end of the day, the Torah is telling us to be different from those around us. Whether it was the Egyptians and Canaanites of old or the hedonists and sensualists of today, the message is the same. Holiness means distinctiveness. A Jew must march to a different beat. It doesn't matter what the rest of the world is doing. We are a people apart.

Our differentness is expressed in many ways. The same Parshah that reminds us to keep Shabbat also cautions us to keep honest weights and measures in our shops, not to lie, to pay our employees on time, and not to gossip.

The same Parshah that declares boldly "Love Thy Neighbor as Thyself," also warns us not to get too lovey-dovey with everyone—not with your daughter-in-law, sister-in-law, father's wife, anyone else's wife, nor a member of the same sex.

Yes, I do think there is something pretty holy about a young couple exercising self-discipline and waiting patiently until their chuppah in order to express their love for one another. It shows character, nobility, and I have no doubt they will confirm that it was worth waiting for. Yes, I think married couples who work hard to keep their marriages and family life intact, even though it may sometimes be difficult, are acting in a G-dly manner. That, too, is holy.

Far be it from me to make light of holy men and miracle workers. I am a great believer. But before we run to faith healers or buy red strings and holy water, perhaps we ought to consult the Torah and try the bread and butter stuff of Judaism first. Let us live with honesty, integrity, respect, honor, dignity, and discipline. Then we will be holy.

∞∞

איש אמו ואביו תיראו

Every man; your mother and father shall you revere. (19:3)

Eternally Grateful

Respecting our parents seems to become more difficult as we get older. When we were small we didn't really have much choice. We were totally dependent on them. Then we became adolescents. Not easy then to fulfill the Fifth Commandment. "Honor Thy Father and Mother" is much easier said than done for a teenager for whom autonomy is the call of the hour.

But it seems to me that it gets even more complicated as we ourselves become mature adults. What happens when a parent is aging ungracefully? What if they are becoming irritable, cantankerous, or just plain difficult? Becoming old and forgetful isn't pretty. And it can make a child's responsibility quite a challenge.

Perhaps that is why this week's Parsha, Kedoshim, tells us *Ish imo v'aviv tirau—Every man: your mother and father shall you revere. Ish* means a man, or an adult. In other words, the Torah is telling us clearly that even when you are an adult, you still have the moral obligation to show respect and reverence for your parents. It doesn't matter that you are the world's busiest executive or that your social calendar is filled with important events. You are still a child. That person helped bring you into this world, fed you, clothed you, changed your dirty diapers, and educated you. Yours is a lifetime debt of gratitude.

The late Rabbi Yirmiye Aloy *olov hasholom,* the doyen of the South African rabbinate for many years, told an interesting story of when he was visiting the United States and looked up some old friends who were living in an old age home. He asked them whether their children visited them regularly. The old man's answer was a quote from *Tehillim,* the Book of Psalms (68, 20). *Baruch Hashem Yom Yom* ... Blessed is Hashem for every day ... Rabbi Aloy was most impressed. "Every single day your children come to visit you? That's fantastic." "No, Rabbi, you don't understand," explained the old man. "*Yom yom,* two days a year—Mother's Day and Father's Day!" That's what we would call *ah bittere gelechter*—a sad joke.

There is no question that there will be times when the best thing for an older person is a caring, well-run institution. The least we can do then is to visit regularly. And the longer people can be independent, the better.

But without trying to lay guilt trips on anyone, let me share an example I myself saw as a young boy growing up in Brooklyn. My grandmother passed away, and my grandfather came to live with us. I had the privilege of being his roommate, on and off, for some 12 years. At times, I would help him with the accounting for the Gemilus Chesed Fund that he operated from the house. This Community Free Loan Fund was distributing over a million dollars in interest-free loans annually. I also remember helping him cut his toenails that were difficult for him to reach.

But far more than I helped him, he helped me. He was a special role model for me. Though he wore a rabbinical hat and a long beard, he never preached. His presence and his personality were enough of a message to me as a confused adolescent searching for my way in life. I can honestly say that without his quiet inspiration, I would probably never have become a rabbi. He never even knew what a profound influence he had on my life.

So while it may be true that older people can be difficult—I remember Zayde being impatient and irritable at times too—the rewards far outweigh the sacrifices.

Oh, there's one more thing. At the end of the day, the way we will treat our parents is likely to be the way our children will treat us.

෫෩

ואהבת לרעך כמוך
Love thy fellow as thyself. (19:18)

Loving the Unlovable

The most famous golden rule of life is found in this week's reading. *Love thy fellow as thyself* is not only famous, it also sounds like an injunction that is virtually impossible to fulfill. Can one ever hope to reach such an exalted level of saintliness to love anyone else as much as we love ourselves? Is the Torah not being terribly naïve and utterly unrealistic?

Indeed, the classical commentaries grapple with this issue. Some suggest that we are being taught to act *as if* we love the other fellow. If we *behave* in such a way, the actual emotion may well follow in time.

Tanya (Chapter 32) teaches that if one is able to put physical considerations aside and focus on the spiritual, it may actually be within the realm of the possible to achieve true love of another. After all, our petty likes and dislikes are all based on physical preferences. We either approve or disapprove of the way others look, talk, dress, behave, and so on. But those are all material concerns. If we would only remember that all these things are only superficial, external, and of little consequence, we wouldn't take them that seriously.

What matters most is the spiritual. The real person is not the body but the soul. The essence of every individual is not his nose but his *neshama*. So what if he's ugly and his mother dresses him funny? His soul is pure and untainted. Who knows if the other fellow's soul is not greater, holier, and more pristine than mine? No one can say his soul is better than the next person's.

By focusing on the inner identity of a person, we can avoid getting irritated by their outer idiosyncrasies. We might think someone weird, but would we ever accuse him or her of having a weird soul? So if we can rise above the superficial and concentrate on the spirit rather than the body, on the essence rather than on the external, we do have a chance of observing this fundamental mitzvah in the literal sense.

How easy it is to fall into the trap of labeling people, of categorizing them, and writing them off. *Him? A meshuggener! Her? Rotten to the core! That family? They are impossible!*

Many years ago I was trying to help a man organize a *halachic Gett* for his estranged and already civilly divorced wife. The problem was that she refused to cooperate. (Usually, the problem is the reverse.) So I engaged an attorney friend of mine to help with the case. The next day he called me to say it was all sorted out. I couldn't believe my ears. "How did you do it?" I asked incredulously. He answered with such genuine directness that

I was completely taken aback. He replied matter-of-factly, "I called her up and said, *I believe you are not an ogre.* Immediately, I received a favorable response and the deal was done."

Nobody is really an ogre. (Even Shrek was a nice ogre.) If we can learn to give people the benefit of the doubt we might be surprised at how friendly and cooperative they really can be. Individuals with the most notorious reputations aren't half as bad as they are made out to be when we get to know them. Human monsters are rare indeed. The spark of humanity needs but to be aroused, and the G-dly soul is stirred and revealed.

So let's try and be more generous, a little more patient and tolerant. We may well be surprised at how lovable some people can be.

₠₧

Emor

Holy Matrimony?

This is the parsha where we read about the laws applying to a Kohen—that as a Minister serving in G-d's Temple he may not come in contact with the dead, his body should be unblemished, certain marriages are prohibited to him, and so on.

You may not have heard the story of the fellow who visits his rabbi and begs him to make him a Kohen. He just *has* to belong to the priestly tribe, and he's prepared to pay the rabbi any amount of money for the honor. The rabbi patiently explains that neither he nor anyone can make the man a Kohen. It is simply not in the province of the rabbinate to do these things. The fellow is desperate. He offers the rabbi a huge donation if he would only grant him this one favor. The rabbi is exasperated but intrigued and asks the man why it is so important to him that he be made a Kohen. The guy answers, "Rabbi, my father was a Kohen, my grandfather was a Kohen, so I just have to become a Kohen!"

The truth is that as funny as a born Kohen wanting to buy into his own family may sound, being a Kohen is no joke.

In my own experience, I have been involved in a number of human tragedies, all of which emanated from Jewish ignorance about the role of a Kohen and the regulations that pertain to members of the priestly tribe.

While cemetery conduct and protocol for a male Kohen is a very important Mitzvah, failure to comply with these regulations is between him and G-d. It does not affect anyone else, at least not in any earthly, tangible form. However, when it comes to marriage choices there is always someone else involved and, subsequently, very much affected.

Some tragedies are unavoidable. When terror strikes, G-d forbid, it may be impossible to stay out of harm's way. Illness is not something any sane person consciously chooses. But the most frustrating tragedy of all is one that was avoidable. And when ignorance of our traditions leads to human pain and anguish, then familiarizing ourselves with those traditions could go a long way towards preventing tragedy from happening in the first place.

Picture the scene. A young man announces his engagement and arrives at the Synagogue to book his wedding. The rabbi discovers that he is a Kohen and his fiancé is a divorcee, convert, someone previously married out of the faith, or perhaps the daughter of a non-Jewish father. Very sensitively, he advises the young couple that there may be a *halachic* impediment to their union being solemnized in Shul. This week's parsha gives us the basic laws governing whom a Kohen may and may not marry. If he is indeed a genuine Kohen and she does, in fact, belong to one of the above-mentioned categories, we have a problem.

Now my question is, why in the two or three years of their relationship did this issue never surface? The answer is ignorance. Nobody ever told them that there might be a problem.

Who gets the blame? Why, the rabbi, of course. He is accused of being a religious fundamentalist, intolerant, uncaring, rigid, and inflexible. Well, let me assure you that my colleagues and I love to be welcoming and accommodating at all times. There are, however, situations when Jewish law and tradition, which to us is sacred and inviolate, may well appear to be standing in the way of human happiness. And we are not empowered to change the law to suit the occasion.

Personally, I say the responsibility to educate our young people about this particular issue lies with their parents, especially a father who is a Kohen and has passed down that lineage to his son has a moral obligation to advise his son of what it means to be a Kohen. True, there are privileges, like receiving the first Aliyah in Shul, but there are also responsibilities, like choosing marriage partners very carefully.

These types of pain and misery are absolutely avoidable if we educate our children. Well before they become romantically involved, parents should inform their kids to be discerning in whom they date. In the same way that no intermarriage ever happened without prior interdating, no Kohen would suffer disappointment over an unsanctioned marriage if he only dated girls he would be able to marry in Shul. He shouldn't be hearing about it for the first time when he approaches the rabbi with a wedding date.

Marriage today is a tenuous institution. The challenge to remain on the right side of the statistics is enormous. If the Torah tells us that a particular union is not kosher, rather than resenting the interference, we should consider it as if the Almighty Himself came down and whispered a word of loving advice in our ears. "Trust me my child; this one is not right for you." Sometimes we think the Torah is standing in the way of our happiness when the reverse is true. In the long run, it may well be protecting both parties from making a serious mistake with life long ramifications.

The priesthood is as old as the Jewish People. To be a Kohen is something no money can buy. Space does not allow me to expand on the subject here. Suffice it to say, it is a very special blessing. Let's make sure that our children never consider that blessing a curse.

₭℞

וְנִקְדַּשְׁתִּי בְּתוֹךְ בְּנֵי יִשְׂרָאֵל

*And I shall be sanctified amongst
the children of Israel. (22:32)*

Ambassadors Wanted

There was a time when a Jew's faith in the one G-d of Israel was challenged on a regular basis. During the Crusades, for example, many thousands of Jews were forced to choose between "the cross and the sword." Would they be prepared to deny their Judaism and embrace the dominant faith, or would they rather die than desecrate the name of G-d? Indeed, countless Jews gave their lives *Al Kiddush Hashem—in sanctification of the name of G-d.* They became martyrs for their faith and heroes for eternity.

Thankfully, today it doesn't often happen that we have to make that choice. The late Daniel Pearl, *Hashem yinkom domo,* was one notable exception. Tragically, we still have far too many martyrs nowadays: Jews who are blown apart by maniacal suicide bombers for no other reason than that they are Jewish. But they weren't asked to make a choice. They didn't choose martyrdom. It was forced upon them.

The commandments to sanctify the name of G-d and never to desecrate it are found in this week's Parsha (Leviticus 22, 32). Generally, today, the concept of *Kiddush Hashem,* sanctifying the name of G-d, is observed not by dying as Jews but by living as Jews. How does a Jew give G-d a good name? When he or she behaves as a good Jew should. When other people see a Jew behaving honestly and uprightly, that gives Jews and Judaism a good reputation. And ultimately it all goes back to Torah, the word of G-d. G-d Himself gets the credit for the noble behavior of His people.

Some classic scenarios would be returning money if you were given incorrect change in your favor or calling attention to the fact that a client overpaid you. Although it is only right to do these things, the fact is that others might have kept quiet about it, and when a Jew acts with honor, he brings honor to his faith and his G-d.

Sadly, it also works in the reverse. Jewish slumlords do not give Jews, or the G-d of Israel, a good name. "Look at those greedy, miserly Shylocks!" is not something we want to hear—especially when there may be some grounds for the accusation.

Albert Einstein is reputed to have once stated, "If my theories prove correct, the Germans will claim me as a German, the French will say I am theirs, and the Americans will call me their own. If my theories are incorrect, they will all say I am a Jew."

How proud are we when one of our own does something especially noteworthy like winning a Nobel Prize or performing a valiant humanitarian act. Conversely, how ashamed are we if there is a moral or financial scandal involving one of our own.

I once protested to the general manager of a radio station in our community because I felt he was giving far too much exposure to Jews and Judaism in relation to our numbers and, unfortunately, the publicity wasn't always flattering. At first he denied it. But when I presented him with statistical proof, his plain and honest answer was, "Jews are news."

Fair or not, the fact of life is that Jews are scrutinized far more carefully than others. Like it or not, every Jew is representing his faith, his people and his G-d. Ultimately, how we act will bring fame or infamy upon all of us. May we all be successful ambassadors.

৪৩

Time Management

I intended procrastinating, but I never got around to it.

Whether you consider the above quotation wise, witty, or silly, it can actually be quite a sobering thought. How many of us can truly say we don't put off important things we know we should have done yesterday? Don't you just go green with envy when you meet those super-efficient Amazons who are so punctual, organized, and always put together? Don't they infuriate you ... with yourself?

From my own experience I now know that if something is important I better attend to it immediately; otherwise, I simply don't trust myself to "get around to it." I know I could benefit from a time management course. In fact, I once signed up for one but I never made it there. No time. There are still so many new ideas, projects, and plans I'd like to get around to. I know that with better personal discipline, they might actually materialize.

You might be surprised to learn that effective time management is not only professionally effective, but it is also a religious imperative. This week's Parsha details the Jewish Festivals where between Pesach and Shavuoth we read about the Counting of the Omer. Just as the Israelites counted the days after the Exodus in eager anticipation to receive the Torah, so do we count these 49 days annually.

But why count time? Time marches on inexorably, whether we take note of it or not. What value is there in counting the days? The answer is that we count these 49 days to make us conscious of the preciousness of every single day. To make us more sensitive to the value of a day, an hour, a moment. As Rabbi Sholom Ber of Lubavitch once said, "A summer's day and a winter's night is a year."

I heard a classic analogy on this theme in the name of the saintly Chofetz Chaim, Rabbi Israel Meir Kagan, (1838–1933). *Life is like a picture postcard,* he said. Ever had the experience of being on vacation and sending a picture postcard home or to a friend? We start writing with a large scrawl and then we suddenly think of new things to say and before we know it we're at the end of the card and there's no more room. So what do we do? We start writing smaller and then when we're out of space we start winding our words around the edges of the card to get it all in. Before we know it, we're turning the card upside down to squeeze in the last few vital words in our message.

Sound familiar? Isn't life like that? We start off young and reckless without a worry in the world, and as we get older we realize that life is short. So we start cramming and trying to squeeze in all those important things we never got around to. Sometimes our attempts are quite desperate, even pathetic, as we seek to put some meaning into our lives before it's too late. (Maybe that's what a mid-life crisis is all about.)

So the Torah tells us to count our days—because they are, in fact, numbered. We each have an allotted number of days and years in which to fulfill the purpose for which we were created. Hopefully, by counting time we will appreciate it better.

Whatever it is that is important for each of us to get done, please G-d, we will all get around to it before it is too late.

৪৩

Behar

וְשָׁבְתָה הָאָרֶץ

And the land shall rest. (25:2)

Capitalists or Communists?

Karl Marx may have been the pioneer, but many Jews were involved in the quest for Communism in the early days of the Russian revolution. I have no apologies to make for this phenomenon. Having suffered unbearably under successive oppressive regimes, those political activists genuinely thought Communism would be better for the people than Czarist corruption. Their sense of idealism fueled hopes for a better life and a more equitable future for all.

On paper, Communism was a good idea. The fact that it failed—and that the new leaders may have outdone their predecessors' oppression—may reflect on the personalities as much as on the system.

What is Judaism's economic system? Is there one? I think it could be described as "capitalism with a conscience." In promoting free enterprise, the Torah is clearly capitalistic. But it is a conditional capitalism and certainly a compassionate capitalism.

Winston Churchill once said, "The inherent vice of capitalism is the unequal sharing of blessings. The inherent vice of communism is the equal sharing of miseries." So Judaism introduced an open market system where the sharing of blessings was not left to chance or to wishful thinking but was made mandatory.

Our Parsha gives us a classic example. *Shemitta*, the Sabbatical year, was designed to allow the land to rest and regenerate. Six years the land would be worked, but on the seventh year it would rest and lie fallow. The agricultural cycle in the Holy Land carried with it strict sets of rules and regulations regarding the landowner's rights and responsibilities. No planting, no pruning—and whatever grows by itself is "ownerless" and there for the taking. The owner may take some but so may his workers, friends, and neighbors. The landowner, in his own land, had no more right than the stranger. For six years you own the property, but on the seventh you enjoy no special claims.

This is but one example of many of Judaism's "capitalism with a conscience" ideas. There were many other legislated obligations to the poor—not optional extras, not even pious recommendations, but clear, mandatory contributions to the less fortunate. The 10 percent tithes, leaving the corners of one's field, the gleanings and the forgotten sheaves to the poor are all part of the system of compassionate capitalism.

Judaism thus presents an economy that boasts the best of both worlds—the advantages of an unfettered, free market allowing personal expression and success relative to hard work without the drawbacks of corporate greed. If the land belongs to G-d, then we have no exclusivity over it. G-d bestows His blessings upon us but, clearly, the deal is that we must share. Without Torah law, capitalism fails. Unbridled ambition and the lust for money and power lead to monopolies and conglomerates that leave no room for the next guy and widen the gap between the haves and the have-nots. The sabbatical year is one of many checks and balances that keep our capitalism kosher and kind.

Some people are too businesslike. Everything is measured and exact. Business is business. If I invited you for Shabbos, then I won't repeat the invitation until you reciprocate first. If you gave my son $50 for his Bar Mitzvah then that is exactly what I will give your son. What you or I are worth is irrelevant. We should be softer, more flexible, not so hard, tough, and businesslike. By all means, be a capitalist, but be a kosher capital-ist. Retain the traditional Jewish characteristics of kindness, compassion, *tzedokah* and *chesed,* generosity of spirit, heart—and pocket.

May you make lots of money and encourage G-d to keep showering you with His blessings by making sure you share it generously with others.

ഇരുരുള

Bechukotai

"Louder!"

One section stands out from the rest in this week's *Parsha*. It is known as the *Tochecho,* or The Rebuke. There we read a whole litany of disasters that will befall our people should we turn our backs on G-d and abandon His way of life. The tradition is that the *Baal Koreh* (Torah Reader) himself, without being called up, takes this Aliya and when he reaches the relevant section he lowers his voice to soften the blow of these terrible curses.

For 24 years, I produced and hosted South Africa's only Jewish radio show, *The Jewish Sound.* Once, my guest on the air was Rabbi Shlomo Riskin from Efrat, Israel. He told the story that as a child growing up in the Williamsburg section of Brooklyn, one Shabbos he went to *daaven* in the Shul of the Rebbe of Klausenberg. Originally from Hungary, the Reb-be was a spiritual giant of a man who had lost 11 children in the Holocaust and never sat *shiva* because he was preoccupied with saving as many lives as he possibly could. After the war, he settled in America and developed a large following. Subsequently, he relocated to Israel and, among other things, set up the Laniado Hospital in Natanya.

That Shabbos, the Rebuke, was being read. When it came to the part of the curses, the Reader did what he always did. He lowered his voice and read in a softer tone. Suddenly, the Rebbe shouted in Yiddish, *"Hecher!"* "Louder!" The Reader was confused. He was simply following the tradition of generations. Perhaps he was not hearing right, so he continued reading in the softer tone. *"Hecher!"* "Louder!" thundered the Klausenberger Rebbe. "Let the Almighty hear what is being read! All the curses have already been fulfilled. Now there must be only blessings for our people." (*"Zol Der Ribono shel Olom heren! Alle klolois zenen shoin mekuyem gevoren. Yetzt darf men nor brochos."*)

Many of our sages have described the Holocaust as the birth pangs of Moshiach and the ultimate redemption. Never will there be a repeat of such calamities. We have endured more than enough of exile, wanderings, pogroms, and persecutions. The curses, in all their tragic, cataclysmic imagery have actually materialized. Now there must be only goodness, happiness, and blessings for Am Yisrael.

At the end of The Rebuke, G-d says, *And I will remember My covenant with Jacob, and also My covenant with Isaac, and also My covenant with Abraham will I remember, and I will remember the Land.*

Not only will the Almighty remember us, the Jewish People, He will also remember His Holy Land, our Land of Israel. Perhaps we might interpret this as a message to the anti-Semites of the world who hide behind their anti-Zionist or anti-Israel rantings and ravings.

I will remember the Land—a message also to the nations of the world who claim to be our friends, the shrewd manipulators who are expert in political backstabbing in Washington and London. *I will remember the Land*— a message to our own Jewish fantasizers who would undermine their own brothers with their hopeless attempts at appeasing mortal enemies. To all of them the G-d of Israel says *I will remember the Land.* I will never forsake My land or My people.

And as He remembers us, let us remember Him and our covenant. May we prepare for Shavuot and the Giving of the Torah with earnestness and joy. May G-d and His people always remember each other. *Amen.*

ॐ

Jews by Choice?

Are converts looked down upon in Judaism? Is conversion to our faith frowned upon? To be sure, I have been privy to plenty of disparaging remarks over the years—ironically, often made by people who themselves are far from religiously observant. "A leopard doesn't change its spots," is one of the milder ones I've heard. But never mind what certain individual Jews may say. What does Judaism say?

The simple answer is that the classic, age-old definition of a Jew has always been "one born of a Jewish mother or one who has converted to Judaism according to Halacha." So, provided the conversion process was supervised and performed by a valid, authentic rabbinic body, a convert is just as Jewish as any born Jew. Those who would look down upon converts should remember that some of our greatest Torah sages were descended from converts, including the legendary Rabbi Akiva.

Furthermore, the Midrash contends that a genuine convert is more precious in G-d's eyes than one who was born Jewish. Why? Because one born of a Jewish mother had no choice in the matter. If your mother is Jewish, you are Jewish. Period. You cannot surrender your birthright. Like it or not, it is a biological and spiritual fact of life. You can attempt to convert out of the Jewish faith, but Judaism does not recognize such artificial alterations. A Jew is a Jew is a Jew. If you were born a Jew, you will die a Jew.

But a convert did not have to become Jewish. No one forced him or her into it. If anything, those electing to join the Jewish faith are aware of something called anti-Semitism. Do they need it in their lives? Are they suicidal or just plain stupid? Why would anyone in their right mind go looking for *tzorris?*! Says the Midrash, one who does make that conscious, deliberate choice to embrace the G-d of Abraham despite the unique unpopularity of the Children of Abraham, is someone worthy of G-d's special love. A Jew by choice is a Jew indeed.

There remains a difficult passage in the Talmud (Yevamos 47b) that begs some elucidation. "Converts are as difficult for Israel as a blight!" Not a very flattering depiction. A simple explanation might be that when converts are insincere and they are not really committed to living a full Jewish life—perhaps they converted for ulterior motives, like to marry a Jew—then their failure to observe the commandments brings disrepute to Judaism and may have a negative ripple effect on other Jews.

But there is also an alternative interpretation. Some understand the suggestion that converts are a blight upon Israel to mean that they give born Jews a bad name. Why? Because all too often converts are more zealous than any other Jews in their commitment to the faith. Have we not seen converts who are more *frum* and more passionate about Judaism than most born Jews? A blight upon Israel would then mean that their deeper commitment and zealousness puts the rest of us to shame.

This week, we read the *Tochacha*—the Rebuke. A series of dire warnings to the Jewish People not to stray from G-d's ways and the curses that will befall us if we should are always read shortly before Shavuot, the Season of the Giving of the Torah. That moment at the mountain, when we stood at Sinai and experienced the great Revelation and the Ten Commandments, was the moment when we became constitutionally enfranchised as a nation. Shavuot marks the day when we were transformed from a family—children of Abraham, Isaac, Jacob, Sarah, Rebecca, Rachel and Leah—to a nation. That is the day we all converted to Judaism. We all became Jews at Sinai. This is one of the reasons why we read the Book of Ruth on Shavuot, as she is the paradigm of the righteous, sincere convert.

So, every year at this time we read the sobering Rebuke to prepare us for the reliving of the historic event when we, too, became "converts," so that we should enter into our covenant with G-d sincerely and genuinely, in reverence and in awe.

May all of us, those born or those who have become, be true Jews who will be true to our faith, our Torah and our tradition. May we accept the Torah anew with the passion and zeal of one who has just made that momentous choice, the choice to become a Jew.

ಬೊCಌR

Is G-d Punishing Us?

My cholesterol is sky high, the boss is unhappy with my performance, my wife is threatening to leave, and now the lousy car broke down. For G-d's sake, why does everything happen to me? Do I deserve this? Am I really such a terrible person?

Sound familiar? As a rabbi, I have certainly heard this and similar questions asked many times over the years. Implicit in the question is the assumption that any suffering or misfortune that befalls us must be some form of Divine retribution; surely, it must be a punishment from G-d. But if I'm such a good guy, why then do I deserve such punishment? And, if on top of that, we also believe that G-d is good, then this is really too mind-boggling for a mere mortal like me to work out.

So what if I told you that punishment is only one of an infinite number of possible scenarios to explain your predicament? There are a great many possible explanations and interpretations for human suffering. In fact, it might not be a punishment at all. So don't be in such a hurry to make all these assumptions.

In the portion of Bechukotai read this week, we come across a section known as the Rebuke. It is an ominous warning of the troubles that will befall Israel should we stray from the G-dly path. The mystics teach that even those frightening punishments are, in reality, hidden blessings that cannot be perceived at face value.

I remember hearing an interesting analogy on this theme from the well-known author Rabbi Dr. A. J. Twerski. A mom takes her toddler to the doctor. The doctor prepares to give the child a vaccination that is done by injection. The kid isn't stupid. He sees trouble coming, so he doesn't make it easy for the doctor. In fact, mom must hold the child down while the doctor administers the injection, and throughout, the kid is screaming and shouting. Not a minute later the child is suddenly burying his face in mom's shoulder, desperately seeking solace in his mother's embrace. And the question is why? Isn't mom a traitor to the cause? Didn't she side with the opposition just a moment ago? Was she not an accomplice to the crime when she held him down while the doctor attacked him? Why is this child suddenly finding comfort on mom's shoulder? She is the enemy!

The answer is that every child knows intuitively that his mother loves him and wants only the best for her child. Even if there be a momentary lapse, he knows it will be short-lived. After the fleeting test of faith, the innate and essential bond of love between mother and child is quickly reestablished.

And so it is with our Father in Heaven. Sometimes we may feel angry; it seems as if he has joined forces with Satan. Why does He allow all these terrible misfortunes to befall us? And yet, we know that He really and truly does love us. After all is said and done, we are His children. Does the mother in the clinic hate her child? Is she punishing him? G-d forbid. Does the doctor want to hurt the child? Of course not (unless he is a dentist or a physiotherapist!). So just as a child is pacified by his mother, so is the Jew comforted by the knowledge and conviction that G-d loves us. And if there is pain and suffering, then it must be some form of injection, which is short-term pain for long-term benefit.

To us it may remain a mystery, but to G-d there is always a cosmic connection and a vast eternal plan. The child doesn't understand or appreciate an injection and neither can we adults fathom the divine vaccinations we must put up with from time to time. Nevertheless, we accept in good faith that somehow there is a reason—and even a good reason—behind all our problems. It may not be revealed to us in this world, only in the next. So we do need a fair amount of patience. Personally, I'm prepared to handle living in suspense.

In our moments of misery and days of distress, let us remember that our loving Father in Heaven is surely no less caring than the mother in the doctor's office.

4

Sefer Bamidbar
The Book of Numbers

Every Jew Counts

Nine of the holiest rabbis cannot make a Minyan. Enter one little Bar Mitzvah boy, and suddenly the Minyan is complete! When we count Jews, there are no distinctions. We don't look at religious piety or academic achievement. The rabbi and the rebel, the philanthropist and the pauper—all count for one; no more, no less.

This week in Bamidbar, we read of the census of the Jewish People. This portion is always read on the Shabbat before Shavuoth, the Season of the Giving of the Torah. One important and obvious connection is that in the Torah, too, every letter counts. One missing letter invalidates the entire scroll. Likewise, one missing Jew leaves Jewish Peoplehood lacking, incomplete.

If we count Jews because every Jew counts, then that implies a responsibility on Jewish communal leadership to ensure that no Jew is missing from the Kehilla, from the greater community. We must leave no stone unturned to keep those Jews on the periphery inside. Make sure they feel that they belong and are welcome—even if they haven't paid any membership fees.

It also means that the individual Jew has commitments and obligations. If you're important, make sure you don't get lost. You are needed.

Once there was a small town consisting of only a few Jewish families. Between them, they had exactly ten men over the age of Bar Mitzvah. They were all dedicated people, and they made sure that they never missed a Minyan. One day, a new Jewish family moved in to town. Great joy and excitement: now they would have 11 men. But a strange thing happened. As soon as they had 11, they could never manage a Minyan!

When we know we are indispensable, we make a point of being there. Otherwise, we may say "count me out."

Today, we are losing a lot of Jews to ignorance. But sometimes we also lose them because we didn't embrace them as we could have. At a time when they were receptive, we didn't make them feel welcome.

Other faiths, ideologies, and cults are using "love bombs" to entice Jews to their way of life. Yes, very often they prey on the weak and vulnerable among us. Anyone desperately seeking warmth, love, and a sense of belonging will be an easy target for such groups. But there are lots of ordinary, stable people who crave these things too. Don't we all? If the Jewish community doesn't provide that warm welcome, we may very well find them going elsewhere.

Some years ago, we had a visiting rabbi from Canada speaking in my Shul. His talk was about the very real threat of Jews for J. and Hebrew-Christians who preyed on unsuspecting Jews by using Jewish symbols and even so-called "Shuls" or Messianic Synagogues, which are really nothing more than churches in disguise. He described how these individuals make every deceitful effort to confuse ignorant Jews into believing they are going to a "Jewish" house of worship.

A woman in the audience then asked, "Rabbi, if I am travelling in North America and want to go to Shul, how will I know if I am going to a *real* Shul or one of these impostor synagogues?"

The rabbi laughed and said, "When you go into these places, they bombard you. As soon as they see a new face, a dozen people will come over to welcome you and give you a seat and a book and make you feel at home. But what happens when you go into a *real* Shul? Nobody greets you. Nobody looks at you. And the first person to say a word to you growls at you because you're sitting in his seat!"

Ah bittere gelechter! A sad joke indeed.

Of course, we need to do more than just wait for people to come to Shul in order to make them feel they belong. We need to go out and find our people wherever they may be. Certainly, though, when someone does show a spark of interest—a soul seeking its source—we need to be there: as an organized community, and as individuals.

Indeed, every Jew counts. So let's count them in.

ജറ

Wisdom from the Wilderness

"Numbers" might be how we call the fourth of the Five Books of Moses, but in the Hebrew original it is known as Bemidbar, or, In the Wilderness. It is interesting to note that this parsha is always read before the festival of Shavuot, the season of the Giving of the Torah. What is the connection?

The rabbis taught that it is not enough for G-d to *give* us the Torah; we have to be ready to *receive* the Torah. What makes us worthy recipients of this most precious and infinite gift from G-d? This is where the Wilderness idea comes in. A wilderness is a no-man's land. It is ownerless and barren. Just as a desert is empty and desolate, so does a student of Torah need to know that he is but an "empty vessel."

Humility is a vital prerequisite if we are to successfully absorb divine wisdom. So long as we are full of ourselves and our preconceived notions, we will not be able to assimilate and integrate Torah into our being. Even if are already somewhat accomplished in our Torah studies, we still need to remember, as the Kotzker Rebbe put it, that "As much as you know, you are still an undeveloped desert."

Then there is the idea that an ownerless desert is there for anyone to stake his claim. No man or group of men has a monopoly on Torah. It belongs to each and every single Jew, not only the rabbis or the Yeshiva students, or the religiously observant. "The Torah that Moses commanded us is the heritage of the entire Congregation of Jacob." While we acknowledge that there is much hard work ahead of us if we are to acquire the Torah and make it ours, we also know that with diligence and effort we can succeed. Indeed, some of our finest Torah scholars throughout the generations have hailed from the simple, ordinary folk—tailors, cobblers, and the like.

Maimonides in his Laws of Torah Study (Chapter 3, 1) states: "With three crowns was Israel adorned—the Crown of Torah, the Crown of the Priesthood and the Crown of Royalty. The Priesthood was the privilege of Aaron. ... Royalty was the privilege of King David ... the Crown of Torah is there ready and waiting for all of Israel ... and it is the greatest crown of all." However, while it may be "free for all," we must surrender to it rather than attempt to adjust it to our own circumstances and lifestyles.

And then too, like the empty, uninhabited wilderness, the Torah personality may well find himself alone and isolated. Most rabbis will confirm that it can be very lonely at the top. We might express our strongly held values and beliefs only to discover that we stand alone, very much the "odd man out." We might display the courage of our convictions and find ourselves, like Abraham, "on the other side" of the whole world. Our principles may well prove unpopular, especially should they stand on toes or upset apple carts. No matter. Being true to G-d and His Torah means standing by it—no matter what—under any and every circumstance.

May the literal title of our parsha and all the many lessons it conveys serve as a fitting prelude for the beautiful festival of Shavuot and may we receive the Torah with joy and earnestness so that this important Yom Tov will be meaningful and memorable.

₧ℂ

Missing Jews

How many Jews are there in the world? 13 million? Perhaps 14 million, if you're feeling generous. How many Jews were there before World War II? Apparently the number was around the 19 million mark. Well then, if we deduct the six million wiped out in the Holocaust, we are down to 13 million—which is exactly where we are today. So the colossal question is this: where are all the missing Jews? Or, specifically, why since 1945 have we not made up our losses?

The truth is that we all know the reasons. Success, affluence, and life-styles that encourage sophisticated selfishness—why spend money on kids when we can enjoy it ourselves?—have all encouraged overzealous adherences to Zero Population Growth. In fact, at 1.8 children per Jewish family, we aren't even replacing ourselves.

Then, of course, there are the ravages of assimilation. If every other young American Jew is marrying out, what chance do we have at increasing our numbers?

Now it is true that, traditionally, Jews were never into playing the numbers game. G-d Himself said so in the Bible when he told us, *Not because of your great numbers have I chosen you, because you are the smallest of nations.* That does not mean, though, that we should be complacent about disappearing Jews. We read in the Book of Numbers how G-d orders the census of our people. And it doesn't matter what the size of our beard is or what type of Yarmulke we wear or don't wear; at the end of the day G-d counts what is precious to him. So if the Almighty values every single Jew, then how can we allow that Jew to write himself out?

Some years go when I was hosting South Africa's only Jewish radio show, I interviewed a prominent leader of the World Jewish Congress. We got talking on this subject. I asked him if he was not perturbed by the dire predictions being made then about the shrinking Jewish population. His answer was that we would probably have a smaller Jewish community but that it would be a stronger one. Those who resisted assimilation would be proud, committed Jews.

I couldn't argue the point, but what disturbed me deeply was a seemingly nonchalant attitude and an almost "matter of fact" tone in his voice. It was almost as if to say, "So what! We will be smaller but stronger." So what?! The Torah says every Jew is important enough to be counted. The mystics teach that every one of us has a *Neshama*, which is a veritable part of G-d. We lost six million in the Holocaust and a Jewish leader says "So what?!"

Only now are people beginning to realize what a visionary the Rebbe truly was when back in the 1950s, at the start of his leadership, he initiated the concept of Jewish Outreach. He sent young rabbis and

Rebbetzins to places that were far away, geographically and spiritually. Even in the '60s and '70s other Jewish movements laughed and scoffed at the idea. They ridiculed the notion of sending young religious couples to somewhere like UCLA in California. "They'll eat them for breakfast." "He has no chance of changing anything." "They won't even be able to remain religious themselves."

Well, as I write these lines, thank G-d, there are hundreds of Chabad centers throughout the state of California. And today, thank G-d, those same movements who initially thought the Rebbe's ideas ludicrous are themselves in the business of Jewish outreach. Indeed, it is gratifying to see his trailblazing efforts being followed by so many, including those who were very cynical in the early days.

In 2005, my daughter and son-in-law established the first Jewish center in Table View, Cape Town. It is an area which has attracted many young Jewish families, but there was absolutely no Jewish infrastructure or communal presence in the area. Assimilation was a serious reality. In her first visit to the local public school, she was able to meet with the Jewish children. When she asked a boy of 12 about plans for his Bar Mitzvah, she was told, "My parents said I don't need to have one."

Needless to say, his was the first Bar Mitzvah celebrated at The Shul of Table View.

But you don't have to be a professional at Outreach to bring a fellow Jew closer. Bring a friend to Shul. Just get him or her there and let the rabbis know so they can welcome them and make them feel comfortable. You don't have to be a Rebbetzin to invite an uninvolved Jewish family to your Friday night table. If you know Alef, teach Alef to someone who doesn't. If you know Bet, guaranteed there is someone out there who does not. You can be a teacher and an inspiration even if you are not a rabbi. In fact, many uninitiated Jews are intimidated by rabbis and might well prefer a friend for moral support and a smooth entrée to Jewish life.

Please G-d, we will all fulfill the responsibility and privilege to help rebuild the lost generation and the vanished communities of Eastern Europe. Please G-d, our nation will be strong and will grow in numbers until every lost Jew will find their place and stand up and be counted among our people.

℘ Q∫

Naso

Stalemate or Stale Mate? Finding Solutions

"Nothing new under the sun," wrote King Solomon in Ecclesiastes. And so, we discover this week that infidelity and other marital problems aren't exactly a new societal phenomenon.

One of the main features of our Parsha is the story of the *Sotah,* a woman accused of adultery. In the ancient Biblical tradition, the husband would bring his wife to the Temple where the Kohen would enact the ceremony of the Bitter Waters. The relevant passages from the Torah were written on a scroll and dissolved in the "curse-causing waters." The name of G-d appeared in these passages and, therefore, every possible alternative was explored first in order to avoid the erasure of the Divine Name. If, indeed, there was no alternative, then the ceremony would be concluded, and in the process Hashem's name would, in fact, be erased. If the woman was guilty, she would die prematurely. If innocent, she would be blessed, and her marriage would enjoy a blissful future.

Thus, Jewish tradition teaches that no stone ought to be left unturned to make peace between man and wife. Even if it mean taking the drastic step of erasing the name of G-d! To save a marriage, it is worth it.

How much effort do we put in to our marriages today?

Interestingly, the jealous husband in the Parsha is also chastised should he overreact and run to the Kohen unnecessarily.

Today, I fear, we run to the lawyer much too quickly.

Too many young marrieds, after the inevitable first argument, come to the premature conclusion that they must have made a mistake. "We had a fight!" "He shouted at me." "Let me quit while I'm ahead."

It may well sound ridiculous, but in my own rabbinic experience I have seen it all too often. There is a name for it. It's called "unrealistic expectations." We forget that some of the best marriages on earth had rocky beginnings and that it is normal and natural to take time to settle down and settle into a marriage.

Why is it that we expect our marriages to cruise along smoothly without the slightest hiccup when we have no such presumptions about any other area of life? Say a business shows a loss in the first quarter. Do we close up shop? Of course not. We sit down, we strategize, we find new ways of doing things and with time and effort things turn around. Why then do we close down our marriages with such alacrity at the first signs of tension or difficulty?

Then there are those who are married for years but are locked in loveless marriages. They see no hope for a better future and are resigned to living out their lives, as Thoreau put it, in "quiet desperation."

I'm here to tell you that it needn't be that way. Many a marriage has hit rock bottom and then rebounded into a beautiful, sensitive, mature relationship.

Here are a few important points to be aware of. (1) Help is available. There are highly qualified counselors in every community. (2) There should be no stigma whatsoever in going for help. If you have the flu, you see the doctor. It's curable. So is an ailing relationship. (3) It is never too late. I've seen people embark on a fresh, new path after 18 or 25 years of marriage and they've never looked back. (4) Fixing your existing relationship is by far the best option available to you.

Why is going for help the best option? Ask yourself honestly: is getting divorced and then looking for a new partner better? What makes you think they are lining up to marry divorced people with baggage? And staying single is no fun either. Loneliness is no picnic. And don't think your miserable ex is going to fall off Planet Earth after your divorce. You will still have to engage him/her on family issues, especially if there are children. So you get to keep most of the headaches with little or no compensation.

For too many people, *work* is a four-letter word to be avoided at all costs. But if we would invest half the amount of work into our existing relationships that we will surely need to survive a divorce, we could have a marvellous relationship.

A woman I know is now on her third marriage. I tried to counsel her during her first marriage. But she was determined to end it. Today she freely admits that had she known then what she knows now, she would never have divorced husband number one. Because, with all his faults, compared to husbands numbers two and three, he was an angel!

Marriage and family life are part and parcel of life. They can bring contentment and happiness to each of us—if we work at it. Our lives can be rich and satisfying in that deep, wonderful way—provided we are big enough to seek help and improve the existing stalemate. If we look at things more objectively, we'll probably find that we are both somewhat stale mates.

Judaism has much to offer to revive tired relationships. While the Mikveh system should not be regarded as a panacea for all marital ills, it can have a profoundly positive influence. Take the plunge. Call for an appointment to see your favorite rabbi or Rebbetzin. They can also direct you to good professional counselors who are committed to making marriages work.

The Torah teaches us how sacred marriage is in the eyes of G-d. Let us show a little more respect for our marriage vows. And perhaps we ought to spare a thought for that "significant other" who does so much for us every day, which sadly, we take for granted.

If we invest more time and effort into our current relationships, we may be assured that Hashem will bless the work of our hands with success, happiness and *nachas.*

Then, families will be whole and wholesome, and G-d's Name will be complete.

ℯℂ

Nazirites and Nunneries

The mightiest man in the Bible was, of course, Samson. He took on the most savage of beasts and leveled a stadium with his bare hands. In the end, Samson was undone by Delilah, who cut his hair. So why should such an innocuous event have sapped his strength? The answer is that Samson was a Nazirite. And as we read in this week's Parsha, the sacred vow of the Nazirite precludes him from cutting his hair, coming into contact with the dead, and drinking wine.

At the end of a person's Nazirite period, there were certain atonement offerings he needed to bring to the Temple. The Talmud asks why should a Nazirite, who essentially was taking upon himself voluntary prohibitions beyond the letter of the law, be required to seek atonement. What sin did he commit? One Talmudic opinion suggests that because he denied himself the pleasure of drinking wine, it is considered sinful.

Now the question is why is it wrong to deny oneself anything? Just because the Creator allows us to enjoy the fruit of the vine, is it wrong to decline? Will I really be held accountable for every product that bears a Kosher certification that I choose to do without? Just because a popular ice cream was recently approved by the Kashrut authorities, am I a sinner for sticking to sorbet? And if I haven't yet made it to that fancy kosher restaurant in Manhattan, am I desperately in need of some atonement?

The answer, it would appear, has more to do with attitude and perspective than with blatant iniquity. What is the right way to live? What should be our approach to G-d's creation and the material world? Do we need to divorce ourselves from society in order to be holy? Should we reject anything that isn't wholly spiritual because we fear it may interfere with our piety?

There are ideologies that preach celibacy and revere those who sequester themselves from the daily grind of worldly activity. They see the body as unclean and marriage is a less than ideal concession to human frailty. Then there are some who climb mountains to escape to the spiritual realms. The heavens are far more blissful and sublimely beautiful than the crass street corners and alleyways of city life.

Judaism sees it differently. We follow neither rejectionist nor escapist theologies. Rather, we embrace and engage with G-d's world. Of course, there are clear guidelines, even rules and regulations. But within the Torah framework we should work with the Almighty's universe. "In the beginning G-d created heaven and earth." Earthiness, too, is part of His vast, eternal plan. That plan is that earthly beings, men and women, should invest their time, energy, wealth, and wisdom to infuse G-dliness into the material realm.

Every *mitzvah* we do achieves just that. We take the physical and transform it to the spiritual, not by breaking it or running away from it, but by confronting it and molding it into something sacred and purposeful. "Jews have no nunneries," goes the proverb. A Yeshiva is not meant to be a monastery but a school that will teach and train our students to add spiritual value to the material world. So the Nazirite who, in his quest for heightened spirituality, found it necessary because of his own moral weakness to distance himself from that which the Creator has permitted us is somewhat sinful after all. And his attitude does indeed require some correction, even atonement.

Judaism calls upon us to live a higher, otherworldly life within this world. Rather than allowing the emptiness of a society to bring us down, we are challenged to assertively insist on changing our society for the better. The Creator gave us the spiritual strength to engage with His world. That is why we must.

By all means drink the wine, but make sure you make Kiddush and say L'Chaim.

₧⌘

The Self-Made Man?

"He is a self-made man who worships his creator." Who said it? About whom? Well, it doesn't really matter, as long as we make sure the description doesn't fit us.

This week's Parsha details the offerings of the princes of the twelve tribes. These gifts were brought at the time the Mishkan, the portable sanctuary in the wilderness, was completed. Previously, towards the end of the Book of Exodus, we had read that Moses blessed the people when they finished their work. What blessing did he give them?

May it be G-d's will that the Shechinah, the Divine Presence, should come to rest upon the work of your hands. He also blessed them with the phrase that would become part of Psalm 90. *May the pleasantness of my L-rd, our G-d, be upon us ... may He establish for us the work of our hands.*

But why pray at this time? Surely the time for prayer was before the sanctuary was built. Then it might have been needed to inspire the people to bring in their offerings and contributions, to execute the huge amount of work that was required to create this new, sacred structure. But now the work is done, everything is in place; why pray now?

The answer is that Moses understood that building G-d's sanctuary is not in our hands alone. Sure, we can create a structure. That's the easy part. The question is, will G-d see fit to live there, to make it His home? For this, a special prayer was called for. We needed a blessing upon the work of our hands.

How often people imagine that they do it themselves—all by themselves. How many boast that they are self-made men? Is anyone who didn't have a rich father before him a self-made man? Do you really believe that your success is all your own doing? Are you convinced that all it takes is hard work, business acumen, or clever trading techniques? Are these the only secrets of success? Where does our wisdom and ability come from? Every one of the skills and talents we possess are G-d-given gifts we should acknowledge and be grateful for. And that's not humility. It's reality. You were born with that natural talent and flair. Give credit to your creator. No matter how many "rags to riches" stories I may hear, I will continue to insist that there is no such thing as a "self-made man." Every individual who makes it in their chosen field of endeavor has made it thanks to the innate faculties or aptitudes that G-d implanted inside his or her character from birth. Sure, we learn new tricks and perfect our skills and talents, but where did they come from in the first place? I will happily recognize and give credit to people for their achievements. They, in turn, should thank He who endowed them with the intellectual or emotional wherewithal that got them there.

There are lots of clever people out there who did not find the success they had hoped for. There are also many less intelligent individuals who are very successful. Clearly, there are higher forces at work.

A friend of mine was once laid up with a bad back. What happened? He picked up a little bicycle for his 5-year old. A tiny nonsense, but it left him flat on his back for weeks.

I remember some years ago catching some kind of "bug" and losing my voice for quite a while. There I was, the rabbi, the preacher, the speaker and the radio show host—the man of words whose entire profession is built around his ability to say the right thing for every occasion, and suddenly he is absolutely speechless, thanks to a tiny germ. Overnight, I was rendered useless and unproductive—all by a little virus.

To get sick takes a minute; to get well can take weeks and months. We all need to remember our frailties and limitations. No matter how strong, clever or talented we may be, we are all subject to higher forces. Nobody can do it alone. There is no such thing as a self-made man.

And so Moses reminds us all that even when our work is done, we still need that blessing from Above. Even when we work hard, concoct the most intricate business schemes, or present the most wonderful proposals, ultimately our success needs a prayer. We need to recognize the hand of G-d in our lives and, hopefully, in our success. Let us do our work as best as we can, and then let us not forget to ask Him to bless the work of our hands.

୫୬

Behalotecho

למה נגרע
Why should we lose out? (9:7)

Path of Least Resistance?

By now you have surely recovered from Pesach so we can break the news to you that there is also a Second Pesach. But don't worry; you won't have to do it all over again.

This week's Parsha tells the story of a group of men who were unable to bring the Passover offering on Erev Pesach in the wilderness and approached Moses with a sincere request. "Why should we lose out?" It so happened that they had been occupied with a good deed—according to some it was nothing less than carrying the remains of Joseph from Egypt en route to his final resting place in Shechem—and because of their contact with the dead were spiritually unfit to participate in the Paschal lamb service.

Moses consulted G-d and was told that, in fact, the men were quite right. Henceforth, those who were spiritually impure or far away at the time the Passover offering was brought on the 14th of Nissan would be given a second chance exactly one month later on the 14th of Iyar to make good their lost opportunity.

There are many important lessons from this law, known as Pesach Sheini, such as, "It's never too late." There are second chances in life for all of us. Or, that G-d sometimes waits to see if we really want something badly enough to demand it and only then does He give it to us.

But now I'd like to share with you an important message I once heard from the former Rosh Kollel of Johannesburg, the late Rabbi Mordechai Shakovitzky *olov hasholom.* He said that what those men in Moses' day did was actually quite inspiring. You see, they didn't really have to come and plead with Moses for a second chance. After all, they had the perfect alibi. They could have simply said, "Sorry, we were busy with another *mitzvah.*" They were *tamei* and spiritually unable to participate. They had no reason to feel guilty. They couldn't be faulted. And yet, it did bother them. They felt left out and genuinely desired to be together with their brethren in the observance of another *mitzvah,* the Pesach offering. People who had every opportunity to be free of obligation and willfully choose to actively seek such obligation are indeed deserving of honorable mention. It is right that they should be singled out in the Torah for their sincerity and devotion to the word of G-d.

Lots of us make excuses lots of times. It's too cold, too hot, too expensive, too difficult etc, etc. Too many of us take the path of least resistance. Parents arranging a Bar Mitzvah for their son sometimes look for the easy way out. "Can we have it at Mincha, Rabbi? That will be less demanding on our son. He's very active in the school sports program and won't have that much time to learn." Brides and grooms don't always appreciate the beautiful way of life Judaism can offer our most intimate relationship. "Do we have to attend the classes, Rabbi? Is the Mikvah compulsory?"

"The difference between a success and a failure is that a failure makes excuses and a success makes a plan."

Let's not look for excuses. Don't opt for the easy way out. Let us learn from the men in the wilderness who could have had every excuse in the book and yet happily chose to look for a new *mitzvah* and to share in the good deed of their community.

ഏരൂ

וארון ברית ה' נוסע לפניהם
And the Ark of the Covenant of
Hashem journeyed before them. (10:33)

Timeless Torah

I believe, you believe, we all believe. Otherwise, you wouldn't be reading this. Yet, not all believers necessarily practice every one of the observances that are part of our belief system. We subscribe to the ideology. We don't necessarily advocate moving the goal posts. But not all of us are quite ready to put into practice all the wonderful ideals our faith espouses.

What is the underlying argument that allows us the comfort of such obvious rationalization? One which, in a moment of frankness, we might admit is somewhat inconsistent with our own stated beliefs?

I get the distinct impression from many people that the subconscious criticism of the traditions they have not yet embraced is that they consider them to be somewhat out of touch with contemporary society. We happily accept those practices we identify with but pronounce the others as old-fashioned, obsolete, and out of step with the modern world. "Rabbi, once upon a time these traditions made sense, but today, do you really expect me to turn the clock back?"

So some will argue that in an age of government inspection and accepted hygiene standards, Kashrut is obsolete. Others will claim that if G-d really intended man to walk to Shul on Shabbos, Henry Ford would never have invented the automobile. (A Jewish humorist who had a fear of flying once said that if G-d intended man to fly, surely He would have made it easier to get to the airport!) And still others contend that today our sexual mores can only be determined by consensus, and as long as it's consenting adults, who cares what people are doing in their bedrooms? The fact is that for many of us the laws of the Torah feel every bit of their 3,300 years! Are we really and truly expected to adhere to this ancient code so out of touch with the modern reality?

Fair enough. So let's think about it. Are we suggesting that G-d who gave us these laws in the first place only had them in mind for those poor Israelites traipsing through the Sinai Desert? Do we really believe the Infinite Creator, the Master of the Universe to be so myopic that He cannot see beyond His Jewish nose? As a rabbi once told an atheist, "The god you don't believe in, I don't believe in either." Unless we accept that G-d could have seen the world as it is today, I would refuse to believe in Him too. A real G-d sees past, present, and future and is equally comfortable in our day as He was in the days of Moses. And the promised land of California is no more challenging to His credentials than ancient Canaan.

This week's Parsha tells us "And the Ark of the Covenant of Hashem journeyed before them ..." Rashi interprets this to mean that the Ark, which housed the Tablets, would miraculously prepare the groundwork for their future encampments. What it also is telling us is that, in fact, the Torah (as embodied by the Tablets) is way ahead of the game. It goes before us. It is not only timeless; it is ahead of its time. I can think of so many values and lifestyles which have become trendy now that Torah has been encouraging for centuries.

Not so long ago, a *Time* magazine cover story focused on a new, developing trend. Young moms are putting successful careers on hold in order to stay home and nurture their children when they need them most. This is new? From the beginning, Torah exempted women from time-bound mitzvahs like Tefillin or running to Shul three times a day so that they could fulfil the more important *mitzvah* of raising the next generation.

The Jewish tradition of sitting *shiva* when one loses a family member is today recognized by non-Jewish psychologists as being excellent bereavement therapy. Jews have been doing this for some 4,000 years. When Jacob was cooking those lentils that his brother Esau so desired, it was actually for his father Isaac, because he was then a mourner sitting *shiva* for Abraham. Today, our mourners eat bagels and eggs; then, the round foods symbolizing the cycle of life was lentils.

Whereas a generation ago, women spurned Mikveh as demeaning, today's woman is embracing it as a supreme acknowledgment of her sexuality and the most beautiful spiritual experience available. But there were mikvehs in Masada and long before.

The whole explosion of a society in search of spirituality, with celebrities and pop icons studying the *kabbalah,* only serves to validate the teachings of Jewish mysticism, which are indeed of ancient days.

Bell bottoms have come and gone and come back again and recede until another season comes. Paisley ties were once compulsory, then became *verboten.* Fads and fashions come and go, but G-dly values, the morals of *menschlichkeit*, and the mitzvahs of Torah are not behind the times. If anything, they are ahead of the times.

As He is beyond time, so are His commandments. If they appear in our mortal eyes as anachronistic, then that is our challenge—to relate Torah to our own realities and to shape our lives according to its standard. He intended it for us and our world too, so obviously it can be done.

The Torah is neither old nor new. Coming from an eternal supreme being, it is beyond time or space. It is timeless and, therefore, always timely.

ဆၣ

Pain or Privilege?

Okay, I admit it. I'm not sure how I would have behaved if I were in the position of the Jews back in the wilderness. We always criticize their lack of faith in G-d and the rough time they gave Moses. Even as G-d was providing them with the most incredible miracles—bread from heaven and water from rocks—they were busy moaning and groaning throughout. But would I have acted differently? Who knows? You think it was easy to live in a desert, even with all the miracles in the Bible? So I'm not all that confident that I would have never complained myself. I suppose a lot depends on a person's attitude and perspective in life.

I once heard a powerful insight in the name of Rav Moshe Feinstein, one of the outstanding *halachic* authorities of our time (he passed away in 1986). He was speaking of the generation of Jewish immigrants to the United States who spawned what became known as the "lost generation." Why was it that the children of parents who were religious, or at least traditional, moved so far away from the Yiddishkeit of their parental homes?

Reb Moshe argued that it could be summed up in one simple question of attitude. Did those parents convey to their children that Judaism was a burden or a boon, a pleasure or a pain? Was the constant refrain these children heard at home, *Oy, es iz shver tzu zein a Yid!* (Oy, it's hard to be a Jew!) or *Ahh, es iz gut tzu zein a Yid!* (Ahh, it is good to be a Jew!) Was being Jewish in those early days in America something to *krechtz* and sigh about, or something to celebrate and sing about? Whether children grew up hearing that Judaism was a pain or a privilege would determine whether they embraced it happily or escaped from it at the first opportunity.

According to Reb Moshe, on that question hinged the success or failure of an entire generation.

Indeed, we know of many Jews who survived the Holocaust and because of their horrific experiences perceived being Jewish as a "death sentence." There were those who sought to run as far away as possible from Europe. Many found their way to Australia and became "closet Jews." Some never even told their children that they were Jewish.

It was for this reason that the late Chief Rabbi of the United Kingdom, Rabbi Immanuel Jacobovits argued that while Holocaust education was very important, there was a danger in overemphasizing the Holocaust in Jewish Day Schools. We want our children to see that Judaism is a blessing, not a curse. Our Jewishness should not be dark and depressing, but bright and joyous.

I remember having a discussion with a group of businessmen some years ago where we were trying to put together a slide show to promote one of our local institutions. We were looking for a particularly powerful scene. One prominent doctor suggested that, for him, the single most powerful scene in Jewish life was the rabbi walking into the house of mourning carrying his bag of prayer books. To him, that may have been powerful, but for me—as a rabbi—I'd never heard anything so depressing. What am I, the Angel of Death?!

The Jews in the wilderness had their own issues. We should try and learn from their mistakes and be more faithful and trusting in the leadership of the Moses of our own time. But beyond that, let us not whine and whimper about the challenges of Jewish life. Let us convey to our children that Judaism is a joy and a privilege. Then, please G-d, they will embrace it for generations to come.

ಬಂದ

Shelach

Minority Rules

In democracies as well as in Jewish Law, majority rules. According to the Mishna in Sanhedrin, a Beth Din must always consist of an odd number of judges lest there be a hung jury. But the fact is, sometimes the majority gets it wrong.

This week's story of the 12 spies sent by Moses to the Promised Land is a case in point. Only two of the dozen, Joshua and Caleb, remained faithful to their leader, to the purpose of their mission, and to G-d's assurance that it was a good land. Despite the fact that they were really only sent on a reconnaissance mission to determine how best to approach the coming conquest, 10 of the 12 spies soured. Their negative report was designed to intimidate the people and discourage them from entering a ferocious, "inhabitant-devouring land." Instead of suggesting the best way forward, they came to the categorical conclusion that "we cannot ascend."

And the people responded accordingly. They cried out to Moses, lamenting their very departure from Egypt. "Why must we now die by the sword?" And G-d decreed that this generation was not worthy of His precious Promised Land. Furthermore, this day of weeping, where they cried for no good reason, would become a time of tears and a day of weeping for generations. Indeed, our sages explain, that day was Tisha B'Av, the day that would become a time of mourning for the destruction of our holy temples and many other national calamities throughout history.

Now, the question I'd like to pose here is why did the people not follow the two good spies, Joshua and Caleb, instead of the others? The obvious answer? They were outvoted and outnumbered, 10–2, no contest. Majority rules.

Tragically, though, they backed the losers. And the result was an extended vacation in the Wilderness for them and a tragedy for all of us to this day.

So although we may be staunch democrats and believers in the democratic process, clearly, there will be times when the minority is right.

The saintly Rabbi Yisroel Meir HaKohen Kagan, better known as the

Chofetz Chaim, was once challenged by a fellow Jew who was a somewhat educated cynic. "Rabbi," he argued, "doesn't the Torah itself say that we must follow the majority? Well, the overwhelming majority of Jews today are not religious. So you religious Jews must come over to our way of thinking!" The Chofetz Chaim replied with a story.

"Recently, I had occasion to be traveling by coach back home from an important trip. On route, the coachman distributed generous measures of vodka to his passengers to keep them warm and content. The coachman, too, helped himself to much more vodka than he should have.

"When we came to a crossroads, there was confusion as to which way to turn. Most people argued that the left road was the correct path. I was one of the only sober passengers on board, and I knew without a shadow of a doubt that we needed to take the road to the right. So I ask you, my friend, should I too have followed the majority? They were hopelessly drunk, and their judgment was very impaired. Thank G-d I prevailed."

All too often, the values and judgment calls of The Big Wide World are simply wrong. No matter how outnumbered moral people may be, we will continue to follow the path of decency and sanity because so much of the world is intoxicated with all sorts of new ideas, and their judgment is faulty. We Jews have never played the numbers game. Always, we have been the smallest of nations. We are not known for our majority but for our morals.

Some years ago, at the time of the fictitious Jenin "massacre" where Israel was accused of atrocities against the Palestinians, then-Secretary General of the United Nations Kofi Anan questioned, "Can it be that the whole world is wrong and Israel is right?" Guess what. He was spot on. The whole world was wrong and Israel was right. It was subsequently proven beyond a shadow of a doubt that there simply was no massacre. It was all fraudulent propaganda promulgated by our enemies.

For many years, my wife taught in a girls' high school. Once, a former student of hers asked if she could speak to her privately. She needed some guidance. She was now a young adult woman and everyone was telling her she was crazy for insisting that she be a virgin at her *chupah*. She was seeking my wife's affirmation that she hadn't lost her sanity.

All too often it is the big, wide world that is stark, raving *meshugga*, veering drunkenly out of control. It takes substantial strength of character to resist the pull of the drunken majority.

Please G-d; we will be men and women of stature and spirit. May we be inspired with the courage to stand up and be counted, even if it means being that lone voice in the wilderness. Otherwise, we may never get to our destination.

ജര

לא נוכל לעלות

We cannot ascend. (13:31)

Draw Your Own Conclusion

Some conclusions are more obvious to come to than others. Sometimes the most obvious conclusion isn't necessarily correct. Drawing our own conclusions can often be a risky business.

Take the case in this week's Parsha. The spies sent by Moses return from their reconnaissance mission of the Promised Land with a frightening report about the fierce warrior nations of Canaan. The Jewish People are dejected, frightened, and even weep at the thought of their impending invasion, convinced it can only be a suicidal mission impossible. The Almighty is angered, the people are punished for their lack of faith in His promise, and the spies go down in history as the villains in the story.

But why? What, in fact, was their sin? Moses asked for a report of the land. They came back and reported exactly what they had seen. They told no lies. The land *was* formidable. The inhabitants *were* huge and powerful. The fruits *were* extraordinarily large. They even brought back samples to prove it. So if it was all true why were they punished?

The answer lies not in the report but in their conclusion. The facts as the spies presented them were entirely accurate. The sin was their conclusion, *Lo nuchal la'alot*—"We cannot ascend to that people for it is too strong for us." Moses had sent them on a fact-finding mission. Their job was to bring back information. Nobody asked them for their personal opinions. The whole point of their mission was to gather the data necessary for the Israelites to find the best way of conquering the land. That it was going to happen was a given. G-d had promised them the land, told them of its natural beauty, and assured them of success.

The same G-d who just miraculously delivered you from Egypt, the mightiest superpower on earth, who split the sea for you and revealed Himself in all His glory to you at Sinai has now said that the Promised Land is there waiting for you. And after all He has done for you, you turn around and publicly doubt His power to help you succeed. This is not only a mistake in judgment. This is shameful, sinful, and faithless. The spies' report was correct, but their conclusion was disastrous.

A high school teacher once decided to demonstrate to his class the dangers of alcohol abuse. So he conducted an experiment. He took one glass of water and one glass of whisky. He then took a little worm and dropped it in the glass of water. The worm had a nice little swim in the glass and then the teacher removed the worm unharmed. He then dropped the worm into the glass of whisky. In no time at all, the worm was dead. He then turned to the class and asked them what the experiment proved. Whereupon one wise guy at the back piped up and said, "Sir, it proves conclusively that if you drink enough whisky you will never suffer from worms!"

The facts are there for all of us to see. The question is how to interpret them. If we have a preconceived position and then manipulate the data to draw conclusions that suit us, we may come off clever at first, but in the end we may well go the way of the spies.

Without faith, even the most accurate information can lead to the wrong conclusion.

৪৩৫৪

וראיתם את הארץ
And you shall see the land. (13:18)

והי' לכם לציצית וראיתם אותו
And it shall be Tzitzit for you that you may see it. (15:39)

Heads Up!

Perspective. What a difference it can make. How we look, where we look, and the way we look at things always colors our impressions. In this week's Parsha, the word *Ur'eetem—And you shall see,* occurs twice. The first is at the beginning in the story of the spies sent by Moses to investigate the Promised Land, and the second time is at the very end, in the chapter of *Tzitzit.*

In the first verse, Moses instructs the spies *And you shall see the land, what is it … are the people strong or weak … is the land fertile or lean … are the cities open or fortified?* In the second verse, we are commanded concerning the fringes on our *Tallit* and told, *And you shall look upon them and remember all the commandments of G-d and fulfill them.*

The same word, *Ur'eetem,* is used both times, yet look at the stark contrast between these two chapters. The first time, with the spies, it turned tragic. Their negative report of the Promised Land caused the people to cry for no good reason, and G-d said that day would become a time of "weeping for generations." Indeed, it was *Tisha B'Av,* and the resulting 40-year delay in entering Israel was to be the first of many national calamities to befall our people on that same day. The second time, however, it was a good thing. Looking at the Tzitzit fringes is a way to remember all G-d's commandments and to observe a G-dly life.

It all depends on how we look at things. It all comes down to where we go looking. To see the land is to see earthiness, a materialistic perspective.

To see the *tzitzit* is to gaze at a *mitzvah* of G-d, a heavenly perspective.

Ever watch an army of ants at work? Isn't it fascinating how they march in a straight line? Such disciplined workers; it is quite amazing. Apparently, ants have only one-dimensional vision. That's why they follow their noses and the guy right in front of them. They have no peripheral vision and therefore no distractions from their single-minded, though limited, perspective.

I remember a *farbrengen* in Yeshiva in Montreal when I was a student. Our Mashpia and mentor, Reb Velvel Greenglass, was waxing lyrical on the difference between a human being and an animal. The animal was created in a horizontal line. That is why the cow, naturally, looks downward, at the grass. Munching grass is its full-time occupation. All a cow thinks about all day is its food. Ever see a cow looking up at the sky and pondering the meaning of life? Human beings, however, were created in a vertical line. It is much easier for humans to look upward, to be pensive, and to contemplate that which is higher and more meaningful. (I guess that's why the chimps and baboons that stand vertically think they are "human"—*gantze mentschen.*)

To be people of vision we must look upward. There is a higher purpose to life. There is a deeper meaning to what meets the eye. The whole concept of Kabbalah and Jewish Mysticism is based on the principle of the metaphysical. This fundamental idea is that there is not only the self-evident body but also the invisible soul; not only the universe but also a cosmic plan and a profound reason for every experience in life, whether it be obvious to us or not.

If we only look at the land and that which is earthly and material, then the world is crass and careless, helter-skelter, and hollow. But when we raise our sights and lift our heads heavenward, we can see so much more. When we utilize our unique human mind power and spiritual potential, we can better discern the wood from the trees, the lofty from the low. The sages of the Talmud noted that by looking at the *tzitzit*, we not only see the commandments of G-d, but we discover G-d Himself, hence the singular *Ur'eetem Otoi.*

I guess where you look will usually determine what you find.

⁎⁎⁎

Korach

כולם קדושים
Everyone is holy. (16:3)

"Everyone is Holy!"

Despite all the drama of a world in turmoil, I sometimes get the feeling that we live in a boring world. Everyone is so politically correct. G-d forbid, we should say what we really think!

I once attended a dinner for a local organization, and the entertainer was a comedian. He got up and told the audience that the rabbi of the organization had called him and made him promise he wouldn't use any material that was "below the belt." Then, another committee member reminded him not to be racist or anti-religious or gender discriminatory. A third made him promise not to offend any minority groups. Having been duly stripped of every opportunity for satire, the comedian just said "Ladies and gentlemen, good night," and walked off the stage.

The argument of Korach, the mutineer in this week's reading, smacks of such inane political correctness. Korach accuses Moses and Aaron of nepotism, of grabbing positions of power for themselves. In doing so, he insists that "the entire community is holy. Why do you exalt yourselves over the congregation of G-d?"

In fact, the very same argument could be used against Jews in general. "Who do you think you are? Chosen People! Aren't all men created equal?"

The fact is that Jews are different. Ask any anti-Semite and he'll confirm it. The blatant hypocrisy of the nations of the world and the international media in constantly holding Israel to a higher standard of morality than it does its Arab neighbors only reaffirms that Jews generally adhere to a value system that is distinctive and unique.

Indeed, we do. The Chosen People concept means greater responsibility, not privilege. Far from being pompous and condescending about it, it has molded Jews into the most sensitive, humane nation on earth. And that is precisely why if we do occasionally veer from those principles, it is such an aberration that it is considered front page news.

Our belief in and respect for the inherent worth of every human being does not contradict our conviction that Judaism is unique. Does not every single religion maintain that its path is the correct one? Almost all, besides Judaism, actively evangelize to graciously save the lost souls of other faiths. We Jews do not seek converts because we believe that "the righteous of all nations have a share in the world to come," and they don't need to become Jews to get a slice of paradise.

Some years ago the University of Cape Town was considering building a student religious facility which would unite all three major faiths in one house of worship. It was to service Muslims, Christians, and Jews in a combined Mosque-Church-Synagogue to be known as a *MosChura-Gogue.* I was asked by a local newspaper what I thought of the idea. My answer was that the mistaken presumption in the founders' thinking was that three separate faiths could not possibly get along. There was therefore a need to join them into one composite. The fact is that we are each distinct with our own set of beliefs and practices, but there is no good reason why each specific faith should not respect the other. Why must we suppress individuality to achieve harmony?

My saintly mentor, the Lubavitcher Rebbe, whose Yahrtzeit is usually observed around the time we read this Parsha, thus explained the Midrashic account of Korach's rebellion. Korach gathered his men, and they donned prayer shawls made of the *tcheles* blue wool used for the *tzitzis.* "Does a Talis made of *tcheles* still need *tzitzis?*" they challenged Moshe. Moshe answered in the affirmative, and they laughed and mocked him. "If one strand of *tcheles* exempts an entire Talis, does not a whole Talis of *tcheles* exempt itself?" Said the Rebbe, this was precisely the argument of Korach. The whole Talis, that is, the entire congregation, is holy. We are all *tcheles,* holy wool. There is no need for distinctions between us. Why do you, Moses and Aaron, appoint yourselves leaders and exalt yourselves over us?

The fact is, however, that distinctions are a necessary reality of life. While we don't look to create divisions between people, not everybody is a doctor. Imagine if every fellow who felt like playing physician would hang up a sign outside his house and start dispensing medicine! We'd have a very sick society.

The Rebbe was a great humanitarian. He was concerned about every nation and every single individual—Jew or Gentile—and tried to make a difference to the broader society, as evidenced by his efforts for a sacred Moment of Silence in American public schools and his emphasis on education for all. Simultaneously, he was adamant that Israel needs to be uncompromising in its territorial strategy to safeguard the security of its citizens. Humanitarianism need not mean blurring all the lines. *Imagine,* John Lennon's peace song where there are no more religions, is not only impractical and anarchic, it is a denial of truth. We don't all have to be the same to get along.

Within our own people, some are Kohanim, others Levyim, while most of us belong to the rest of the tribes of Israel. There are doctors and lawyers, priests and prophets. The challenge of those who hold legitimate, genuine high office is to keep the distinctions from disintegrating into divisiveness. It is possible to be holy, distinctive, special—and sensitive.

ಕಾ

Inside/Outside

Some arguments are petty affairs between small people who aren't big enough and so need to stand up for their perceived honor or imaginary status. Other arguments are classic differences of opinion between people of stature, where each has an opinion worthy of consideration. We need to be able to discern the subtleties beneath the surface of any debate before formulating our own view.

This week's Parsha tells the story of the mutiny of Korach, a cousin of Moses, who challenged his authority. In the end, Korach and his henchmen were swallowed by the earth in a Divine display of rather unearthly justice.

The Midrash reveals some of the behind-the-scenes dialogue and debate between these men. Remember, Korach was no pushover. Besides being of noble lineage, he was clever, wealthy, and quite charismatic. One of the questions Korach put to Moshe was this: Does a house full of holy books still require a Mezuzah? Moshe answered that it did. Korach scoffed at the idea, ridiculing Moshe. The little Mezuzah contains but two chapters of Torah, the Shema Yisrael. A whole houseful of books with the entire Torah won't do the trick and a little Mezuzah will? It doesn't make any sense, argued Korach.

Why was Moshe's answer correct? What indeed is the significance of a small parchment on the doorpost in relation to a library inside? The Rebbe explained that it all depends on location. The books are inside. The Mezuzah is outside. When there are Jewish texts inside our study and living rooms, this indicates that the home is a Jewish home. This is good and as it should be. But what happens when we leave the comfortable confines of our home? Do we cease to be Jewish?

The Mezuzah is at the threshold of our homes, at the juncture and crossover between our inner lives and outer lives. As we make the transition from private person to public citizen, we desperately need to be reminded of who we are and that we take our identity with us wherever we may go. There is only One G-d, says the little scroll, whether in our private domain or in the big, wide world outside.

One of the many works by well-known author Herman Wouk is an autobiographical novel called *Inside, Outside* in which he portrays his own inner struggles straddling two conflicting worlds. His pious Talmudist *zayde* had a profound influence on him but so did Hollywood and Broadway. It took him a long time to find his way and settle into an observant Jewish lifestyle while still writing bestsellers. Being Jewish "Inside" relatively easy. It's when we hit the "Outside" that we encounter temptation and turmoil. The challenge every Jew must face is to remain proudly Jewish even in the face of conflicting cultures, curious looks and often hostile attitudes.

In the German-Jewish community of old there was a slogan that has long been discredited. *Yehudi b'veitecha v'ish b'tzeitecha.* "Be a Jew in your home and a man outside." The Nazis did not distinguish between Jews who looked Jewish or those who had removed any visible identifying marks. Today, traditional dress reflecting a national character is common, accepted, and respected—from Scottish kilts to Arab kaffiyehs. The outlandish hairstyles of sportsmen and celebrities are not only accepted, they are mimicked by millions of mindless wannabees.

Is it too much to expect a Jew to assert his Jewishness in unfamiliar corporate territory or to keep the Yarmulke on his head even when he walks out of Shul? Moshe rejected Korach's argument with good reason. The Mezuzah does not replace the need for Jewish libraries, but it serves as a perennial reminder on our doorways. As we step out of our home to enter the outside world, it beckons us to take our G-d and our Torah, our values, and our traditions along with us.

৪৩১৪

Sportsmen or Spectators?

Are you a spectator or a participant? Do you only watch the sporting events or do you sometimes kick a ball yourself?

A few years ago, it was decided to widen the seats at Wimbledon. Apparently, the problem was rather simple—obesity. It appears that the fans that admire the tennis stars in action don't get much exercise. The chairman of the British Sports Council was prompted to state, "If only the admirers of sport would practice it themselves."

The Parsha this week is named after Korach, cousin of Moses and a revolutionary who attempted to usurp the authority of Moses and Aaron. His ill-fated rebellion came to a bitter end when the earth opened and swallowed Korach and his followers, demonstrating to all that Moses and Aaron were truly chosen by G-d. But why name a parsha after a villain? Korach was a sinner and is surely not a role model for us to emulate.

The Rebbe, offered a novel approach. There is one area where Korach can, indeed, be a good role model. What was Korach's burning desire in life? It was to be a Kohen Gadol, the High Priest. He coveted Aaron's position of honor. Now, being a High Priest meant much more than just fame and fortune, glory, or privilege. Many sacred responsibilities came with the job. It was no easy task to be a Kohen Gadol. There were numerous restrictions: where he could go, what kind of activities he could be involved in, whom he could marry, etc, etc. Yet, Korach was absolutely single-minded in his aspiration to become the High Priest. Said the Rebbe, this is something we can all learn from Korach: the yearning to serve G-d in the holiest capacity, the craving to be a Kohen Gadol.

Would it be that all of us shared similar aspirations to holiness. Wouldn't it be wonderful if each one of us longed to live a life of sanctity dedicated to the service of G-d? How often we are only too happy to allow others to handle the sacred stuff. "You can put on Tefillin for me, Rabbi." And your Bobba can keep kosher for you and the ADL can fight anti-Semitism for you and the Chabad'niks will save the world for you. And what will you yourself do? Watch them?

It is interesting that in many parts of the world, much of the financial support for religious institutions comes from people who themselves are not religious. It has, in fact, been suggested that this phenomenon may well be a form of vicarious Judaism. These are fine people who really do believe in the truth of Judaism, but they haven't got sufficient commitment to practice it all that seriously themselves. Nor do they believe their own children will do it. Who then will defend the faith and perpetuate Judaism and the Jewish People? So they sponsor a religious institution to do it for them.

I recall hearing a pertinent story from the late Professor Velvel Greene of Ben Gurion University. A young man signed up to join the paratroopers. On his first training flight the instructor has him in his parachute huddled at the door of the airplane and starts counting down. "5, 4, 3, 2, 1, —JUMP!" The candidate is paralyzed with fear and doesn't move. "Okay, it happens to the best of us," says the instructor sympathetically; "we'll try again." The second attempt, however, is no better, nor the third or the fourth. The would-be paratrooper is simply too petrified to jump. Exasperated, the instructor asks him, "Tell me, son, if you are so scared to jump, why on earth do you want to join the paratroopers?" The young man answered, "It's true. I am scared out of my wits. But I just love to be around people who are not afraid."

It is wonderful to support and encourage the activists among us. But let us learn from Korach who wanted so badly to be a High Priest himself. Let's not be content with being spectators as others do it for us. Let each of us participate in the Jewish idea. And let us do it personally.

ജ

Chukat

Conduct Unbecoming

A life sentence for jaywalking? Twenty years for chewing gum in public?! Singapore notwithstanding, surely that's over the top.

Well, was it so different for Moses, who, in this week's reading, is punished and denied entrance to the Promised Land for the seemingly minor infraction of hitting the rock instead of speaking to it?

The people are clamoring for water in the wilderness. Hashem tells Moshe to speak to a certain rock (he was meant to ask nicely) and promises that, miraculously, water will flow from the rock. Commentary enlightens us as to the behind-the-scenes reasons for Moshe actually striking the rock, but in the end the miracle happens anyway, and the people's thirst is quenched.

So if your average rabbi today would make a rock produce water, even if the rock needed more than mere gentle persuasion, surely it would be hailed as the greatest miracle of the century, and the rabbi would win the Nobel Prize for chemistry! But for Moses it is a problem? Even if it would have been a greater sanctification of the Divine had he only spoken to the rock, still, for such a minor infraction such a severe penalty?

The answer, we are told, is that responsibility is commensurate with the individual. If a child messes up, it is entirely forgivable. For an adult who should know better, we are less likely to be as forgiving. Likewise, among adults, from a person of stature we expect more than from an ordinary fellow. A blemish on a coarse garment is not nearly as bad as it is on a piece of fine material. A stain on a pair of denims is not only acceptable, it is absolutely desirable. In fact, some people pay a premium for pre-stained jeans. Put the same stain on a silk tie, and it's simply unwearable.

Moshe was like the finest silk and, therefore, even the smallest, subtle hint of sin was considered a serious breach of conduct, and the repercussions were severe.

I recall reading in one of Rabbi Dr. A. J. Twersky's early books an exposition on the well-known Yiddish expression *es past nit—it is unbecoming*. When he was a child and his father would admonish him for doing the wrong thing, he would say *es past nit*, that is, for you, this sort of behavior is unbecoming. Not only did such a rebuke not shatter the child's self image, it reinforced it. A wise father was telling his child, "You are special; you are important; for someone like *you*, this sort of conduct is unbecoming." There are behavior patterns that are not necessarily criminal or sinful. Yet for someone from an esteemed family background, *es past nit*, it is unbecoming. This was the kind of criticism that could actually build a child's self-esteem. How beautiful, that even in chastisement, one can find validation and praise.

As I write these lines, I think of the Chupah ceremony when I officiate at a marriage. After reading the Ketubah in the original Aramaic, I usually read an abstract in English. There in the text one finds the antiquated expression, "even as it beseemeth a Jewish husband to do." The groom's obligations to his bride are reflected in that old, quaint turn of phrase reminding him that he will be expected to conduct himself appropriately—"as it beseems a Jewish husband to do." Yes, we Jews do expect more from our husbands. There is a historical ethic and a sacred tradition we are all held to. No matter what the rest of the world may get up to, for a Jewish husband, *es past nit*, it may be unbecoming.

Moshe was the greatest prophet that ever lived. For him, the standard could be no higher. Luckily for us mere mortals, we will not be held to that exalted benchmark. But we will be held to our own standard. The standard of Jews who were called upon by G-d to be "a kingdom of priests and a holy nation."

છાજી

Where There's a Will There's a Why

Why do certain people find satisfaction in Judaism while others are bored stiff? Why is faith exciting for some and irrelevant for others; a joy for one guy and an absolute burden for the next? One fellow cannot imagine going to work without first putting on his Tefillin, and the other hasn't seen his Tefillin since his Bar Mitzvah 40 years ago. This woman can't wait to get to Shul, and the other can't wait to get out.

Why?

This week we read about the ultimate *mitzvah* of faith, the Red Heifer. It is a statutory commandment whose reason still remains a mystery. I must admit, to take the ashes of a red heifer and sprinkle them on a person so he may attain spiritual purification is, indeed, rather mind-boggling.

According to the Midrash, the Almighty promised Moses that to him He would reveal the secret meaning of this mitzvah, but only after Moses would initially accept it as a Divine decree. If he would first take it on faith, thereafter more rational understanding would follow.

The truth is that there are answers to virtually every question people may have about Judaism. Intelligent skeptics I meet are often amazed that what they had long written off as empty ritual is actually philosophically profound with rich symbolic meaning. But the skeptic has to be ready to listen. You can hear the most eloquent, intellectual explanation, but if you are not mentally prepared to accept that this may in fact be a worthwhile exercise, chances are you won't be impressed. Once we stop resisting and accept that there is inherent validity, suddenly Judaism makes all the sense in the world.

It is a psychological fact that we can grasp that which we sincerely desire to understand. But if there is a subject that we have no interest in, we will walk into mental blockades regularly.

The previous Lubavitcher Rebbe, Rabbi Yosef Yitzchok Schneerson, said that this can explain why some very astute businessmen may sit at a Talmud class and find themselves struggling to grasp basic principles of rabbinic reasoning. Why is it that the same person who can concoct the most brilliant schemes in the boardroom fails to follow straightforward logic in the Talmud class? The answer, he says, is that this businessman is really not that interested in the subject. But if it was half as important to him as making money, he might well become a Rosh Yeshiva!

So, in the same way that G-d told Moshe that he could come to comprehend the meaning of the red heifer but only after he accepted it, similarly today, those who genuinely wish to understand Judaism will succeed, but only if they buy into the product on some level first.

When I was studying in Yeshiva, I would always try to attend the annual Encounter with Chabad weekends for university students. These were organized to expose Jewish students to Judaism over a Shabbat, and there were lectures by leading rabbis and religious academics. Once a young man shouted back at the lecturer, "How can you expect me to put on Tefillin if I don't believe in G-d?!" Very calmly, the speaker replied, "First put on Tefillin and I promise you will see that you really do believe in G-d."

We all have a G-dly faith inside us. It just needs to be revealed. As illogical as it may sound, if we start by observing a *mitzvah*, we find that our faith will follow through and begin to blossom. It has been shown to be true again and again. If we are genuinely searching for truth and we are objective, there are ample answers. If we are not interested, no answer will be good enough. As they say in the classic advertisement, *Try it, you'll like it.*

৪৩

אַל תִּירָא אֹתוֹ

Do not fear him. (21:34)

Who's Afraid of Big, Bad Og?

Believe it or not, there was a time when Moses was afraid. Yes, the greatest leader of all time—the man who fought and vanquished Pharaoh, split the sea, challenged the angels on High for the rights to the Torah—this spiritual colossus was afraid. Who and what could possibly frighten Moses?

The end of Parshat Chukat tells us that G-d reassured Moses and said, *Do not fear him.* Why did Moses need reassuring? The story is this. The Israelites were about to go into battle against Og, King of Bashan, a mighty warrior, a man who was, literally, a giant. And Moses was afraid to such an extent that the Almighty had to assuage his fears.

Why did Og inspire such dread in the great prophet? Surely he had dealt with more formidable threats in his career? According to Rashi, the story goes back many years. Og (or according to some commentaries, the ancestor of the current king), escaped from battle during the days of Abraham. This refugee then came to Abraham and informed him of his nephew Lot's capture in battle. Abraham immediately went into action, fought the kings, and successfully rescued Lot. Says Rashi, Moshe was afraid to do battle with Og lest the merit he had acquired when helping Abraham might stand him in good stead.

In other words, the fact that Og had done a kindness to Abraham all those years ago might be considered of such special significance that he would be spiritually protected from harm in the merit of Abraham, the beneficiary of his good deed.

But was it really such a good deed? The same Rashi in his commentary on Genesis (14, 13), informs us that Og's motives were not altogether altruistic. Apparently, by telling Abraham that his nephew Lot had been taken captive Og was actually hoping that Abraham would attempt to rescue his nephew and be killed in battle so that Og could then take Abraham's beautiful wife, Sarah, for himself—hardly an act of magnanimous righteousness! Why would Moses be worried about the spiritual merit of conduct tainted by such ulterior motives?

The answer, it would seem, is that although Og's motives were far from unselfish, the fact is that he had done Abraham a kindness. Abraham was grateful for the information and was, indeed, successful in saving Lot from his captors. So, although Og's reasons were less than noble, the end result of his deed was good and Abraham considered it a favor. That's why Moses was afraid of Og, lest his spiritual credits protect him. And that is why the Almighty needed to put Moses' mind at ease. *Do not fear him, for into your hand have I given him, his entire people and his land.*

It is an incredible lesson in the power of *chesed*, acts of loving kindness. That one good turn, performed so many years back, and out of sinister motivation on top of it, could cause Moses himself so much anxiety is surely proof positive of the awesome and long-term positive effects of a single act of kindness.

Clearly, from a spiritual point of view, deeds of goodness and kindness have the power to protect us from harm. Performing a single act of compassion or helping someone in need really does have the capacity to shield us. So, if you think about it, in the end, we are not only helping them but helping ourselves.

Let this story inspire us to be a little more considerate to each other, a little more helpful to those around us, and may our benevolence protect us and our families from any harm.

৪০ল্ড

Balak

חטאתי כי לא ידעתי
I have sinned because I did not know. (22:34)

A Lousy Excuse

"Ignorance of the law is no excuse," we are told. Try explaining to the traffic cop that you simply never knew crossing a red light was an offense. It won't get you very far.

This week, we read the strange but famous Biblical narrative of the heathen prophet Balaam and his talking donkey. At one point, an angel blocks the donkey's path and the animal stops in its tracks. Balaam is frustrated and strikes the donkey. *And Hashem opened the mouth of the donkey and it spoke to Balaam saying, "Why did you hit me?" ... And then Hashem opened the eyes of Balaam and he realized there was an angel in the way.* So Balaam apologized to the donkey and said, *"I have sinned because I did not know."*

So if he genuinely didn't know, why was it a sin? The answer is that for a prophet who is able to communicate with the Divine, not to be aware of an angelic presence right in front of his nose is indeed sinful. A man of his spiritual stature should have known better.

There is no question that in many communities where organized Judaism is weak and not easily available, ignorance of what being Jewish entails may still be a valid excuse. For millions of Jews who grew up in the former Soviet Union under an atheistic regime, ignorance of Jewish law and lore is, undoubtedly, understandable and even justifiable.

But for those of us who live in Jewish communities that are alive and vibrant, for those who are aware enough to be reading these lines, surely ignorance as a rationalization no longer holds water.

In my own community of Johannesburg, South Africa, thank G-d there are educational opportunities too numerous to mention. Not only Day Schools for children but adult education programs too. Some of our own Shul lectures and symposia attract hundreds of men and women regularly. The Internet, with all its serious flaws and dangers, is providing unparalleled opportunities for Jews, even in the remotest outposts, to connect with their heritage. So today, while Jewish ignorance still remains Public Enemy Number One, there are thankfully ample avenues for Jews who were never exposed to Judaism, its teachings and its relevance, to become more aware and better educated.

I remember an advertising campaign that ran in the United States years ago for what was then known as the United Negro College Fund. The Fund was established to provide a university education to promising black students from underprivileged backgrounds. To this day, I can still visualize that photograph of a young man studying and underneath it, the slogan: "A mind is a terrible thing to waste."

Why do rabbis become rabbis? To teach. The word *rabbi* means *my teacher*. Sure there are many facets to a spiritual leader's position, but the main incentive for me, as for so many of my colleagues, is the privilege of educating Jews about Judaism—especially those who, through no fault of their own, were not raised with that awareness.

In no way do I minimize the importance of the pastoral role a rabbi plays in his community. Helping people in times of distress, as on joyous occasions, can be deeply gratifying. Counseling troubled souls or ordinary people with moral dilemmas is equally significant. But the most stimulating part of the job for me is teaching Jews how to be Jewish. Teaching Torah and introducing it to the previously uninitiated. The privilege of opening a Jewish mind to the beauty of Jewish wisdom and to the eternal relevance of the Jewish way of life is what led me to the rabbinate.

During my tenure thus far I have officiated at many hundreds of Bar Mitzvahs, weddings and, sadly, at as many funerals and unveilings. While I always treat each case with the sensitivity and respect it deserves and do my best to make these milestones meaningful rites of passage, my real "job satisfaction" comes when a young person comes to see me for advice on how to explore his or her Jewish identity. Rabbis get a real "high" when young couples take the initiative and ask for guidance on how to establish a really successful Jewish home and family. That's a rabbi's *nachas*.

So wherever you are reading these lines, follow the wise counsel of Ethics of the Fathers and "Acquire for yourself a rabbi," a teacher.

In our age of the information explosion, ignorance has become a lousy excuse.

∞∞

מה טובו אהליך יעקב
How goodly are your tents, O Jacob. (24:5)

Keeping Up With the Cohens

"That's some new kitchen Sandra just had done. State of the art!" "Psst ... did you see the new car Mark just took delivery of? It's got every gadget in the book!" Common conversation. Rather routine, everyday talk.

They tell of a traveling salesman who had broken all records for sales in his company. When asked the secret of his success, he explained that the first thing he said when someone opened the door was, "Did you see what your neighbor Mrs. Jones just got?" That trick never failed him.

This was never the Jewish ethic however. We were taught differently. And our ancient value system is as relevant as ever in contemporary life. Privacy, modesty and discretion are all characteristics our people have cherished since we became a nation.

Balaam raised his eyes and saw Israel dwelling according to its tribes. Rashi offers one interpretation of the verse to mean that the doorways of the Israelites in the wilderness were designed so that they did not face each other. That way, one person was not able to see into his neighbor's tent, and their privacy was protected. In fact, this is one of the explanations of Balaam's famous praise of the Jews, *Ma Tovu Oholecha Yaakov— How goodly are your tents, O Jacob.* The heathen prophet was extolling the Jews' virtues in their town planning whereby they took precautions in safeguarding their privacy and modesty and protecting their personal family lives from would-be busybodies and peeping toms, otherwise known as *yentas* and *nudniks.*

But another possible interpretation of "not looking into your neighbor's tent" might be this: do not look into your neighbor's tent to help you decide what you should be doing. Your decisions in life should not be based on what other people are, or are not, doing. Certainly not on what your neighbors have or do not have.

Social workers today will painfully testify that family breakdowns are often a result of financial difficulties and the stress that puts on marriages. Many of those stresses are self-imposed. Their clients confessed that they didn't really need the new kitchen or the new car, but once their friends were moving up in the status stakes, they felt under pressure to maintain their social standing.

Whether it is the kitchen, car, vacation, or the latest digital technology, if we allow ourselves to be judged by other people's criteria, we lay ourselves open to a lot of unnecessary stress. Even a *simcha*—a wedding or Bar Mitzvah—can get us into "keeping up with the Cohens" mode, from the 7-layered designer invitation hand-delivered to every guest down to the posh dinner-dance replete with chopped liver sculptures.

Why? All because we are busy looking over our shoulders or peering into the next-door neighbor's place.

The principle even applies to Tzedakah. There is an appeal for the Shul or a Jewish charity and how do we respond? "Well if so and so who is a multi-millionaire only gave $10,000 then all I should give is $10!" But what difference does it make what someone else gave or didn't give? You should give what you can, irrespective of what others gave.

How much resentment, bitterness, disappointment, and *fardrus* we would avoid if we didn't try to measure ourselves by other people's standards. We would be much happier people if we looked into ourselves and achieved what we could and should without drawing comparisons with others.

If you want to enjoy the blessing of "goodly tents" or even just good housekeeping, keep your eyes and your nose in your own tent. Then you will be content too.

෫ඁ෬

Pinchas

הנני נותן לו את בריתי שלום
Behold I give him My covenant of peace. (25:12)

Is Everything Okay?

Once upon a time, in the days of Moses and the Jews in the Wilderness, the Moabite women were seducing young Jewish men. The Almighty was angered and sent a plague upon His people. Jews were dying left, right, and center. To compound matters, Zimri, a Prince from the Tribe of Shimon, was himself consorting with a Midianite Princess named Kozbi and flaunting their illicit relationship in the face of Moses.

Enter Pinchas, a young Jewish zealot, and in true zealot tradition he kills both Zimri and Kozbi. Suddenly, the plague stops. No more Jews die. And G-d declares Pinchas to be not a murderer but a hero, a defender of the faith, and bestows upon him the world's first peace prize. "Behold I give him My covenant of peace." He is appointed to the priesthood and, as befits a hero, gets a whole portion of the Bible named after him, this week's parsha, Pinchas.

Now I have serious reservations as to whether Dale Carnegie would use Pinchas as a role model for How to Win Friends and Influence People. I would not quite suggest that we root out all sinners and put a spear through them. What was appropriate in ancient times is not necessarily appropriate today. The way to stop the internal hemorrhaging of our people through assimilation and intermarriage is clearly not the way of Pinchas.

The Jewish prince Zimri was rebellious with intent. He knew full well that what he was doing was wrong. It was a deliberate provocation on his part. Most people who turn their backs on Judaism today, though, do so out of ignorance. They simply don't know. Nobody taught them. It's not their fault. We cannot condone it, but such people don't need a whipping; they need a whetting of their spiritual appetite. They need an education, urgently. They need a lot of love and warmth and for people to reach out to them and share the beauty of a Shabbos or an inspirational Shul experience. Show them their own Jewishness and how meaningful it truly is, and they will no longer want to give it up.

What then is the message of Pinchas for our time? Perhaps it might be that sometimes, even today in our super sensitive, tolerant society we do need to take a stand. There will be issues that demand that we put our foot down, that we insist, that we say "No!"

It might be different issues for different people. For some it may be Jerusalem; for others, Yom Kippur; and for still others, it might be insisting that their daughter's boyfriend cannot sleep over. Somewhere, surely, there has got to be a bottom line.

Generally, diplomacy and positive encouragement work much better than fighting. We are not trying to train Jewish holy fundamentalists to go around killing infidels. But inevitably there will be occasions when even pacifists like us will need to adopt the zero-tolerance approach of Pinchas.

Sooner or later, we will be required to stand up and be counted. There will come a time when we, too, will have to say, "I'm sorry. I cannot accept this kind of behavior. This is wrong. Stop!"

Even in our OK Generation, not everything is okay.

80CR

What's Your Bottom Line?

This is the Parsha of Pinchas the Zealous. The courageous young priest stood up against idolatry and immorality and, in the end, saved Israel from a devastating plague.

While Pinchas's radical response made him a hero worthy of having a Torah section named after him, we wouldn't necessarily suggest to our children that they emulate his behavior. Those were extraordinary times. Today, violence dare not become our norm. So, Pinchas—hero though he may be—cannot become our role model. At least not when it comes to the details of what he did.

Nevertheless, Pinchas does give us something very important to consider. What is it that would arouse *our* righteous indignation? What, in Jewish life today, would get us emotionally worked up? What would it take to galvanize us into action in defense of that which we consider sacred and inviolate? Is there something that would incense us? Anything?

I am reminded of a famous saying attributed to Rabbi Yosef Yitzchak Schneerson. He said, "A Jew is neither willing nor able to allow himself to become divorced from G-d." In other words, once a Jew becomes consciously aware that what he is contemplating doing will cause him to be alienated from G-d and that which is holy, he simply will not—and cannot—do it. Even if he is not remotely "religious," it is something that comes from his inner essence, his spiritual DNA. It is in his very being.

How many true stories we all know that validate this principle. One that springs to mind is of a Jewish actor during the Holocaust. In those days especially, the stage was not the place where one would find "nice Jewish boys," at least not nice, Jewish, *religious* boys. When the Nazis invaded the town, they desecrated the synagogues and—painful as it is to write these words—they unraveled the Torah scrolls and rolled them out in the gutter. To add insult to injury, they ordered this fellow, the actor, to urinate on the Torah. He was not at all religious. He probably hadn't looked into a Torah in many years. Yet, he could not bring himself to commit such sacrilege. He refused. The savage beasts killed him on the spot. He gave his life *al Kiddush Hashem,* sanctifying the name of G-d, and he went down in history as a holy martyr.

For the Jewish actor, that was his bottom line. What is ours? Religiously, is it Shabbos, Yom Kippur, intermarriage? Marrying out on Yom Kippur with a pork chop reception? Morally, is it insider trading, fraud, Ponzi schemes, or murder? Nationally, is it the West Bank, Jerusalem, or Tel Aviv? Where do we draw the line?

Our politically correct rules of etiquette promote such unparalleled tolerance that people's democratic right to do anything they may wish has become the defining principle of our generation. The Ten Commandments are obsolete. "Thou shalt not violate my democratic right" is the first and last commandment.

Of course, in any democratic country people may choose their own lifestyles as they wish. But when there is absolutely nothing that arouses our passion, nothing that raises our blood pressure, nothing that sparks any kind of protest, then we have become an insipid, innocuous, characterless society.

The story of Pinchas and his brave stand for G-d, Torah and morality gives us cause to consider and an important point to ponder. You don't have to be a zealot to have a bottom line. What is *my* bottom line? What would *I* get passionate about? Is there *anything* in Jewish life that inspires me, excites me, or incenses me enough to take a stand?

Please think about it.

ഇൽ

Destiny Beckons

How did an unknown youngster suddenly rise to prominence? Pinchas, the hero of this week's Parsha, was previously unheard of. Though as a grandson of Aaron he belonged to the "royal family," he was an unseeded young man, who, with a single act of bravery was catapulted to stardom.

The Talmud (Sanhedrin 82a) tells the behind the scenes story. Zimri, a prince of the tribe of Shimon, publicly flaunts his intimate relationship with a heathen Midianite princess. Moses is momentarily stymied. Pinchas respectfully reminds Moses that he himself taught the principle that one who behaves as Zimri did may be executed by the zealous. Moses responds that since Pinchas remembered this, he, Pinchas, should be the one to actually carry it out. Pinchas duly does just that, and the terrible plague that had taken the lives of thousands is stilled. G-d blesses Pinchas with His Covenant of Peace, and he goes down in history as the hero who saved the day. But why did Moses forget what he himself had taught? Apparently, Divine Providence saw fit that the great prophet should suffer a temporary memory lapse in order that young Pinchas assume his destined status.

Now Pinchas could have made a simple calculation. Here stand Moses and Aaron, as well as other prominent elders and leaders, and they are all silent. In the face of such brazen moral travesty all these great men stand back. Who, then, am I to step forward? How can I, little old me, a new kid on the block, stand up and say what I believe in their august presence? Surely I must keep quiet and hold my peace.

But Pinchas did not say that. And thank G-d he didn't. Had he kept his silence, the plague might not have been averted, and Pinchas would have remained a non-entity.

This serves a powerful lesson to all of us. If you witness a situation where you feel that you can make a difference, then you must. And the fact that greater people than you seem paralyzed should not necessarily mean that you too should remain idle. Perhaps this is your unique chance to do something historic. Perhaps you are earmarked for greatness, and G-d is opening your window of opportunity. Deny yourself this moment, and you deny destiny.

Sometimes the moment is yours. Sometimes greater people may vacillate and the responsibility and opportunity rest with you and you alone. Each of us has so much unlocked potential. Rare and precious are those crossroads of life when the chance to unleash that inner calling presents itself. This is your baby, your moment of glory, your own personal calling, and you dare not desist from it.

Such was the case with Pinchas, and such may be the scenario that every one of us may find ourselves playing out one day.

In the story of Purim, the Megillah records how Queen Esther is asked by Mordechai to intercede with King Ahasuerus on behalf of her people. She explains that she fears this may be absolutely suicidal for her. Mordechai responds with rather strong words. *Relief and deliverance will come for the Jews from elsewhere and you and your father's house will perish.* What Mordechai was telling Esther was that the chance to single-handedly save one's entire nation doesn't present itself every day. It is a unique moment and ought to be seized. If you won't do it, someone else will, but this once-in-a-lifetime opportunity may be lost to you forever.

Pinchas reminds us that when opportunity knocks, we should open the door quickly. Do not hesitate. Destiny may be beckoning.

৪০৫

Matot

ככל היוצא מפיו יעשה

Whatever issues from his mouth he shall do. (30:3)

Promises, Promises

I have always been intrigued by the traditional way in which diamond merchants seal a deal. They shake hands and say "Mazel and Brocha" (Good fortune and blessing). Once those few words have been said, the industry considers it a done deal, and it has all the power of a legal, contractual transaction. It is a tribute to the diamond fraternity that in their fraternity a word is a word. In some other industries, even a contract isn't worth the paper it's written on. Here, the spoken word is deemed to be binding and irrevocable. Interestingly, the Mazel & Brocha principle has been upheld in arbitration cases throughout the world.

This week's Parsha, Matot, opens with an injunction about the sanctity of our words. *And Moshe spoke to the heads of the tribes ... if a man takes a vow ... he shall not desecrate his word, whatever issues from his mouth he shall do.*

A word is a word. Promises are promises. And the words we utter are sacred and inviolate. If we disregard what we say, we have profaned and desecrated our words. That's why many people are careful to add the words *bli neder* ("without vowing") whenever they say something that might be construed as a vow. Should they be prevented from fulfilling their promises and be guilty of sacrilege, the words *bli neder* stipulate that their undertaking does not have the full force of a vow, making the offense less grave. Nevertheless, that legal loophole in no way diminishes the regard we hold for our words. On the contrary, the fact that we are so concerned that we should not violate a vow attests to the gravity we attach to our words.

The question, though, is why was this commandment given to the heads of the tribes? Surely, it applies to each and every one of us. I suppose the simple answer is that since it is usually leaders who make the most promises, therefore it is they who need the most cautioning.

Politicians are infamous for campaign promises, which—once they are elected—are rarely fulfilled. Like the candidate who promised to lower taxes if he was elected. As soon as he took office, though, he actually raised taxes. When he was challenged by the people about his unkept promise, he actually admitted that he had lied. "Wow! What an honest politician!" The naïve electorate thought that was quite a genuine confession and promptly decided that he was the most honest politician they had ever met. We are a gullible people indeed.

Many books have been published on the subject of business ethics. While there are a great many laws and nuances to this theme, at the end of the day, the acid test of business ethics is, "Did you keep your word?" Did you carry out your commitments, or did you duck and dive around them? It makes no difference how other companies are behaving. It matters little whether our competitors are corrupt. We must honor our promises, and that is the ultimate bottom line.

Whether in our business relationships or in the *Tzedakah* pledges we make to the synagogue or to other charities, our word should be our bond. Even if we are worried about the immediate financial costs, we can be assured that with the passage of time, the reputation we will acquire by speaking truthfully and keeping our word will more than compensate any short-term losses. So, leave the spin doctoring to the politicians. A Jew's word should be sacred.

৪৩০৪

בנו לכם ערים לטפכם וגדרות לצנאכם

*Build for yourselves cities for your
children and pens for your flock. (32:24)*

Priorities and Price Tags

Is it the money or the man, the cash or the kids? What is most important in our lives? Of course, no one ever admits to putting money ahead of their children, but is it not an all-too-common phenomenon? Aren't most parents, even good parents, guilty of making that mistake now and then?

In this week's parsha, the Jewish People are preparing for the conquest of Canaan. In anticipation of entering the Promised Land the tribes of Reuben and Gad make a special request of Moses.

They had abundant herds of livestock, and the land east of the Jordan River was especially fertile and suitable for grazing. They asked Moses if they could inherit this land rather than the land west of the Jordan. In making this request they expressed themselves thus: "Pens for the flock shall we build here for our livestock and cities for our small children." Immediately, Moses chastises them and corrects their mistake. "Build for yourselves cities for your small children and pens for your flock." Moses turns around their sequence, putting the children ahead of the animals.

Rashi observes that those tribes appeared to be more concerned about their money—livestock—than they were about their sons and daughters. Moshe needed to give them a lesson in values and priorities. Put family first. Possessions come later.

The veteran American spiritual leader, the late Rabbi David Hollander, was renowned for always finding an appropriate anecdote to fit the message. Concerning this Parsha, he once told me the story of a fellow who somehow managed to get himself locked in inside a big department store after they closed up for the day. To compound the problem, it was over a vacation weekend. As it was before cellphones were invented, all his attempts to get out proved futile. So he decided to give vent to his frustrations by taking revenge on the store management. He spent the time of his incarceration swapping price tags on the merchandise. The result? A mink coat was now priced at $29.99, a necktie at $999.00. Furniture was going for the price of peanuts, the latest hi-fi for a song, and a set of underwear was absolutely unaffordable! Imagine the chaos when the store reopened.

The question is, are our own price tags correctly marked? Do we value the things in our own lives correctly? Are our priorities in order? Or do we, too, put the cattle and the sheep—the car and the office—ahead of our children?

How many workaholic husbands have told their wives, "Honey, I'm doing it all for you and the kids?" But the businesses we are busy building for them actually take us away from them in the most important and formative years of their lives. Rightly has it been said, "the best thing you can spend on your kids is not money but time."

I've seen many people become "successes" over the years. They achieve professional success, career success, business success growing their fame and fortunes. Too many in the process have become family failures. At the end of the day, our deepest satisfaction in life comes not from our professional achievements but from our family—the growth, stability, and togetherness that we have nurtured over the years—what our Jewish parents and grandparents simply called *Nachas*.

"Jewish wealth is not measured in property portfolios or stocks and bonds" (to paraphrase a holy rabbi of yesteryear). True Jewish wealth is being blessed with children who walk in the ways of G-d. For that, we need to be there for them and with them.

I once spoke about this idea in Shul on Shabbos, and after the service a congregant walked up to me and proclaimed, "Rabbi, I am a millionaire!" I knew the man to be of modest financial means but he immediately explained, "I'm a millionaire in *Nachas!*" I wish it upon you.

࠸ꗄ

Massei

The Power of Prayer

A fellow was boasting about what a good citizen he was and what a refined, disciplined lifestyle he led. "I don't smoke, I don't drink, I don't gamble, I don't cheat on my wife. I am early to bed and early to rise and I work hard all day and attend religious services faithfully." Very impressive, right? Then he added, "I've been like this for the last five years, but just you wait until they let me out of this place!

Although prisons were not really part of the Jewish judicial system, there were occasions when individuals would have their freedom of movement curtailed. One such example was the City of Refuge. If a person was guilty of manslaughter, but not murder, the perpetrator would flee to one of the specially designated Cities of Refuge throughout Biblical Israel where he was given safe haven from the wrath of a would-be avenging relative of the victim.

The Torah tells us that his term of exile would end with the death of the Kohen Gadol, the High Priest. Commentary tells of an interesting practice that developed. The mother of the Kohen Gadol at the time would make a point of sending gifts of food parcels to those exiled so that they should not pray for the early demise of her son to which their own freedom was linked.

Now this is very strange. Here is a man who, though not a murderer, is not entirely innocent of any negligence either. And the rabbis teach that G-d does not allow misfortune to befall the righteous. If this person caused a loss of life, we can safely assume that he is less than righteous. Opposite him stands the High Priest of Israel, noble, aristocratic, and, arguably, the holiest Jew alive. Of the entire nation, he alone would have the awesome responsibility and privilege of entering the inner sanctum of the Holy of Holies in the Holy Temple of Jerusalem on the holy day of Yom Kippur. Do we really have reason to fear that the prayers of this morally tainted prisoner will have such a negative effect on the revered and exalted High Priest to the extent that he may die? And his poor mother has to go and *shlep* food parcels to distant cities to soften up the prisoner so he should go easy in his prayers so that her holy son may live? Does this make sense?

But such is the power of prayer—the prayer of any individual, noble or ordinary, righteous, simple, or even somewhat sinful. Of course, there are no guarantees. Otherwise, I suppose, Shuls around the world would be overflowing daily. But we do believe fervently in the power of prayer. And though, ideally, we pray in Hebrew and with a congregation, the most important ingredient for our prayers to be successful is sincerity. "G-d wants the heart," we are taught. The language and the music are secondary to the genuineness of our prayers. Nothing can be more genuine than a tear shed in prayer.

By all means, learn the language of our Siddur, the prayer book. Improve your Hebrew reading so you can follow the services and *daaven* with fluency. But remember, most important of all is our sincerity. May all our prayers be answered.

₧⁂

אותי עזבו...לחצב להם בארות נשברים אשר לא יכלו המים

They have forsaken Me ... to dig broken cisterns
that hold no water. (Haftarah, Jeremiah 2)

Flirting With Futility

The Jewish calendar and the Parsha are somehow always synchronized. There is a deep connection between the two, and it is never coincidental that a particular Parsha is read at a particular time of the year. This week's parsha is always read during the Three Weeks of Mourning when we recall the destruction of our Holy Temple.

I am not going to focus on these latent connections here but prefer to look at the *haftarah* and the message of the Prophet Jeremiah (Chapter 2), which is also especially chosen for this week. The prophet castigates the Jewish People: *Listen to the word of G-d, O House of Jacob ... what wrong did your fathers find in Me that they distanced themselves from Me and went after (gods of) emptiness and became empty themselves?* (Verse 5).

They are guilty on two counts, laments Jeremiah. *They have forsaken Me, the spring of living waters, (and furthermore) to dig for themselves wells, broken cisterns that hold no water* (Verse 13). What is the prophet saying? If you exchanged G-d and Torah for some other noble, exalted philosophy or for another highly principled ideology, *nu*, at least there might be some imaginary justification. But for what have you exchanged the lofty moral truths of G-d and Torah? For *hevel*—futility, emptiness, and nothingness. This is a terrible double blow.

Those who pursue a path of emptiness become empty people. Their lives are filled with nothing more than empty materialism—zero content and zero meaning. At least people like Warren Buffet gave it away. His single-minded focus on amassing wealth has been more than vindicated by his unprecedented philanthropy. But materialism for its own sake, with no higher purpose whatsoever, is futile and empty and can only lead to those practicing it becoming empty-headed themselves. Some generations sinned by denying G-d. Jeremiah weeps for a generation that worships nonsense and empty escapism.

What is the worst thing in the world that can happen to a teenager today? To be home alone on a Saturday night without a date! And the teenager's parents need to chill after all the pressures of the workweek. So we build ourselves huge and magnificent entertainment edifices, towers of trivia, centers of senselessness. And we fill the void and the vacuum in our lives with escapist pleasures—drinking and gambling, smoking and snorting.

Generations ago, Jewish parents cried bitter tears because they lost their children to communism, socialism, a strain of anti-religious secular Zionism, hippie-ism, or other anti-establishment ideologies. The tragedy of our time is that we are losing our youth not to any form of political activism or social consciousness, but to emptiness and futility, to drugs and raves. At least the misguided young rebels of old believed in a cause. Right or wrong, they were trying to build a better world. Today, it's "to hell with the world, pass the beer!"

Jeremiah pleads with us to forsake this fling with futility and empty cisterns and to embrace the eternal spring of living waters, the authentic truths of Torah and the way of G-d. Let us lead our children towards meaningful spirituality and sanctity. Sanity must surely follow.

5

Sefer Devarim
The Book of Deuteronomy

Jewish Survival Course

What is the biggest miracle of our generation? The fall of Communism? The electric-powered car? The Internet?

Surely for us Jews, indisputably, the greatest miracle of all must be that after the Holocaust the Jewish People picked themselves up and rebuilt Jewish life, Jewish communities, and especially, the Jewish Homeland. Is there anything more extraordinary than that Jews who were singled out for extermination because of their faith should nonetheless want to embrace that same faith and still be Jewish!

This parsha of Devarim always coincides with Shabbos Chazon, the Shabbos before Tisha B'Av, our National Day of Mourning. On that day, we remember the destruction of both our Temples and pray for Jerusalem to be restored to all her former glory.

In *Eichah,* the Book of Lamentations, which we read on Tisha B'Av, there is a verse (3, 22) that reads, "Hashem's kindness surely has not ended, nor are His mercies exhausted." Rashi offers an alternative interpretation. Not only that His kindness had not ended but that it is by Hashem's kindness that *we* have not come to an end. That He took out His wrath on the wood and stones of the Temple structure. True, His House was destroyed but His People survived. Despite all the destruction, the nation of Israel lives. So this is an appropriate time to reflect on Jewish survival. After all the suffering and dispersions, notwithstanding the Holocausts that have decimated us through the ages, how *did* we survive? How *do* we survive? And, most importantly, how *will* we survive?

Of course, the simple answer is that G-d will never allow us to disappear. We live by the ongoing miracles of Divine intervention. But in the face of the demise of all the great ancient civilizations and empires—Egypt, Babylon, Greece, Rome, Persia, and more recently the Third Reich—what is the unique secret of Jewish survival?

Let us take a quick tour of history to see if we can put our finger on the most important ingredient in our unbelievable tenacity of spirit.

Some people might say it is our national Homeland that has been the one key element in our continuity. Indeed, Israel is our eternal homeland, and we pray for the Return to Zion three times a day and more. It is central to everything we believe in; it is our heart and soul. It unites us wherever we are and wherever we have been. It is in our dreams, hopes, and aspirations.

But while we will never relinquish our eternal claim to it, the reality is that we have been away from our homeland longer than we've been in it. The fact of the matter is that, even today, there are more Jews scattered around the world than there are in Israel. So, as uncompromisingly committed as we are to our Homeland today and as critical as it is to our global stature and security, geography alone could not have been the main factor in our survival throughout history.

Is it perhaps a common language? Indeed, Hebrew is our national language and is still the language of our Prayer Book. But are there not people reading these lines who could not read them if they were in Hebrew? Certainly the vast majority of Jews today do not speak Hebrew, and I shudder to estimate the percentage of intelligent Jews who are Jewishly illiterate. Throughout history we had a variety of vernaculars. Aramaic, Greek, and even Arabic were, at one time, the most popular languages in Jewish communities of old. In more recent generations, Yiddish or Ladino, as English today, have been the preferred vehicles of communication for most Jews. The fact is that we simply cannot claim a common language to be the overwhelming factor in our continued uninterrupted existence.

How about culture? Well, have you ever tried offering a Sephardic Jew gefilte fish? Or an Ashkenazi Jew couscous? Food and music are cornerstones of any culture. In both, it will vary markedly between East and West. A regular Shul goer from Golders Green will probably be totally lost at a Shul service in Singapore. And vice versa. To the Ashkenazi Jew, Sephardic music sounds Arabic; to the Sephardic Jew Ashkenazi music sounds more European than Jewish! Honestly speaking, we actually do not have one common culture. We have adapted many nuances of style in food, music, and dress from our host societies. Different environments have influenced us differently.

So if we are open and objective, we will come to the certain conclusion that the one and only feature absolutely common to all our people all the time, the uniquely unifying entity that has gone beyond borders, across continents, cultures, languages, and lifestyle has been ... the Torah! Whether Israel or Babylon, Minsk or Madrid, Sydney or San Francisco, Johannesburg or Jerusalem, the Jewish Way of Life as enshrined in our holy Torah and its commandments has been the single most important element in keeping the Jewish spirit alive and vibrant. And not some vague, sentimental sense of "Yiddishkeit" either, but a clearly defined value system that has been transmitted faithfully down the generations wherever we have lived.

The clearest proof of this idea is the fact that where there has been an abandonment of the traditions of Torah, assimilation has followed almost immediately—and with tragic consequences. Those pockets of Jews have simply not survived.

Of course, G-d is the ultimate miracle maker of Jewish survival. But there's no magic at work here. G-d has given us the secret. We hold His key in our hands. Just being Jewish by birth does not guarantee survival of any kind. Only where there has been a concrete commitment to the study of Torah, to teaching it to our children, and to the fulfillment of its eternal practices, have we seen this miracle happen.

May our dedication to Torah grow so that Jewish survival and the flourishing of Jewish life may be assured forever. Please G-d, our prayers for the rebuilding of Zion and the wholeness of our land and our people will soon be answered. Amen.

₧₧

Memory

Devarim is the Parsha associated with Tisha B'Av, the Jewish National Day of Mourning. On this Shabbos, we hear the famous Haftarah of Chazon, the Vision of Isaiah, always read immediately prior to Tisha B'av. And after Shabbos, we will recall the destruction of our holy temple nearly 2,000 years ago.

But why remember? The world cannot understand why we go on about the Holocaust, and that was only in the last century! For over 19 centuries, we have been remembering and observing this event, and it has become the saddest day in our calendar. Why? Why not let bygones be bygones? It's history. What was, was. Why keep revisiting old and painful visions?

They say that Napoleon was once passing through the Jewish ghetto in Paris and heard sounds of crying and wailing emanating from a synagogue. He stopped to ask what the lament was about. He was told that the Jews were remembering the destruction of their Temple. "When did this happen?" asked the Emperor. "Some 1,700 years ago," was the answer he received. Whereupon Napoleon stated with conviction that a people who never forgot its past would be destined to forever have a future.

In the words of Elie Weisel, "Jews never had history. We have memory." History can become a book, a museum, and forgotten antiquities.

Memory is alive, memories reverberate, and memory guarantees our future. Even amidst the ruins, we refused to forget.

The first temple was destroyed by the Babylonians. As they led the Jews into captivity, they sat down and wept. "By the rivers of Babylon we sat and wept remembering Zion." What did they cry of? Their lost wealth, homes, and businesses? No. they cried for Zion and Jerusalem. "If I forget thee O Jerusalem, let my right hand lose its cunning. If I fail to elevate Jerusalem above my foremost joy, then let my tongue cleave to its palate." They were not weeping for themselves or their lost liberties but for the heavenly city and the holy temple. Amidst the bondage, they aspired to rebuild; amidst the ruins they dreamt of returning.

And because we refused to forget Jerusalem, we did return. And because we refused to accept defeat or accept our exile as a historical fait acompli, we have rebuilt proud Jewish communities the world over, while our victors have been vanquished by time. Today there are no more Babylonians, and the people who now live in Rome are not the Romans who destroyed the second temple. Those nations became history while we, inspired by memory, emerged revitalized and regenerated, and forever it will be true that *Am Yisrael Chai.*

I remember the late Reb Shlomo Carlebach telling a story from the Holocaust of a Torah scholar and his nephew. In the concentration camp, they studied the Talmud together. They were learning *Gemorra Moed Katan,* a part of the Talmud that, ironically, also discusses the laws of mourning. And when the time came that the uncle saw himself staring death in the face, he said to his nephew, "Promise me that if you survive you will finish studying this book of *Moed Katan.*" Amidst the misery, desolation and tragedy, what thought preoccupied his mind? That the Talmud should still be studied. This was his last wish on earth. Was it madness, or is it the very secret of our survival?

Only if we refuse to forget, only if we observe Tisha B'av, can we hope to rebuild one day. Indeed, the Talmud assures us, "Whosoever mourns for Jerusalem, will merit to witness her rejoicing." If we are to make it back to Zion, if our people are to harbor the hope of being restored and revived, then we dare not forget. We need to observe our National Day of Mourning every year. Forego the movies and the restaurants. Sit down on a low seat to mourn with your people and perhaps even more importantly, to remember. And, please G-d, He will restore those glorious days and rebuild His own everlasting house. May it be speedily in our day.

ა◌ლ

Are We Really Independent? (Tisha B'Av)

Tens of thousands of Jews will converge on Jerusalem's Western Wall this week as our people mark Tisha B'Av, our National Day of Mourning. On this day in history, both our Holy Temples were destroyed, and a host of other calamities occurred throughout the centuries.

Some may wonder, why do we still mourn? Don't we have a sovereign state of Israel? Isn't Jerusalem united under Jewish rule today? Why are we still mourning?

The fact is that no Israeli rabbis have ever suggested that Tisha B'Av be deleted from our calendars. Nor have the staunchest, most zealous Zionists ever proposed doing away with the custom of breaking a glass under the Chupah. This tradition has always reminded us that our personal joy is incomplete until our nation's joy is reestablished. And that requires the total restoration of our national life, including Jerusalem rebuilt.

Thank G-d, since 1967 we are again able to visit the Western Wall. But as important as that sacred shrine may be, it is only a pitiful remnant of a glorious temple that once stood inside those walls. In fact, according to *halacha*, when we visit the Wall, we should rend our garments like a mourner because we are witnessing the site of the *churban*, the destruction of our holy temple.

So the reality is that although we have a Jewish state operating in our eternal homeland, the national state of exile is more than just geographical. Exile, *galut*, is a state of being and not a place on the map. It does not mean the Diaspora, as if to suggest that only Jews living outside the borders of Israel are in exile. Whether we live in Jerusalem or Johannesburg, we are all in exile. Until the era of Redemption arrives and the Temple is rebuilt, the exile isn't over. You might live in an apartment in the old city of Jerusalem overlooking the Western Wall but you, too, are in exile because the entire Jewish People is still in a state of exile.

It is not only a question of place; it is a question of time. At this time in our history, the redemption has not yet arrived. We still pray three times a day that the Temple be rebuilt speedily in our time. And until those prayers are answered, I'm afraid we are all still in *galut*.

Sure, it would have been wonderful if David Ben Gurion's announcement in 1948 spelled out not only a *Declaration* of Independence but also real, practical, and total independence. The truth, however, is that we are far from independent. Israeli prime ministers have proudly proclaimed that Jews may buy any property they wish in any part of Jerusalem, East or West and thank G-d they did. But while we proclaim our sovereign rights, the rest of the world still seems to be on its own mission, and we are still very dependent on America, Europe, public opinion, on the media, and even, to a degree, on the United Nations.

We are certainly not yet independent of Hamas, Hizbollah, or Ahmadinejad, who threaten our very existence as I write these lines. When Jewish lives are being lost to terrorist armies, when our neighbors still dream of driving us into the sea, when they still deny us our basic legitimacy, when the international media challenges our right to defend our citizens, can we claim that we are really and truly independent?

Thank G-d we have an army, navy, and air force. Thank G-d; they are fighting valiantly to thwart our mortal enemies' murderous machinations. But true independence means that our national security is no longer threatened and that a genuine and lasting peace has been achieved. No wonder *Moshiach* is called the Messenger of Peace. Who else can we turn to for that long-awaited dream? Political schemes certainly do not seem very promising.

And so we still observe Tisha B'Av. And unless Moshiach comes before that day, we will fast and sit on low chairs in the manner of mourners. We will mourn the destruction of our temple and the state of exile it created. And we will pray for our full return to Jewish sovereignty and total independence. A time when our cities and towns will be free of enemy rockets and our children will feel safe and secure. May that time be now.

৪৩৫৪

Vaetchanan

Ten Commandments Checklist

Everyone has an opinion on the Ten Commandments, even the U.S. Supreme Court. So often, I hear people say, "Well, I am not all that religious but I do keep the Ten Commandments." I'm tempted to say, "Really? You do know that The Ten Commandments are not multiple choice." I sometimes wonder if the people who glibly make that claim actually know what the Ten Commandments are. Seeing as in this week's Parsha, Moshe reviews the Big 10, why not go through the list so we can all get a better idea and see how we score.

1. I am the L-rd Thy G-d.

Basically, this is the command to believe in One G-d. I have every confidence that you all get full marks on this one.

2. Thou shalt have no other gods before Me.

Okay, so you don't make a habit of bowing down to that bust of the Buddha in your living room. The question is, should it be there in the first place? And isn't it interesting that today we have all these Idols competitions being run around the world. Then, of course, there are all those well-established contemporary idols we tend to ogle and worship, the celebrities and pop icons of the day.

3. Do not take the name of G-d in vain.

This is not only about taking the oath or swearing in court. What about swearing in the street? How many choice four-letter words are in your vocabulary? And why drag G-d into those graphic expressions?

4. Observe the Shabbos day to keep it holy.

Interestingly, the Ten Commandments appear twice in the Torah. In Exodus, the fourth Commandment begins with *Zachor*—Remember *the Sabbath day to keep it holy.* This week, we read *Shamor*—Observe *the Sabbath day.* "Remembering" is achieved through positive acts such as Kiddush, candle lighting etc. "Observing" Shabbos, to guard it from any desecration, is the hard part. It may cramp our current lifestyles. Being a Shomer Shabbos takes true commitment.

5. Honor thy Father and thy Mother.

Many people do indeed fulfill this Mitzvah in exemplary fashion. I stand in admiration of sons, daughters, and often daughters-in-law, who care for and tend to the needs of an aged parent or parent-in-law. They *shlep,* they cook, they humor, and often tolerate irritable, cantankerous elders. This commandment seems to get more difficult as time progresses. Yet the Torah makes no distinctions based on age. It is our responsibility to look after our parents when they are dependent on us as they looked after us when we were dependent on them. As they age, this commandment becomes more challenging.

6. Thou Shalt Not Murder.

Well done. Here's another easy one to fulfill. I'm sure not one of you reading this ever murdered anyone. You *thought* of doing it, you *almost* did it but, in the end, Jews are not the murdering type. You can safely tick another one.

7. Thou Shalt Not Commit Adultery.

According to Torah it does not matter if it is between consenting adults. If a woman is married, she is off limits to anyone but her husband. Next!

8. Thou Shalt Not Steal.

Strictly speaking, this refers to kidnapping in particular. However, all white-collar crimes apply.

9. Thou Shalt Not Bear False Witness.

How truthful are we? Even if we are not under oath, our word should be sacred. I remember hearing an old rabbi being introduced to a group of university students simply as a "man who never told a lie." Not simple at all. How many of us could make that claim?

10. Thou Shalt Not Covet.

Not easy either. Commentary defines this injunction as a prohibition on badgering someone, or conniving, to acquire—even legally—that which belongs to another. Go get your own. Why must it be *his* wife, house, or car?

There you have it. Did you score full marks? Did you pass, or are you in the forty percent or less bracket? Worth working on, isn't it? Hopefully, we can all improve our score and one day claim with justification that we really do observe the Ten Commandments.

ജ്ഞ

קול גדול ולא יסף
A mighty voice that did not end. (5:19)

The Never-ending Voice

The Ten Commandments are repeated in this week's Parsha as part of Moses' review of the last 40 years. He describes how G-d spoke those words in a *mighty voice that did not end.* One of the explanations offered by Rashi is that Moses is contrasting G-d's voice with human voices. The finite voice of a human being, even a Pavarotti, will fade and falter. It cannot go on forever. But the voice of the Almighty did not end, did not weaken. It remained strong throughout.

Is this all the great prophet had to teach us about the voice of G-d? That it was a powerful baritone? That it resonated? Is the greatness of the Infinite One that he didn't suffer from shortness of breath, that He didn't need a few puffs of Ventolin? Is this a meaningful motivation for the Jews to accept the Torah?

Let's look at this phrase a little more broadly. Moses was the greatest of all prophets. He foresaw what no other prophet could see. Perhaps he wasn't only speaking to his own generation but to every generation of Jews in the future.

Perhaps Moses saw his people becoming caught up in the civilization of ancient Greece, in the beauty, culture, philosophy, and art of the day. And they might question, is Torah still relevant?

Perhaps he foresaw Jews empowered by the Industrial Revolution where they might have thought Torah to be somewhat backward. Or, maybe it was during the Russian Revolution, where faith and religion were positively primitive.

Maybe Moses saw our own generation with space shuttles and satellites, television and technology. And he saw young people questioning whether the old Torah still speaks to them.

And so Moses tells us that the voice that thundered from Sinai was no ordinary voice. The voice that proclaimed the Ten Commandments was a voice that was not only powerful at the time but it did not end! And it still rings out, it still resonates, and it still speaks to each of us in every generation and in every part of the world.

Revolutions may come and go, but revelation is eternal. The voice of Sinai continues to proclaim eternal truths that never become passé or irrelevant. *Honor Your Parents,* revere them, look after them in their old age. Never abandon them to some decrepit old age home. *Live moral lives;* do not tamper with the sacred fiber of family life, be sensitive to the needs and feelings of others. Dedicate one day every week and *keep that day holy.* Stop the madness. Turn your back on the rat race and rediscover your humanity and your children. *Don't be guilty of greed, envy, dishonesty, or corruption.*

Are these ideas and values dated? Are these commandments tired, stale or irrelevant? On the contrary. They speak to us now as perhaps never before. The G-dly voice has lost none of its strength, none of its majesty. The mortal voice of man declines and fades into oblivion. Politicians and spin-doctors come and go but the heavenly sound reverberates down the ages.

Moses knew what he was saying and whom he was talking to: Torah is truth, and truth is forever. The voice of G-d shall never be stilled.

ഔൽ

וְאָהַבְתָּ אֵת ה' אֱלֹקֶיךָ
Love G-d...with all your might. (6:5)

"Your Money or Your Life?"

Judaism's most famous Prayer comes from this week's Parsha.

Shma Yisrael Hashem Elokeinu Hashem Echad. Hear O Israel, Hashem is our G-d, Hashem is One.

The verse continues, "And you shall love Hashem your G-d with all your heart, with all your soul, and with all your might."

Rashi, the great Biblical commentator, interprets this last word (in Hebrew, *Meodecho*) to mean "with all your resources," that is, your money. This, of course begs the question, if we have already been commanded to love Hashem with all our heart and soul (i.e., to be prepared to give our very life for G-d), then why the rather mundane command about money? Surely, if we are prepared to give our lives for G-d, then sharing our money is a small thing to ask?

Rashi explains that in reality there are some individuals who value their money more than their lives. Such people need to be told specifically to love G-d with all their money.

Jack Benny, the well-known American entertainer from long ago, used to joke self-deprecatingly about his frugality. Once, he told of walking down a New York street late at night when he suddenly felt cold, hard metal pointing into his back and a gruff voice barking, "I said, your money or your life!" When he didn't immediately respond, the gun at his back pressed deeper into his flesh and the voice from behind became more menacing, "I SAID, your money or your life!" Benny replied, "I'm thinking, I'm thinking."

There are actually quite a few real-life situations today that prove this is no joke. Take the many private security personnel working in the political and military hotspots of our world at any given moment. Nobody drafted them. They are simply there to make a quick buck. What about the threat to their lives? What of their colleagues who have already been murdered? It would appear that some people really do love money more than life. How about those who have elected to remain in their countries of residence when the political winds of change have wreaked havoc and put their lives in serious danger? Many fled the country, but not all. It's not easy to walk away from your life's work and only source of income— even if your life may be in danger.

So the Torah insists that we must love Hashem with all our heart, soul, life, and resources—whatever it is that we value and cherish most, we should be prepared to dedicate in love to G-d.

How many workaholics do we know who are so busy making a living that in the process, they forget to live. Remember, no one was ever heard lamenting on their deathbed, "Oy, if only I'd spent more time at the office."

So the Shma reminds us that whatever our core values may be, they should be directed to Hashem and His service. Even for those who aren't overly thrifty, money is an issue.

The reality is that Judaism costs. It's not cheap to be Jewish, certainly not to live Jewishly. Whether the price of Synagogue membership, the additional expenses of making Pesach, buying a Sukkah, Tefillin, Mezuzahs, or kosher food, all these things require a commitment from us financially. When we make that commitment with love and don't complain about the high cost of being Jewish, then we are observing the mitzvah of loving Hashem with all our might, money and resources.

The good news is that the love is reciprocated by G-d. Hashem loves us too.

₲₳

Ekev

כי לא על הלחם לבדו יחי' האדם
Man does not live by bread alone. (8:3)

Bread, Bucks and Making a Living

Man does not live by bread alone. A famous line but what does it mean?

The verse comes from this week's Torah reading and is a reference to the miraculous Manna, which fell from heaven daily during the Jewish People's sojourn in the Wilderness. The conclusion of the verse is that man lives by the word of G-d. Thus, it is reminding us about the true source of human sustenance.

Contrary to popular belief, it is neither our earthly toil nor the sweat of our brow nor all those conferences, meetings, and sales seminars that ensure our success. The reality is that it is G-d who sustains us and looks after us. In the very same way as our ancestors trekking through the desert were totally dependent on Him for their daily bread, believe it or not, so are we. Wealth is a G-dly gift. At the end of the day, it is not our hard work or business acumen alone that provide our prosperity but the blessings from above that endow our efforts with success.

Ask anyone in sales. How often have their best-laid plans and pitches come to naught and then, out of the blue, a big order comes in with little or no effort. Of course, it's not the rule, and we must be prepared to put in effort if we are to succeed. But when it does happen, it reminds us that there are higher forces beyond our control at work.

I confess, I like a good ad. Some years ago, McDonald's was running a campaign, and in the center of the full magazine page was a big, fat, juicy double burger. It was literally bursting from the roll on either side. The bread was dwarfed by the beef, and the caption read, "Man does not live by bread alone."

A good ad indeed. But no ad agency will convince me that Scripture meant to teach us that bread is inadequate and what man really needs in life is a burger! What the Torah is teaching us is something about the nature of men and women and the spirit of humanity. The human spirit is such that we crave more than bread.

Now "bread" colloquially means money and symbolically refers to all things material. So *man does not live by bread alone* means that Man simply *cannot* live by bread alone, that human beings cannot possibly be satisfied with bread or money or materialism alone.

Money is important, but we cannot live by money exclusively. What about job satisfaction? I know a number of individuals in our community who willingly gave up lucrative positions for less rewarding ones because they found their work unstimulating. They were making lots of cash, but there was no emotional reward.

I also know people who have it all financially but who are nonetheless unhappy people. They are highly successful ... and equally miserable. The successes we achieve do not guarantee our happiness. After we've bought the house of our dreams and our fantasy sports car and the latest mechanical toys we tire of them all. For satisfaction to be lasting it must be more than material; it must be spiritual. We need more than bread and money; we need stimulation and a sense of meaningful achievement. To know that our lives have purpose and that somehow we have made a difference. We want to be assured that our work is productive and will have lasting value.

They tell the story of an old Russian labor camp and a long-term prisoner whose job it was to turn a heavy wheel attached to a wall on the prison boundary. For no less than 25 years this poor prisoner worked at his backbreaking manual labor. What kept him going mentally was the conviction that this wheel must be attached to a mill on the other side of the wall. He assumed that his revolving wheel turned the mill and a watering pipe must have been irrigating many fields. His work was thus helping yield plentiful crops of grain to feed and nurture thousands of people. After 25 years of hard labor when he was about to be released to freedom, the prisoner asked to be shown the mill and the apparatus behind the prison wall. Tragically, he discovered to his shock that there was nothing! The wheel was just a wheel—the crass authorities' instrument of manipulation and torture for no useful purpose. The man collapsed in a dead faint, absolutely devastated. His life's work had been in vain.

Men and women need to know that their lives are purposeful, physically and spiritually. When we understand that every good deed is attached to a complex spiritual apparatus, that our every action meshes with a systematic structure of cosmic significance, then our lives become endowed with a deeper sense of meaning and purpose. We desperately need to know that, in some way, our work is helping others—that we are making a contribution to society beyond our own immediate and often selfish needs. Then we are living. Then we are happy.

Man does not live by bread alone. We cannot. We dare not. There's got to be more to life than bread and money.

∞∞

במדבר הגדול והנורא
That great and awesome desert. (8:15)

What Will the World Say?

Much has been said and written about the *Galut Mentality,* the subservience felt by generations of Jews living in the Diaspora. As second-class citizens for so many generations in Eastern Europe and in the Arab countries, Jews, allegedly, came to lose their self-esteem. Finally, in our own time, the old ghetto Jew would be replaced with a proud, strong, independent Israeli. No more would *Moshke* the Jew cower before his *Poretz,* the country squire. Jews would now walk tall.

In our Parsha, Moses reminds his people never to forget that it was G-d who took them out of Egypt and who led them through the wilderness into the Promised Land. And he describes the wilderness as *that great and awesome desert.* The wilderness before we reach the Promised Land represents the state of exile. And the problem with this wilderness is that we are impressed with it. In our eyes it is *great.* The big, wide world out there is great, powerful, impressive, and all too overwhelming to the Jew.

I think we sometimes forget that the real *Galut Mentality* is not necessarily living in a ghetto, but considering the non-Jewish world to be so great. The real exile is the exile within, the exile inside our own heads and hearts. When we attach so much significance to the outside world, then we are still living in a state of exile and with a *Galut* mindset, no matter where we may be geographically.

And once we start attaching greatness to this wilderness, our sense of self-worth is further eroded, and we begin considering this wilderness not only *great* but also *awesome,* even terrifying.

But why? What is so great and awesome about this outside world, about this wilderness? Why does what the non-Jewish world think so unsettle us? Why do we get so upset, so disturbed by what the world's media says about us? Why does a cartoonist's poison pen distress us so?

The new Israel was supposed to be different. No more weakness, no more cowardice, gone with the old world syndromes. So why do we still care what they say? If we are convinced that justice and morality are with us, then it shouldn't bother us what others may say. If they have a problem with an Israel that can defend itself and stand up and fight its own battles, then that's their problem, not ours. We will do what we need to do.

Why should I respect a world that has so lost its moral bearings that genocide in Africa or Asia goes unnoticed, and the most immoral country on the globe is an Israel that defends its civilian population from terror? Why should we be intimidated by a world that smiles upon state-sponsored terrorism while heaping abuse upon us? Why does it still pain us when we hear them say we are guilty of disproportionate responses and excessive force? Why do we suffer anxiety attacks every time the United Nations condemns us?

The answer is because the big, wide world is the wilderness we live in. And that wilderness is perceived by us as *great and awesome*. And as long as a corrupt, hypocritical, morally bankrupt world impresses us, we will continue to be demoralized by its negative opinion of us.

So know, Jew, that there is nothing whatsoever to be impressed with— that this world is nothing but a wilderness and a moral wilderness at that. The world's presidents and prime ministers with all their moral indiscretions give us precious little to be overwhelmed about. The princes of the wilderness society are paupers of the spirit.

Anti-Semitism is a fact of life, and the sooner we accept that reality, the healthier and saner we will all be. By all means, wage the diplomatic war; do battle with media bias. Don't tolerate the blatant hypocrisies. But don't fret if you fail to turn around public opinion. Remember that the first step in leaving the exile is to stop being impressed by it. In order to redeem our land and our people, we must first redeem our own souls and our own self-respect.

May we never forget where our true strength lies. When we remember who took us out of Egypt and led us through the wilderness and who is truly the Great and Awesome Being of Beings, then we will be able to truly walk tall and stand proud forever.

₭)ℛ

Me, You, and Us

Who is more important, the Jew or the Jewish People? Is it *Reb* Yisroel or *Am* Yisrael? In last week's Parsha we read the first chapter of the Shema. This week, we read the second. Yet there are so many similarities between the two. In fact, certain sentences are virtually identical. Why would the Torah, normally so cryptic, be so repetitive?

If one examines the text closely, a significant distinction between the two chapters becomes immediately discernible. The first chapter is in the singular, and the second is in the plural. Teach Torah to your *son* in the first and to your *children* in the second. Put Tefillin on your *hand* in the first and on your *hands* in the second. But why the need for both? Why not use one or the other? Why a paragraph for each expression?

One important answer is that G-d speaks to the individual but G-d also speaks to the community. He addresses the Jew and also the Jewish People. The first paragraph of the Shema teaches us that each and every single individual is important, even critical, and G-d addresses every individual personally. The second paragraph reminds us that there is also a sum of all the parts, that together, individuals make up a community. And communities, too, are very important. A community is not only a motley collection of disparate individuals. A community is an important entity in its own right. In some ways, a community is supreme; in others, we acknowledge the supremacy of the individual. Yes, there is a tension at play here.

The Talmud captures these seemingly conflicting notions when it examines why humankind was created differently from the animal kingdom. Whereas they were created in herds, only one man and one woman were created initially. Says the Talmud, this is to teach us that (a) it was worthwhile for the Almighty to create the world for but one man and woman, that is, one single individual, and (b) so that no human being could boast that his or her pedigree was better than anyone else's. We *all* came from Adam and Eve, so you are no better than me nor I than you. On the one hand, the individual human being is king, while on the other, humanity reigns.

Over 800 years ago, Maimonides, the great Rambam, ruled that communal leaders were obliged to safeguard the community and ought not to pay exorbitant ransom monies if one of its members was taken hostage. On the other hand, though, should a dangerous enemy demand that Jewish leaders hand over to them a particular individual lest they attack the entire community, it is not permitted to sacrifice even one individual for the sake of the community.

So we need both sections of the Shema, because both are important, the individual and the community.

In approximately six weeks' time we will usher in the New Year. And the ongoing tension between the single and plural will manifest itself very blatantly. "Why must we pay to pray?" some will demand. They will decry the shameless commercialism of organized religion. And, yes, they have a point. A Shul should have a heart. And our Houses of Prayer should not be allowed to become materialistic and mercenary, lest we lose the young, the poor, and the idealistic. At the same time, individuals need to be understanding and sympathetic to the hard facts of congregational life. We cannot take for granted or take advantage of our established—and costly to maintain—infrastructures. The tension is sometimes tangible as we struggle to balance these two, seemingly exclusive, imperatives of Jewish life.

Statistics vary. In some communities, not more than 30 percent of Jews are officially affiliated. In others, the figure is much higher. The community must be sensitive, welcoming, and embracing of every individual who seeks to belong. Still, individuals must be fair too. If everyone demanded a free ride how would a congregation support itself?

Let us keep reciting both chapters of the Shema. Then we can look forward to healthy Jews and wholesome communities.

ഔൽ

Re'eh

ראה אנכי נותן לפניכם היום ברכה וקללה
See, I present before you today a blessing and a curse. (11:26)

Virtue, Vice, and Vision

Blessings and curses. Stirring stuff from the Bible this week as Moses again cautions his congregation. The great prophet reminds them that living a life of goodness will bring them blessings, while ignoring the Divine call must inexorably lead to a cursed existence.

Moses prefaces his admonition with the Hebrew word *Re'eh*, "See." *See, I present before you today a blessing and a curse.* But why see? What is there to see? Did he, in fact, show them anything at all? The Torah does not use flowery language just because it has a nice ring to it and sounds poetic. What was there to behold? Why *Re'eh?*

One answer is that how we *look* will, in itself, determine whether our lives will be blessed or cursed. How do we look at others, at ourselves? Our perspective, how we behold and see things, will result in our own lives being blessed or, G-d forbid, the opposite.

The saintly Rabbi Levi Yitzchak of Berditchev once chanced upon a strong, young man who was brazenly eating on Yom Kippur. The rabbi suggested that perhaps he was feeling ill. The fellow insisted he was in the best of health. Perhaps he had forgotten that today was the holy day of fasting? "Who doesn't know that today is Yom Kippur?" responded the young man. Perhaps he was never taught that Jews do not eat on this day? "Every child knows that Yom Kippur is a fast day, Rabbi!" Whereupon Rabbi Levi Yitzchak raised his eyes heavenward and said, "Master of the Universe, see how wonderful Your people are! Here is a Jew who, despite so many opportunities, simply refuses to tell a lie!"

The Berditchever was always able to look at others with a compassionate, understanding, and benevolent eye. How do we view the good fortune enjoyed by others? Are we happy for them, or do we look at them with begrudging envy? How do we look at ourselves and our own shortcomings? Are we objectively truthful or subjectively slanted? "He is a stingy, rotten good for nothing. Me? I am just careful about how I spend my money." "She is a bore of bores, absolutely anti-social. Me? I am a private person who just happens to enjoy staying at home." "He is as stubborn as an ox! Me? I am just very determined."

Clearly, the manner in which we look at our world and those around us will have a major impact on the way life will treat us. Quite justifiably, Moses says *See.* For how we will see things in life will undoubtedly affect life's outcomes.

Rabbi Yosef Yitzchak Schneerson (1880–1950) once told how, when he was a young child he asked his father: why does a person have *two* eyes? The right eye, his father replied, is to be used lovingly, when looking at a fellow Jew; the left eye is to be used discerningly, when looking at candies, sweets, or other objects that are not that important in the grand scheme of things.

When I was in Yeshivah, the same building also housed a synagogue where we would often interact with the adult men who would come to the daily *minyan.* One particular gentleman, may he rest in peace, always seemed to us rather cantankerous, what you might call a grumpy old man. I cannot remember whether he was actually a bit cross-eyed or not, but we referred to him as "left-eyed Sam" because he always seemed to be looking at us students with that proverbial left eye.

The Parshah that is entitled *Re'eh,* "See," is a perennial reminder to all of us that even our vision alone can bring virtue or vice. Let us look at the world correctly and invite the blessings of G-d into our lives.

℘℘℘

Blessings and Curses

Does it always go right for you if you are religious? Does *frum* equal good fortune?

See, I give you this day a blessing and a curse. The blessing that you will hearken to the commandments of Hashem your G-d … and the curse if you do not and you stray from the path that I command you today to follow the gods of others …

Do you actually believe these words from the opening verses of this week's Parsha? Are all righteous people blessed and all godless people cursed? Does it really work that way in the real world? The truth is the Talmud states categorically "the reward for Mitzvot is not in this world at all." Ultimate accountability is reserved for the world to come.

What then is the Torah telling us here?

Well, one answer may be that it is teaching us that living a G-dly life is *itself* a blessing. And that leading a life where Hashem's value system is irrelevant is in *itself* a curse. Virtue is its own reward, and the reward for a Mitzvah is in the Mitzvah itself.

Perhaps once upon a time we needed faith to believe this. Today, I honestly think it is self-evident. In our generation, we see empirically that a life dedicated to Torah values is blessed and, sadly, other lifestyles bring the opposite of blessing in their wake. Let's examine a few areas in society today and see if we can discern some truth in these verses.

Divorce:

It is now some time since the Jewish community has reached level par with the rest of the world in the divorce statistics. We, too, have passed the one-out-of-three rate, and virtually every other marriage is ending in divorce. Because of this unacceptably high failure rate, in my own community we have instituted very successful marriage preparation programs for brides and grooms, which, thankfully, are making positive inroads.

However, if we look at the observant Jewish community, while there are indeed more divorces now than ever before, the rate is still way below the rest of the community. Now cynics may argue that it is because among religious people there still exist certain stigmas and taboos and therefore a reluctance to split so that many people remain in unhappy marriages. I might agree to an extent, but I am convinced that there are many positive factors contributing to the higher success rate among observant couples.

To name a few: religious people share common values and aspirations. Many of the things others argue about are not issues of difference among observant individuals. Religious people are far from perfect but, statistically, they mess around a lot less than others. *Shalom Bayit* is a religious imperative. A happy family life is a social necessity in religious communities. Then there are Mitzvot that help in tangible ways. Just keeping *Shabbat* is one mitzvah that brings with it quality family time and togetherness in ways that would have necessitated heroic efforts to achieve otherwise. And, of course, the *Mikvah* is a Mitzvah that directly impacts on marriages, enhancing the intimate relationship immeasurably.

Violent Crime:

Unfortunately it is not unheard of for Jews to have been involved in white-collar crime. Fraud and embezzlement are not things we are proud of. But today, even violent crimes are being perpetrated by Jewish people in a way that was always foreign to our people. Road rage now happens in Israel on a regular basis. And there have been some highly publicized cases of Jew-on-Jew violence in the United States and Israel.

But in the religious community, while white-collar crime is unfortunately not unknown, violent crime is a rarity. In fact, when Yigal Amir assassinated Prime Minister Yitzchak Rabin, it sent such shockwaves across the world not only because he was a Jew, but precisely because he was a *kippah*-wearing Jew! And the same can be said for other terrible murders that have been perpetrated by people who were members of the religious community.

Dennis Prager poses an interesting hypothetical question: If you were walking down a dark alley one night and saw three burly young men wearing leather jackets, sunglasses, and chains around their necks you would no doubt be petrified, right? Now what if you were told that these young men had just come from a Bible class? Would you be alarmed or relieved? Perhaps in other faiths, religious fundamentalism breeds violence. With Jews it is the opposite. (Okay, I did hear of a case where a fellow in Shul who didn't get an Aliya punched up the Gabbai! But you must admit, that is an exception.)

Social Ills:

While drug abuse and HIV/AIDS are not entirely unheard of, they are certainly the rare exception in religious circles. In the wider community, these scourges of our generation are affecting Jews in large numbers. We are, after all, totally integrated into the fabric of our society. Our degree of susceptibility depends almost entirely on the choices we make in schools and social environments.

Please don't think me smug and condescending about religious people. Obviously, there are no guarantees. Every individual faces the same challenges and choices in life. There are no clones in religious enclaves. And tragedy, G-d forbid, can strike anywhere. If we are objective, though, we cannot dismiss these tangible pieces of statistical evidence that our Parsha does have a point. That the G-dly way of life is not only a pathway to Paradise in the Hereafter, but is in itself a blessing for us in the here and now.

If we want the blessings of this world for our families and ourselves we should seriously consider a Torah lifestyle. The choice is ours.

ৰেওৎ

לדעת הישכם אוהבים את ה׳ אלקיכם בכל לבבכם ובכל נפשכם

*To know whether we do, in fact, love G-d
with all our heart and soul. (13:4)*

The Tests of Life

Will the real prophet please stand up? There are false prophets out there, always have been. Way back in the Bible (Deuteronomy 13), the Torah was already warning us that we would encounter individuals who looked like prophets. They might even seem to make miracles like prophets, but, in truth, they are really false prophets. Why then would G-d allow a false prophet to make a miracle or do wondrous things that are really impressive? (I mean, you've got to admit that walking on water is pretty awesome.)

The answer, says our Parsha, is that G-d is testing us. If we really and truly love G-d with all our heart and soul, then we won't be impressed by any fancy wonders or miracles. The acid test will always be, does this would-be prophet encourage us to follow G-d's laws or to ignore them? And if this "prophet" is not faithful to the word of G-d, then he is no prophet at all but an imposter and a false prophet.

So how can a false prophet look so amazing? Because it is a test of faith for us.

If you think life's tests were over when you finished school, guess again. There are many tests in life, and they can be much more difficult than chemistry or physics. And there isn't that much homework we can do to prepare for these kinds of tests either. Poverty is a big test of faith. Even affluence can be a test that's tougher than we think. Failing health is no easy one, and real tragedies are worse. Every individual faces his or her own unique tests and challenges. We might wish the other fellow's tests upon us, but our tests are ours and ours alone to deal with. What tempts one person may not tempt the next. What is difficult for me might be simple for you and vice versa. If we remember that the challenge of the moment is, in fact, a test we might be better able to handle it and pass the test.

But we don't always realize that this may just be our very own personal, spiritual challenge, perhaps even the most important one of our entire existence. We don't necessarily appreciate that our souls might have come down to this world for the express purpose of passing these tests.

So we rationalize: *If there is a G-d in the world, where was He at Auschwitz? If G-d didn't intend for me to take the money, why did the boss leave the cash register open? If this relationship is wrong, why does it feel so right? This poor woman is locked in a loveless marriage. Isn't she entitled to a little happiness? Shouldn't I be there for her? If G-d really wanted me to keep Shabbos, why is my biggest turnover on Saturday? If a yarmulke was meant for me to wear, why am I bald? I can't even find any hair for the darn clip!* But if we accept the concept of a test of faith, then it becomes easier to deal with the challenges, as formidable as they may be.

The question remains, why does G-d test us? Is it really *to know whether we do, in fact, love G-d with all our heart and soul?* Doesn't G-d know all that already? How will we enlighten Him one way or the other? Is there anything G-d does not know?

The answer, according to Rabbi Shneur Zalman of Liadi in his classic *Likutei Torah,* is that these tests are not for *G-d* to know but for *man* to know. Of course G-d knows. But He deliberately places tests and obstacles in our path so that when we overcome them, we develop and bring to the fore the inner, latent love of G-d that was always there inside our hearts and souls. We are stronger after conquering the hurdles than we were before we faced them. When we pass life's tests, we discover that we do have that inner strength after all, that we really are believers who are profoundly connected to G-d and that our commitment is true and genuine. In passing life's tests we become more confident in our own moral strength and enriched and ennobled with a higher awareness of G-d.

We don't go looking for tests. Every morning in our prayers we ask G-d *lead us not to temptation.* But if it does come our way, we must appreciate that it is critical to our success as moral human beings and as committed Jews that we face up to the challenge.

May we never be tested. But if we are, let us remember that it is a test. Please G-d, we will pass with flying colors.

ഇരൽ

Shoftim

Here Comes the Judge

Don't be judgmental. Unless, of course you happen to be a judge. Then it's your job.

This week's Parsha, Shoftim, lists the Biblical command for judges to be appointed in every city and town to adjudicate and maintain a just, ordered, civil society. Interestingly, it occurs in the first week of Elul, the month in which we are to prepare in earnest for the Days of Judgment ahead, Rosh Hashanah, and Yom Kippur.

There are, however, some significant differences between earthly judges of flesh and blood and the heavenly judge. In the earthly court, if after a fair trial a defendant is found guilty, then there really is no room for clemency on the part of the judge. The law is the law, and it must take its course. The accused may shed rivers of tears, but no human judge can be certain if his remorse is genuine. His feelings of regret may be touching but are still futile.

You see, a human judge may only make a decision based on "what the eye can see." The misdeed was seen to have been committed. The remorse, who knows? Perhaps he is worthy of an Oscar and is only acting contrite. The Supreme Judge, however, does know for a fact whether the accused genuinely regrets his actions or is merely putting on an act. Therefore, He alone is able to forgive. That is why in heavenly judgments, *Teshuvah* (repentance) is effective.

The great Maharal of Prague gave another reason. Only G-d is able to judge the whole person. Every one of us has good and bad to some extent. Even those who have sinned may have many other good deeds that out-weigh the bad ones. Perhaps even one good deed was of such major sig-nificance that it alone could serve as a weighty counterbalance. The point is, only G-d knows. Only He can judge the individual in the context of his whole life and all his deeds, good and bad.

Our goal is to emulate the heavenly court. We should try to look at the totality of the person. You think he is bad, but is he all bad? Does he have no redeeming virtues? Surely, he must have some good in him as well. Look at the whole person.

A new rabbi came to town, and the very same week Chaim, the town drunkard, resident liar, and horse thief died. The family approached the rabbi and asked him to offer a eulogy at the funeral. Only after the rabbi agreed did he discover what an unsavory character he was going to have to praise. I guess that's why rabbis must be wise enough to find a way out of difficult situations. So, *nu*, what did the rabbi say? He said it as it was. "Chaim was fond of a drink or two, and he liked horses, even if they weren't his own. At times, Chaim may even have used language that was not entirely appropriate. And perhaps he wasn't always fanatical about telling the truth. But I want you to know that compared to his late brother, Chaim was an absolute saint!"

A teacher once conducted an experiment in class. He held up a white plate and showed it to the entire class. In the center of the plate was a small black spot. He then asked the class to describe what they saw. One student said he saw a black spot. Another said it must be a target for shooting practice. A third suggested that the plate was dirty or damaged. Whereupon the teacher asked, "Doesn't anyone see a white plate?"

There may have been a small black spot but, essentially, it was a white plate. Why do we only see the dirt? Let us learn to find the good in others. Let's be more positive, tolerant and less judgmental. Nobody is perfect, not even us. Let's not be so critical. Let's try to see the good side.

৪৩৫৪

לא תשיג גבול רעך
You shall not move the boundary of your fellow. (19:14)

Don't Move the Markers!

Many countries have legislation dealing with unfair competition and monopolies. The term used in *halacha* to describe these offenses is *hasogas gvul.* Literally, the phrase means moving the markers that serve as the boundaries between neighboring properties. The Scriptural source is found in this week's Parsha. *You shall not move the boundary of your fellow, which the early ones marked out.* On a simple level, it means that you mustn't move the markers, pegs, or any other landmarks that were employed to demarcate the boundaries between neighbors' properties. To go in the night and move the landmarks to take some of your neighbor's land for yourself thus carries an additional prohibition over and above the normal laws against theft.

Let's spend a moment, though, looking at some of the boundaries and borders of Jewish life. We, too, have neighbors. Some are friends and some are foreign. Many of us live in communities beyond the ghetto. Many are exposed to cultures, lifestyles, and business environments that are very different to our own. How is a Jew, surrounded by a sea of neighbors who are nice, friendly people but who are, culturally, very different still able to retain his or her Jewish distinctiveness?

The answer is that we need landmarks. We, too, require boundaries and borders to help us draw the lines between being good neighbors, sociable colleagues and losing our own traditions. Otherwise, we become the same as everyone else on the block or at work. When we try hard to be "normal," we run the risk of losing our own uniqueness in the process.

This American Jewish girl joined the Peace Corps and went to do humanitarian work in Africa. After a two-year stint, she returned home to the Bronx. She rings the bell and her mother is shocked to see standing next to her a boyfriend she brought back from Africa. And he's not just any boyfriend. He is a big, black, burly Zulu warrior with bald head, loincloth, beads around his neck, a spear, and a shield. And to top it off, he's carrying a bag of bones in his pouch. The Jewish mother stands there stunned and speechless. Finally, she recovers somewhat and shouts at her daughter. "Idiot! *Meshuggeneh!* I said a *rich* doctor!"

Maybe this story is an exaggeration but similar ones are happening daily: *Ma, I'm in love! What difference does it make what religion he is? He's a great guy and we are both very happy together. So, what's the problem? Dad, all the Jewish girls I meet are spoiled princesses. I finally found someone who cares about me. Please don't stand in the way of my happiness.* And Jewish parents are visiting their rabbis and asking, "Rabbi, where did we go wrong? How can this be happening to us?"

Well, rabbis are also nice guys and aren't looking to cause any more pain and anguish to these distraught parents than they already have. So they don't actually answer the question of where they went wrong. But if they did, it might go something like this: The Torah teaches us not to move the markers. Losing everything begins by losing a little bit at a time. When we move the landmarks of Jewish life, slowly and inexorably we lose our borders and the lines become blurred. Children, in particular, need clear, solid lines to understand the boundaries, the dos and don'ts of living correct and meaningful Jewish lives. G-d gave us certain landmarks to help us see who we are and where and how we live. When we remove those landmarks we lose our borders and we lose our distinctiveness.

Long ago, G-d gave us a *Shabbos,* a day on which the Jew behaves very differently from his neighbors. He gave us *Kashrut* so that we eat differently, too. And He urges us to educate our children Jewishly so that they will understand, feel, and know why they really are distinctive.

But if we move those markers, things become hazy and young people become confused. And then they wonder why we are suddenly putting up barriers that we ourselves previously took down.

A rabbinical friend of mine once asked a prominent international businessman why he, a nice Jewish boy, was marrying out of the faith. Couldn't he have found a nice Jewish girl? The fellow answered in all honesty, "Rabbi, I just don't mix in those circles anymore." An honest answer. But had this entrepreneur retained the landmark of a kosher home, for example, he would have still been mixing in kosher circles. By preserving our landmarks, we preserve our identity.

Let's try to find some of those missing markers in Jewish life. Who knows? We may discover our own distinctiveness, and it may help our children find out who they really are.

₧

מִי הָאִישׁ הַיָּרֵא וְרַךְ הַלֵּבָב

Who is the man who is fearful and fainthearted? (20:8)

Cowards of the World, Unite!

What makes a real-life hero? Are most normal people cowards and only a few crazies who throw caution to the wind the fearless few?

In this week's Parsha, the Torah discusses war and some of the moral imperatives that apply even under fire. Specifically, we read of the exemptions that entitled a soldier to leave the front. One of these was "the man who is fearful and fainthearted." Lest his cowardice melt the hearts of his comrades in arms and demoralize them, the Torah rules that he should rather go home and join the civil service.

Interestingly, Maimonides (Rambam) rules that this exemption only applied to wars which were optional for political or territorial reasons (*milchemet ho'reshut*) but not to obligatory wars where the Torah itself mandated Israel to go into battle (*milchemet mitzvah*), for example, to conquer the Promised Land.

But where is the logic here? Why the distinction? If the problem is that the coward's fear will have a negative effect on his colleagues in combat, then that is a psychological fact of life. What difference does it make if the war is obligated by G-d or by Jewish leadership of the day? Surely a coward is a coward whatever the war!

But Maimonides is sharing with us a striking analysis of human nature. Fear and anxiety are magnified when there is more than one option open to us. When we have the choice of fighting or not, when war is not strictly commanded by G-d and it's only a decision by the government of the day, then I may very well choose to retreat, to live and perhaps fight another day. But when there is no choice, when it is a non-negotiable Mitzvah from G-d that this war be fought, then even cowards become heroes.

I am fond of quoting that famous American philosopher, John Wayne, who once said, "True courage is not the absence of fear. True courage is being scared like hell and saddling up anyway." Now that's a wise cowboy. The fearless few are indeed strange exceptions. Most normal people experience fear in scary situations. Those of good courage face up to the fear and confront it.

I can tell you many stories of ordinary people who became heroes. How? By overcoming their fears and doing whatever deed had to be done. My friends' father, the late Pinne Merkel, once ran into a Shul on fire in the old neighborhood of Doornfontein, Johannesburg to rescue the Torahs from the Holy Ark. The firemen warned him not to, but he ran in anyway. Pinne was not a religious man. But for him saving the Torah scrolls was not up for negotiation. It just had to be done, so an ordinary Jew became a holy hero.

My late congregant's son, Hugh Raichlin, is not a doctor. He's a lawyer. But when his wife was in labor and suddenly things started happening much too quickly, he delivered his own child inside the car in the parking lot of the maternity hospital. He wasn't looking for heroism. He had no option. Heroism found him.

When something just has to happen, we find a way to make it happen. We pluck up the courage and act valiantly. Haven't we heard stories of women lifting heavy cars to rescue their child trapped underneath?

My own father used to be a chain smoker. Thank G-d, he eventually gave up the habit. It often amazed me that the same person who would never be without a cigarette between his fingers six days a week, was able to go cold turkey every Shabbos! For six days he couldn't wait two minutes, but once a week he waited for 25 hours! How?

The answer is that keeping Shabbos for him was simply a non-negotiable commitment, so he had no option and survived. As soon as Shabbos was over, though, he and his fellow Shabbos-observant smokers would make a mad dash for the nearest pack.

It applies to life, to marriage, to business, to everything. If something is so important to us that to lose it would be unthinkable, we discover that we really can make a plan after all. In our Jewish lives, too, when we accept that a particular Mitzvah is a sacred principle and inviolate, we will observe it no matter what the challenge.

So, cowards of the world, unite. Let us be bold and brave and do what we know must be done. That's how ordinary people become heroes.

&)&

Ki Tetze

כי יפול הנופל ממנו

Should any man fall from it. (22:8)

DIY Judaism

Where do I fit in with Destiny? This week in Deuteronomy 22, 8 we read, *Ki tivne bayit chadash ... when you build a new house, you must place a guard-rail around your roof so that you will not bring blood upon your house should any man fall from the unenclosed roof.*

In the olden days, most roofs were flat and people would use them as entertainment areas. The Hebrew wording is *Ki yipol hanofel.* Now, literally, *hanofel* means, "the one who falls," which the commentators say implies that this individual was actually destined to fall off a roof and lose his life. So the question is, if that person was, in fact, preordained to fall, why is it my fault just because it happened in my house? Why am I responsible for him acting out his destiny? Why should his blood be on my shoulders?

Jewish philosophers would answer this question by saying that although we do definitely believe in destiny and that whatever happens is part of the Almighty's vast eternal plan, nonetheless, every individual has an obligation to do his best to prevent tragedy. We must take precautions. Although we *believe* in miracles, we are not permitted to *rely* upon them.

There is a Yiddish proverb that *the man destined to drown will drown even in a glass of water*. But that doesn't mean that you have to be the one to put his head under the hose. In short, we believe in the concept of *bashert* but we mustn't live by it. Otherwise, why go to work? We say in the *Bentching* (Grace After Meals) that G-d is the feeder and provider for all. So if G-d will support us, why must I *shlep* off to work?

Clearly, this is not the Jewish attitude. That's why it is a commandment of the Torah to safeguard our health. Likewise, we are not to live dangerously by leaving roofs unenclosed or swimming pools unfenced or our doors unlocked. "Trust in G-d, but lock your car."

One may ask, is it not an expression of faith to leave it all to G-d? To put our trust implicitly in Him that He will provide? That He will protect and guard us from accidents? The answer is an emphatic NO. "G-d helps those who help themselves." Far from being a heretical statement, this is quite consistent with Jewish belief.

Elsewhere, the Torah states that "Hashem, your G-d, shall bless you in all that you do." Meaning that to succeed in any endeavour, we need G-d's blessing, but He blesses us in all that we *do*. So, in order to merit His blessing, we must first lay the ground work and create the opportunity for Hashem's blessings to work. It's like the farmer who knows that the success of his crop depends on G-d granting rain, but the blessing of rain will only help after the farmer has tilled, ploughed, and planted.

Remember the story of the *shlemiel* who kept praying to G-d three times daily that He help him win the lottery and solve all his financial problems? Day after day he implored the Almighty to grant him his personal salvation via the lottery. When the lottery was drawn, unfortunately our *shlemiel* was not the winner. So he went back to Shul the next day and cried out to G-d bitterly, "Hashem you let me down, I prayed so hard. Why didn't I win the lottery?" And a deep, booming voice rang out from the Heavens saying, "Because you never bought a ticket, dummy!"

This concept applies to everything in life. As Gary Player once said, "The more I practice, the luckier I get." If you want to be *mazel'dig*, don't depend on *mazel* alone. If you want to have *nachas* from your children, don't rely on the luck of the draw that they will marry the right person. Parents have to plough and plant (and pray very hard) for *nachas* to happen.

In the words of the Psalmist that we say in *Shir Ha'maalot (Psalm 126)*, "He who sows with tears, will reap in joy."

שסב

אשר לא קדמו אתכם בלחם ובמים ... ואשר שכר עליך את בלעם

Because they did not greet you with bread and water and...
and they hired Balaam. (23:5)

Can You Afford It?

What do we cherish? What do we truly value? What do we make time for?

There is a rather curious juxtaposition of ideas in our Parsha this week. The Torah cautions us against allowing Ammonite and Moabite men from converting and joining the Jewish People. The reasons? First, *because they did not greet you with bread and water on the road when you were leaving Egypt.* And second, *because they hired Balaam ... to curse you.*

Such a diverse set of crimes lumped together in one verse. In the same breath we are told to shun them because they didn't play the good host when we were a tired and hungry nation trudging through the desert from Egypt and because they hired the heathen prophet Balaam to curse us. How can we possibly compare these two reasons? The first is simply a lack of hospitality, while the second is nothing short of attempted genocide.

The answer is that the two are indeed interrelated. One enforces the other and one proves the sinfulness of the other. If it was merely a question that they didn't show us any generosity during our journey we could possibly justify it by their own poverty. Perhaps Ammon and Moab were in an economic depression. Maybe they were broke and therefore were not in a position to offer hospitality. If they didn't have enough for themselves, how can we expect them to feed others?

But when we see that they hired Balaam the prophet to curse the Jewish People, then we know that money was not the problem. Do you think Balaam came cheap? Balaam was a very expensive consultant. "A houseful of gold and silver" was his asking price. If you found money for him, you could have found a few shekels to give some bread and water to tired, hungry travellers. The fact that they were prepared to pay such exorbitant fees to Balaam proves the enormity of their crime.

Ammon and Moab may be extinct, but their legacy lives on. One of the root causes of the Middle East quagmire is the Palestinian problem. So many live in squalor in refugee camps. It is truly a *rachmonus,* a terrible pity and a crying shame. But why have these people not been accommodated by their brethren over all these years? From the early years, Israel always welcomed Jewish refugees from Arab lands, from Syria, Yemen, Iran, and Iraq. Later, they absorbed many Ethiopian and Russian Jews. Israel is a small country with limited resources, yet no Jew is refused entry. Everyone is welcomed.

So tiny Israel can do it and the combined land and wealth of the Arab world cannot? Saudi Arabia builds palaces and engages in all sorts of royal excess. Have you been to the Dubai airport? They also now boast the richest horse race in the world! Billions are being spent on flippant luxuries, but to help their poor Palestinian brothers and sisters, nobody is home!

Sadly, we have a problem in our own community too. How often is a Jew approached for a worthy cause and he pleads poverty but the very next day he blows a fortune at a casino! We are too busy to come to a lecture at the Shul, but to kill a night playing poker we have plenty of time.

I am reminded of the fellow who asked me if he really needed to put up Mezuzahs on all his doorways inside his house. When I answered that he did, he gave a huge *krechtz.* "Oh Rabbi, but I just built a new house with eighteen rooms. Do you realize how much the Mezuzahs are going to cost?!

We are now in the month of Elul, a time for introspection and correction before Rosh Hashanah, our Judgment Day. Let us reflect on how we spend our money and our time, and let us try our best to be consistent and honorable to G-d and our fellow men and women.

ഔരു

לֹא תִשְׁכַּח
You shall not forget. (25:19)

Who Needs Anti-Semites?

It has been called *the world's longest hatred.* It continues to rear its ugly head across countries and continents. Whether it manifests in the crude bigotry of the lower crass or the snide subtlety of the upper crust, anti-Semitism is a sad fact of life. Of course, we all wish it would finally go away. We even had reason to hope that after Auschwitz it really would. Who among us doesn't want to feel accepted and appreciated?

But there is a strong argument to suggest that, in a perverse sort of way, anti-Semitism has been good for the Jews. The French philosopher Jean-Paul Sartre made that point in his book *Anti-Semite and Jew*. There, he argues that without the constant reminders and threats to our existence, we Jews would have been lulled into a peaceful and passive state of national amnesia. Secure in our comfort zones, we might have lost much of our unique identity.

History records that under regimes that persecuted us, we remained steadfastly Jewish. Whereas under more enlightened, liberal forms of government, we became comfortable in our new found freedoms, gradually embracing a welcoming but dominant culture and forfeiting much of our own.

Back in the '70s, when I was working with Jewish university students, we were struggling to break through a wall of icy indifference towards Judaism. It was so frustrating that my colleagues and I even considered going onto campus in the dead of night to paint a few swastikas on the Student Union building. Maybe that would jolt them out of their apathy. Of course, we never actually did it, but I confess to having been very tempted.

Towards the end of this week's Parsha, we read of the commandment to remember the unprovoked attack by the nation of Amalek against the Israelites when they left Egypt. The command comes in the form of the word *Zachor—Remember* at the beginning of the section. The final words are *Lo Tishkach—You shall not forget*. But why the need for both expressions? And what difference is there between *remembering* and *not forgetting?* Surely one is superfluous?

Commentary suggests that *remember* is a command to the Jewish People. *Do not forget* would seem to be a prophecy concerning the nations that they will not *let* you forget! Should you ever lapse into a false sense of security and forget your Jewishness, the anti-Semites of the world will be there to remind you of who you are and that you have not yet been accepted in their ranks. You are still an outsider, *a people that dwells alone.*

Everything has a purpose in creation. There is nothing redundant, nothing in vain in G-d's world. So what is the purpose of an anti-Semite? Just that, to remind Jews that they are Jewish!

But why wait for the Amalekites of this world to remind us? Do we want or need their taunting? Rather, let us be proactively, positively and proudly Jewish. You can sing the old Yiddish song one of two ways. Either it is *Oy es iz gut tzu zein a yid* (Oh, it is *good* to be a Jew) or *Oy, es iz shver tzu zein a yid.* (Oy, it is *hard* to be a Jew.)

There are a million good reasons to be proudly Jewish. If in the last century being Jewish carried a death sentence, today it is a life sentence—

promising a meaningful and blessed life. And when we decide to live proud, committed Jewish lives, we make a fascinating discovery. When we respect ourselves, the world respects us, too. And that applies across the board, from the individual Jew to the collective Jewish State.

Judaism is a boon, not a burden. We should be staunch about our heritage. It is a badge of honor to wear with noble pride. If you don't know why, go and study, but that's another sermon.

ଞୈ

Ki Tavo

Jewish Joy

Whether we appreciate the blessings in our lives or we take them for granted will always depend on whether we pause long enough to consider life and its blessings, or we just go along our merry way, oblivious to anything but the superficial.

This week we read about *Bikkurim,* the first fruit offerings Jewish farmers in the holy land were commanded to bring in thanksgiving to G-d for the land and its produce. On a basic level, *Bikkurim* remind us never to become ungrateful for the things we are blessed with in life.

Interestingly, the law only took effect 14 years after the Jewish People entered the Promised Land. It took seven years to conquer and another seven to distribute the land to the 12 tribes of Israel. Only when that process was completed did the law of the first fruits become applicable.

But why? Surely there were quite a few tribes who were settled earlier than the others. No doubt, some of the farmers who had received their allotted land had planted and seen the first fruits of their labors. Why then were they not required to show their appreciation immediately by bringing the *Bikkurim* offering then and there?

The Rebbe explains that in commanding this Mitzvah the Torah uses the phrase "And you shall rejoice with all the good that Hashem your G-d has given you." In order to be able to fully experience the joy of his own blessings in life, a Jew needs to know that his brothers have been blessed as well. As long as one Jew knew that there were others who had not yet been settled in their land he could not be fully content. Since *simcha,* genuine joy, was a necessary component in the mitzvah of *Bikkurim,* it could only be fulfilled when everyone had been satisfied. Only then can a Jew experience true *simcha,* a sincere and genuine joy.

Knowing that one's friends and cousins are still fighting—or even not yet enjoying their own stretch of land—somehow takes away the appetite for a party, even if we personally may have reason to rejoice. One Jew's satisfaction is not complete when he knows his brother has not yet been looked after.

I remember reading a story from the annals of the Previous Rebbe's arrest by the Communists back in Russia in 1927. Rabbi J. I. Schneersohn was the heroic spiritual leader of Russian Jewry then, and the Soviets sentenced him to death for his religious activities on behalf of his people. The Previous Rebbe had a marvelous pen, and he described his incarceration and the tortures he suffered at the hands of the most uncouth and sadistic warders in that notorious Russian prison. One of the prison guards was unbelievably cruel. He himself told that when he would beat and torture a prisoner, he would derive so much pleasure watching the man suffer that when he drank his tea he didn't need his usual dose of sugar. Just watching the torture sweetened his tea! Such was a vicious anti-Semite. But a Jew experiences the reverse sensation. He cannot enjoy his tea or his first fruits knowing that his brother is still unsettled. The sweetest fruits go bitter in our mouths, feeling the emptiness of our brethren.

So if you have a job, think of someone who doesn't. If you are happily married, think of those still searching for their *bashert* and try making a suitable introduction. And as it's almost Yom Tov, if you will be privileged enough to buy new outfits for the family, spare a thought for those who cannot contemplate such a luxury. And when you plan your festive Yom Tov meals with your family and friends, remember to invite the lonely, the widow, and the single parent too. In this merit, please G-d, we will all be blessed with a joyous and sweet new year.

ℴ⁗ℴ

ובאו עליך כל הברכות האלה והשיגוך

All these blessings will come upon you and overtake you.
(28:2)

G-d in the Fast Lane

Can we prepare for a blessing? Can one plan to be blessed?

Obviously, we believe that when we live life as G-d intended us to, we will find our lives blessed in many ways. Even if we do not always see the results tangibly or immediately, we certainly are aware of many blessings that come with the territory of leading a G-dly life. But there is a verse in our Parsha that promises us blessings we never even dreamed of.

If you will listen to the voice of Hashem ... and observe the command-ments ... then G-d will make you supreme over all the nations on earth. All these blessings will come upon you and overtake you.

What does it mean that blessings will *overtake* you? Rabbi Ovadia Sforno, one of the classical Biblical commentators, suggests that it means you will be blessed even when you made no effort to seek those blessings. It will come out of the blue, an unexpected windfall.

The story is told of the saintly Rabbi Levi Yitzchak of Berditchev that he once saw a young man running down the street. The Rav stopped him and asked, "Where are you running?" The fellow answered, "To make a living, Rabbi." To which the Berditchever responded, "So how do you know that your living lies is in that direction? Perhaps your livelihood is to be found in the opposite direction?"

Do we ever know for sure? How often do the best laid plans of mice and men come to naught? Haven't we all had the experience of trying our hardest to do a deal with all the planning, strategizing, blood, sweat, and tears and yet nothing whatsoever materialized? And on the other hand, there may have been times when we put no work into it at all, and sud-denly from nowhere we landed the deal of the year! The truth is, we don't know where the blessing of our livelihood lies.

And so it is with spiritual blessings. There are times when we make the effort and remain uninspired, and there are times when we become in-spired effortlessly. According to the Baal Shem Tov, our unconscious soul may hear something on a higher plane, and when it filters down to our conscious soul, we are touched, moved, or inspired.

We live in an era of much confusion. Many are lost, floundering in spir-itual wildernesses. But many are finding themselves, too. There have been many who didn't necessarily go looking for G-d, but G-d found them. "How did you get inspired?" "To tell you the truth, I'm not really sure. I was minding my own business, and I bumped into this rabbi." Or, "I was sitting next to this fellow on the plane ..." Or, "I was just a tourist at the Western Wall, but something moved me." Everybody has a story. In some stories we went looking for G-d, in others He came looking for us.

So if you feel the spirit overtaking you, don't speed up. Slow down. Let it catch up with you. May the blessings of G-d overtake you and transform your life.

❧

וְרָאוּ כָּל עַמֵּי הָאָרֶץ כִּי שֵׁם ה' נִקְרָא עָלֶיךָ וְיָרְאוּ מִמֶּךָ

*And all the nations of the world will see that the name of G-d is
upon you and they will fear you. (28:10)*

Spiritual Security

It was May 1967. Egyptian president Gamal Abdul Nasser had mobilized his troops and was threatening to "drive the Jews into the sea." The United Nations Peace-Keeping Force was dismissed and sheepishly left the region. Abba Eban, Israel's eloquent foreign minister questioned the purpose of an umbrella if as soon as it started raining, one closed the umbrella? Syria and Jordan, too, were preparing to join the war, and Israel was once again threatened with annihilation by its neighbors.

I was in New York. Lag B'Omer fell on the 28th of May. As it was a Sunday, thousands of Jewish school children had assembled on Eastern Parkway in Brooklyn for the Lag B'Omer Parade. The highlight of the event was the address to be delivered by the Rebbe. The Rebbe spoke passionately about the mortal threat to Israel and her people. But his talk was filled with a fiery faith and unambiguous optimism about the outcome. He assured the people that Israel would prevail. Previously, he had instructed all his American Yeshiva students in Israel to remain there and not return home, although their parents were extremely—and understandably—anxious. At the same time, though, he urged Jews the world over to do something practical to help Israel overcome this dire threat to her very existence.

What could we do? Besides material support for the war effort and in addition to tanks and fighter jets, Israel also needed spiritual support. There is a spiritual defense system, too, said the Rebbe. It was then that he launched the International Tefillin Campaign. By as many Jews as possible observing this hallowed Mitzvah, it would contribute in a tangible way to Israel's security. He called upon Jews around the world to encourage their brethren to begin putting on Tefillin, even if they were not religious or hadn't done it since their Bar Mitzvah. People responded instantly and Jewish men, in unprecedented numbers, embraced the campaign.

Nine days later, the battles began. Israel made military history when it decimated the Egyptian Air Force and defeated the armed forces of Egypt, Syria, and Jordan in lightning speed. Jerusalem was reunited under Jewish sovereignty, and the Six-Day War would be recorded for posterity as Israel's finest hour.

Without in any way minimizing the heroic efforts of our brave soldiers or the brilliant military strategies of our High Command, this amazing, miraculous victory surely pointed to a higher force. I firmly believe that the protective cover of G-d was inspired by the many thousands of new mitzvahs performed by our people.

But why Tefillin? Of all mitzvahs, why should the Rebbe have chosen Tefillin specifically to ensure Israel's security?

The answer is in this week's Parsha.

And all the nations of the world will see that the Name of G-d is upon you and they will fear you (Deuteronomy 28, 10). What does it mean that *the Name of G-d is upon you?*

The Talmud (Brachot 6a) quotes Rabbi Eliezer the Great who explained that the verse refers to *tefillin shel rosh*, the Tefillin worn on the head, which bear the *Shin* symbolizing Hashem's name. These are visible to the eye and have the spiritual power to inspire fear in the hearts of our enemies. Indeed, one of the most powerful images of the Six-Day War, still vivid in my mind, is the one of the Egyptian soldiers fleeing the Sinai in total disarray.

Whether they are massing armies on our borders or not, no one can deny that Israel's security is still at very high risk. Thank G-d, since its launch, the Tefillin Campaign has touched the lives of hundreds of thousands, perhaps millions, of our brothers. If Tefillin are not yet part of your daily routine, may this story inspire you to begin observing it now. If you are already a regular, then share the mitzvah with a friend. Besides all the wonderful traditional reasons for wearing Tefillin, contributing to the spiritual security of Israel adds one more important motivation. In its merit, may Israel be safe and secure until the ultimate era of peace on earth with the coming our righteous Mashiach speedily in our day, Amen.

ℬℭ

Nitzavim — Vayelech

ובחרת בחיים
And you shall choose life. (30:19)

Choose Life!

I call this day upon heaven and earth as witnesses. I have set before you life and death, blessing and curse. And you shall choose life, so that you and your children may live. (Deuteronomy 30, 19)

Do we really need the Torah to tell us to choose life? Which person of sound mind would choose death?

Clearly, the answer is that one must make a conscious decision to *live* and not just vegetate. And I don't mean to live it up by living life in the fast lane. To choose life means to choose to live a meaningful life, a life committed to values and a higher purpose. Did it make any difference at all that I inhabited Planet Earth for so many years? Will anyone really know the difference if I'm gone? Was my life productive, worthwhile?

When Rabbi Schneur Zalman of Liadi, wanted to bless his disciple Reb Yekusiel Liepler with wealth, he declined the offer, saying that he was afraid it would distract him from more spiritual pursuits. When he offered to bless him with longevity, he stipulated that it should not be "peasant's years with eyes that do not see and ears that do not hear where one neither sees nor senses G-dliness."

Reb Yekusiel was rather fussy, it seems. The holy rebbe is offering him an amazing blessing, and he is making conditions! Yes, he chose life and he chose to live a life that would not simply be long, but would be purposeful, productive and really would make a tangible difference. He wasn't interested in a long life if, essentially, it would amount to an empty life.

With pain in my heart I think of those tired, sadly pathetic human beings who walk the corridors of old age homes around the world simply waiting for the next meal. They have exhausted their purpose in living. It is simply a question of existing or vegetating, and the most exciting event to look forward to is lunch or supper.

But, sadly, they aren't the only ones. Much sadder is the fact that there are so many younger, able-bodied and able-brained people out there whose lives are also empty and devoid of meaning and fulfilment. There are millions of people of all ages living lives of emptiness, who feel they have no real purpose in life. They are simply surviving the day but, by their own definition, are not being productive or making any significant difference to others or to the world around them. So they feel that their lives are meaningless.

I remember a brilliant poem by Linda Ellis called "The Dash" in which she described a eulogy at a funeral where the speaker focused on the dash, or hyphen, on the tombstone inscription between the year of birth and the year of death of the deceased. That dash represented the years of the person's life and that little dash was the most important part of the entire tombstone. It represented what the person did and accomplished in the years between their birth and death. The dash was, basically, the person's whole life. Did they live a meaningful, productive life, or was it a waste of time, and tragically, a waste of a life?

In the words of Benjamin Franklin, "A long life may not be good enough, but a good life is long enough." Life is not measured in years alone. Chassidim would say, "Life isn't measured by one's passport age." It's what we put into our years that determines the value of our lives.

As we stand just before Rosh Hashanah, let us resolve to choose life. Let us live lives of Torah values and noble deeds. And may we be blessed ı a good and sweet new year.

ഇരുബ

Elul

"Keep Knocking on the Door!"

The other day I was sitting and working in my office at Shul. It was Friday afternoon, the secretaries downstairs had gone home, and I was the only one left in the building. I was preparing my sermon and *shiur* for Shabbos when I heard the bell ringing. Now to be honest, knowing from experience that whoever was ringing the bell was not coming to see me, I had no intention of going all the way downstairs to get involved in someone else's business. Usually at these times, it's either a wedding booking for next year or a congregant wanting to pay an account. I knew I had no appointments, so I carried on minding my own business and kept working on my sermon.

But the bell didn't stop. And then I heard loud banging on the front door. So I thought—what if it's an emergency? Maybe somebody really needs the rabbi, who knows? So eventually when the ringing became quite persistent, I went downstairs to check it out.

Sure enough, it was a young man who had a problem and very much wanted to speak to the rabbi.

I did my best to try to help him and then went back to my office. Before wishing him a Good Shabbos, though, I asked him why he was so persistent. Why didn't he give up when for some time he was receiving no reply? He said very simply that he knew I was inside. I asked how he knew and he answered, "Because I saw your car parked outside." Now I understood why he didn't give up.

I thought to myself; look at the tenacity and determination of this young man. He simply had to make contact and so he did.

How many of us would have given up?

How many of us have tried reaching out to G-d and didn't get an immediate reply or the answer we were looking for and have since resigned ourselves to not hearing from Him forever?

How many have tried to pray now and then and have given up because they didn't get instant results? "What's the use?" we argue. I called out but there was no reply

It reminds me of the new Dial-a-Prayer for atheists. You call this number and it rings ... and rings ... and rings.

The story of that Friday afternoon and the young man who just had to see the rabbi, reminds us not to give up, not to surrender to impatience.

The very act of prayer is beneficial to our inner peace, our serenity, our very soul.

We know G-d is there. Just keep knocking on the door until you get an answer.

We've just entered the month of Elul. Rabbi Schneur Zalman of Liadi compares this season to a time when the "King is in the field." There are occasions when the king leaves his royal palace to visit his subjects. At these times, he travels through the countryside and anyone and everyone is given the opportunity to approach the king and is received with a warm, smiling countenance. Elul is a time when the supreme King of Kings is eminently approachable.

Now, more than ever, He will respond when we call. Please don't stop ringing the bell.

₨ℛ

Haazinu (Shabbat Shuvah)

Teshuvah Fallacies

Usually, this Parsha is read between Rosh Hashana and Yom Kippur on *Shabbos Teshuva* or *Shabbos Shuva*. The title of the Shabbos will depend on whether we focus on the calendar (the season of Teshuvah) or the Haftarah, which begins with the words *Shuva* Yisrael, *Return O Israel*. At any rate, it is a Shabbos dedicated to the theme of Teshuvah, repentance.

There are two popular misconceptions about Teshuvah and, ironically, they come from opposite sides of the spectrum. The first is *I'm too good,* that is, repentance is for sinners, and since I'm no sinner and am basically a good guy and a good Jew, this whole process is irrelevant to me. No need for it on my agenda.

In other words, if I'm okay, I'm exempt from Teshuvah. Right? Wrong! That's the first fallacy. No one is exempt. Even the wholly righteous *klop al chet* (beat their chests in penitence)—either for their own failings on a more subtle level, or for the members of their community whose lives they have not yet succeeded in transforming to a Torah lifestyle. Only those who are 100 percent perfect are exempt from Teshuvah. All others must get to work. So who is perfect? In fact, there is no one as imperfect as he who thinks he is perfect.

I remember many years ago, going to the Berea Shul in Johannesburg to hear a famous Chazan *daaven* on Shabbos Mevorchim Elul. Indeed, the melodies and *nusach* were evocative of the high holy days. Afterwards, I bumped into a well-known *baaleboss,* a prominent shul-going business-man. I said to him, "*Nu,* you really felt Elul during the *daavening,* didn't you?" He shrugged his shoulders and said, "Elul is for sinners. I don't need Elul." How wrong he was. *Oy,* did he need it! People with over-inflated egos can sometimes fool themselves into believing everything they think about themselves.

But there is another Teshuvah fallcy too. This fallacy belongs to the overly humble. The fellow who puts himself down so low that he really believes he is beyond salvation. *I'm too bad for Teshuvah. Too far gone, there's no hope, I'm a lost case. Give up on me Rabbi, I'm too old, too tired, too lazy, too sinful, or just too set in my ways.*

There are numerous true stories of some of the worst sinners in history who found G-d, Torah, and themselves in an instant and returned with a full heart. The renowned Talmudic sage, Reish Lakish, was previously a robber chieftain. Eliezer ben Durdaya was infamous for his immorality (he once boasted that there wasn't a harlot he hadn't patronized), and yet in a moment of inspiration he returned and was accepted, gaining eternal life then and there. And don't we all know people today who have turned around their lives in a most beautiful way?

This is the Shabbos of *Teshuvah* in the week of *Teshuvah.* Please G-d, we will all embrace this mitzvah that applies to every one of us, from the holiest to the most far removed. It is a great equalizer. May our Return be sincere, genuine, and well-received up where it counts.